Radio Canada International

Arthur Siegel

Mosaic Press
Oakville, ON - Buffalo, N.Y.

Canadian Cataloguing in Publication Data

Siegel, Arthur
Radio Canada International: history and development

Includes index.
ISBN 0-88962-620-0

1. Radio Canada International - History. 2. International broadcasting - Canada - History. I. Title.

HE8697.45.C3S54 1996 384.54'06'571 C96-930810-8

Published by MOSAIC PRESS, P.O. Box 1032, Oakville, Ontario, L6J 5E9, Canada. Offices and warehouse at 1252 Speers Road, Units #1&2, Oakville, Ontario, L6L 5N9, Canada and Mosaic Press, 85 River Rock Drive, Suite 202, Buffalo, N.Y., 14207, USA.

Mosaic Press acknowledges the assistance of the Canada Council, the Ontario Arts Council and the Dept. of Canadian Heritage, Government of Canada, for their support of our publishing programme.

Cover and book design by Susan Parker
Printed and bound in Canada
ISBN 0-88962-620-0

In Canada:
MOSAIC PRESS, 1252 Speers Road, Units #1&2, Oakville, Ontario, L6L 5N9, Canada. P.O. Box 1032, Oakville, Ontario, L6J 5E9
In the United States:
MOSAIC PRESS, 85 River Rock Drive, Suite 202, Buffalo, N.Y., 14207
In the UK and Western Europe:
DRAKE INTERNATIONAL SERVICES, Market House, Market Place, Deddington, Oxford. OX15 OSF

TABLE OF CONTENTS

for
Ariane, Alisa and Maura

PREFACE

Habant sua fata Libelli or, in today's English, strange things happen to books. Sometimes even before they are published, as in the case of the history of Radio Canada International.

The Canadian Broadcasting Corporation was celebrating its 50th anniversary in 1996. Early the same year, almost as an afterthought to the celebrations already in progress, the CBC decided that its external service, Radio Canada International should be somehow included in the festivities. Commissioning of its history, as quite distinct from the rest of the corporation, seemed an excellent idea. The intention was to publish the book in about three years time, to coincide with the 45th anniversary of RCI itself.

An author was found and a contract signed. Arthur Siegel, an RCI veteran script writer who left RCI in 1976 to pursue his academic interests at the Social Science Division of York University was commissioned to research and write the manuscript.

To assist Siegel in his research, RCI initiated an oral history project which consisted of a series of taped interviews with a large number of people who played an important role in RCI's creation and development. Former diplomats, CBC and RCI managers and staff shared their experience and talked about the organization and the many facets of its activities. All the tapes were transcribed for easier consultation.

In addition to the oral history project, documents, recordings and other archival materials under RCI's care and control were made available to the author.

The years went by, the book grew but was not completed. Waiting for its history, RCI twice faced and survived threats of extinction.

Radio Canada International: History and Development by Arthur Siegel is not the final history of RCI. It is rich in personalities and intrigues of the early years, it is a collection of fascinating vignettes painting the picture of RCI within the larger canvas of Canadian diplomacy and political pressures, domestic and international.

The bulk of the book deals with the first 20 years or so of RCI's existence including a captivating analysis of the origins of the organization and its early relationship to External Affairs and the CBC.

The later years and the whole broadcasting side of RCI are sketched briefly, more to fill in the reader on what happened next than to report and reflect. The contemporary period of RCI's activities, RCI as part of history of

Canadian radio, RCI's significant and more recent role within the international community of broadcasters still await its literary recognition.

To provide the reader with a review of the most recent developments in the RCI's saga, a brief update of events and a bibliography of articles in the Canadian press were added as a Post Scriptum.

Arthur Siegel's book, in its distinctive format of insightful anecdotes, becomes a first attempt at explaining and understanding a reality which despite all its intricacies is in fact quite simple. Since its inception, throughout various phases of history and into the present, RCI has always been somewhere in the margin of real politics and convenient policies. Its path has been traced by a sum of accidental moves, conflicting personalities, good intentions and sometimes lucky breaks.

Elzbieta Olechowska
Manager, Europe Service
Radio Canada International

April 17, 1996

CHAPTER I

INTRODUCTION

Radio Canada International -- the Voice of Canada in international broadcasting -- was born of war and thrived in times of international tensions. It first went on the air on Christmas Day 1944,[1] four-and-a half months before the end of World War II. The original name was the International Service of the Canadian Broadcasting Corporation. The first home at 1236 Crescent Street in downtown Montreal was in a rundown building that had previously housed a brothel. Nearby was the Forum where the Montreal Canadiens of hockey fame reigned supreme.

Truly great talent moved into the dilapidated building on Crescent Street from which RCI broadcast at first to Europe and later to all the world. Rene Levesque waxed poetic in a down-to-earth manner about his beloved Quebec and the greatness of Canada as a whole. Larry Henderson developed announcing skills that would serve him well when he became the anchorman of CBC television news. Stuart Griffiths left RCI to become a driving force in television in Canada and Britain. Mavor Moore, one of the RCI pioneers became a legendary figure in television, theatre and the arts. Eric Koch, the Voice of Canada for German audiences for many years, became a prominent programmer for CBC television. Glenn Gould, Maureen Forrester and Oscar Peterson made their first recordings from RCI. Among the Godfathers of RCI were Prime Minister Mackenzie King, Lester Pearson and Winston Churchill.

Despite these incredibly impressive connections, the Voice of Canada has almost always been involved in controversy; the external broadcast service could never carry a tune that satisfied its two masters. The joint project of the Government and the Canadian Broadcasting Corporation, created in wartime under the provisions of the War Measures Act, RCI became an instrument of Ottawa's involvement in international politics and brought to the surface a clash of cultures between journalist and diplomat. At the centre of this clash for many years was Lester Pearson who, as Minister for External Affairs and Prime Minister, had difficulties in separating the affairs of journalism and the affairs of government. Pearson supported and defended RCI in public and in Parliament but he never really cared for it; at one time he wanted to get rid of it by giving it away to the United Nations. C.D. Howe, who had a long-running feud with the Canadian Broadcasting Corporation, did not want Canada to become involved in international broadcasting in the first place.

Early Controversy

On January 13, 1943, the Honourable C.D. Howe, Minister of Munitions and Supplies, forced Prime Minister William Lyon Mackenzie King to call back a letter he had written to President Roosevelt.[2] The letter, already in Washington to be hand delivered by Lester Pearson, asked the American leader to personally intervene to help Canada obtain shortwave radio transmitters for use in World War II. The Prime Minister wanted to bring Canada into the war of words -- the radio war -- that had become an adjunct to the war on the battlefields.

Mr. Howe was furious when he learned on January 11 about the Prime Minister's letter to Roosevelt and immediately wrote to A.D.P. Heeney, Secretary of the War Cabinet, seeking to abort Mr. King's initiative. Meanwhile, External Affairs notified Pearson, the Minister Counsellor in Washington, to hold the letter -- "do not deliver" -- until further instructions. At a meeting of the Cabinet War Committee on January 13, the Prime Minister and Howe put forward opposing views: King wanted Canada to become involved in international radio propaganda as quickly as possible and stressed the importance of radio shortwave broadcasting as a weapon of political warfare; Howe, for his part, argued against asking President Roosevelt to intercede personally; shortwave transmitters were not a priority for him.[3] Howe's view prevailed: the War Cabinet instructed Pearson to send the King letter back to Ottawa.

Howe -- the principal architect of Canadian industrialization in wartime -- believed in hard weapons and not "talk", the soft bullets, over the airwaves behind enemy lines. When the argument was made in Canadian newspapers that the price of the shortwave station was about the price of an aeroplane, Howe chose aeroplanes over airwaves. This was a time when radio propaganda was seen by many as a critically important weapon and, as the renowned American broadcaster Edward R. Murrow would recount later, Churchill had "mobilized the English language and sent it into battle to steady his fellow countrymen and hearten those Europeans upon whom the long dark night of tyranny had descended." But even Churchill put bullets ahead of words and sneered at the Nazi propaganda machine: "If words could kill, we would all be dead."

For two years, Howe was a roadblock in the face of British pressure to have a shortwave radio service built in Canada. His objections had been neutralized on September 18, 1942 when the Cabinet formally requested the Canadian Broadcasting Corporation to build an external broadcasting service and operate it on behalf of the Government. Howe, however, was not prepared to jeopardize Canada's shopping practices for war material in Washington; he feared that American officials would resent Prime Minister King's appeal to Roosevelt instead of queuing up and waiting its turn to buy the equipment. Without the personal intervention of the American President, it was a long wait until Canada obtained the shortwave transmitter.

When cabinet authorized the building of the shortwave station, the Allies appeared to be losing the war. Canada had just suffered two serious setbacks: The failed raid at Dieppe which had been planned in large part for propaganda purposes and the failure in Quebec province in the national referendum on conscription.

The Beginning

By the time the Canadian shortwave station went on the air, much of France had already been liberated and the allied victory was assured, although some hard battles were still ahead. RCI immediately became involved in psychological warfare -- the war of words -- in an effort to hasten the German surrender and to bolster the spirits of people in occupied countries; it was low-keyed propaganda; the emphasis was on telling enemies and friends about the on-going battles, the Canadian contribution to the war and the bright future for world peace that would be shaped under the auspices of the United Nations. After Germany surrendered, the principal aims of Canadian broadcasts in the German language were denazification and reeducation.

The broadcast priorities, however, had changed in the two-and-a-half years it took to build the station: The main objective at the end of the war was not the war of words but a radio link between Canada and its hundreds of thousands of troops in Europe who would soon be returning home. The troops learned from these broadcasts about the veterans' benefits they would receive, the sort of training they might take up as they moved into civilian life and how Canada had industrialized and changed dramatically during their absence.

The International Service of the CBC, as it was called until the name was changed to Radio Canada International; in 1972, was a powerful instrument for propaganda and information technically it proved better than expected: It was the loudest voice from North America into Europe. CBC engineers had designed a sophisticated antenna system for two 50 KW shortwave transmitters at Sackville, New Brunswick, which made the Canadian signals stronger than those from more powerful Voice of America stations. Some of the most important personalities in the CBC in the 1940s and 1950s -- including Gladstone

Murray, Augustin Firgon, Davidson Dunton, Alphonse Ouimet, Ernest Bushnell -- unhesitatingly supported the shortwave station. The CBC contribution, however, was in large part confined to technology. True, the CBC provided the first supervisor in Peter Aylen but in wartime the hard-pressed public broadcaster was not in a position to share its editorial force. As the war drew to an end some former servicemen and war correspondents gravitated to the International Service. This was a time of strong enthusiasm for internationalism in Canada and the external broadcaster attracted the brightest and the most enthusiastic including Rene Levesque, Rene Garneau, Jack Craine, Patrick Waddington, Stuart Griffiths, Andrew Cowan, Gerard Arthur, Arthur Phelps, to name but a few.

Refugees from Europe were the broadcasters in the foreign language sections. The sophisticated and elegant foreigners -- especially the Germans and the Czechs -- touched responsive chords in their native lands. Few of them had any journalistic background but they were, what CBC veteran Jack Craine to this day calls 'incredibly intelligent'. The most important contribution in the psychological warfare machinery came from Helmut Blume, a musicologist by profession, who became the dean of the Conservatory of Music at McGill University after he left the CBC. Blume's assistant was Eric Koch, a young Jewish refugee from Germany. Karl Renner, the grandson of the former President of Austria, used information from the letters of German prisoners to provide material for some of the most successful psychological warfare broadcasts directed toward Germany. All three -- Blume, Koch and Renner -- had been shipped to Canada from Britain and were held in detention camps for some time until they were allowed to go free and join the war of words against the Nazis. Dr. Walter Schmolka, who introduced Czech programming, was a lawyer and a gifted musician; he became an acknowledged expert in propaganda. Maja van Steensel, an underground hero in the Netherlands, whose exploits against German occupiers became legendary stories in the corridors of the International Service, came to Canada as a war bride and was soon broadcasting home in Dutch.

The pioneers of the external broadcasting service, whether Canadian or foreign, shared above all a sense of anti-fascism and an obsession to defeat Germany. Ideologically, they were mostly small "l" liberals who would have been most comfortable in the Liberal Party and CCF (forerunner of the New Democratic Party).

Their anti-fascist background made some of the broadcast staff -- Canadians and foreigners -- suspect in the cold war when right wing elements in the United States and Canada pointed fingers of suspicion at CBC personnel, especially International Service employees. Prime Minister Louis St. Laurent responded by dispatching a diplomat, Ambassador Jean Desy, to clean up the

International Service and place it on the correct ideological track. Years later during the Vietnam War, the ideological pendulum swung again and External Affairs expressed concern about a perceived anti-Americanism. Ideology mixed with nationalism, also had its fall out internally: The foreign language sections seemed at times to be continuing amongst each other the wars of old Europe.

The Voice of Canada lost its innocence in the cold war when it was a junior partner in a cooperative effort with the United States and Britain to broadcast into the communist countries of Eastern Europe. There was a sense of mission and RCI was an instrument of foreign policy; it provided Canada the means to comment on the wars in Korea and Vietnam, the Hungarian Revolution and the Suez Crisis of 1956, the Soviet military intervention in Czechoslovakia in 1968, the wars in the Middle East, the Solidarity Movement in Poland, the collapse of the Berlin Wall, the reunification of Germany and the decline of communism. In some international upheavals, Canada was more interested in not saying anything but the absence of comment was deafening. This created difficulties for Ottawa which, the record shows, does more than its share of fence sitting.

Whose Voice?

This book focuses on the history of Radio Canada International as it sought to make itself heard in the hot war against the Nazis, in the cold war against communism and in periods of detente and reconciliation. Whose voice has it been? There were times when it spoke of the Minister for External Affairs as an instrument of foreign policy. At other times, especially in recent years, Radio Canada International was the independent voice of the parent organization; the Canadian Broadcasting Corporation, which although publicly owned, is in many ways insulated from political interference. Should the Voice of Canada speak with a single voice or should it reflect the diversity of a democratic society with a variety of voices -- including English, French, federal, provincial, native peoples -- often not in harmony. In the cold war period the distinction between truth and lies became especially problematic as Canada's external radio voice sought to find a working balance between its journalistic fonctions of information and communication and the interests of External Affairs in disinformation and propaganda. It is remarkable that in the tug of war between journalist and diplomat, it is the journalist who prevailed in the long term.

RCI weathered the storms from outside and the occasional turmoil within. Through the corridors walked former diplomats, writers, composers, esteemed poets, anti-Semites, a 'righteous gentile' and a former KGB agent planted by the Royal Canadian Mounted Police. Even before the service began broadcasting, its first head received training at Camp X -- Sir William Stephenson's famous Ontario training ground for covert activity. External Affairs, for its part, never know quite what it wanted from the external broadcaster and after setting course in one direction would change its mind time and gain. Despite the cross currents and uncertainties, the International Service for many years could lay claim to the best newsroom in the CBC and produced the best commentators on international and Canadian affairs.

Languages

Perhaps the most dramatic use of shortwave broadcasting in recent time -- involving almost certainly some Canadian programming -- came during the ill-fated coup against President Gorbachev on August 19, 1991. On his return to Moscow after three days of detention at his summer home in the Crimea, the Soviet leader said he kept himself informed on developments in his capital through broadcasts from abroad: "We were able to catch some broadcasts and find out what was happening. We got the BBC best of all, Radio Liberty, the Voice of America." Mr. Gorbachev and his personal staff, as is the case with so many millions of other shortwave listeners, were playing around with the dials. The British Broadcasting Corporation transmitters at Skelton, England, which beam to Eastern Europe also carry Canadian broadcasts in the Russian and Ukrainian languages. In addition, Canadian broadcasts can be targeted to what was formerly the Soviet Union via transmitters located in Sines (Portugal), Xian (China), Yamata (Japan) and Kimjai (South Korea). There are also direct transmissions in Russian and Ukrainian from Sackville, New Brunswick on Canada's Atlantic Coast. No other broadcaster penetrates the Soviet Union from so many directions. This heavy interest in reaching Russian-speaking and Ukrainian-speaking audiences has its roots in the cold war and is a matter that will be discussed in some detail. It is significant that during the Soviet crisis, Mr. Gorbachev was not alone in bringing out his shortwave receiver; millions of his fellow citizens were doing the same; one in every four citizens of the Soviet Union was listening to foreign broadcasts. To meet these interests, Radio Canada International increased by 50 percent its transmission time in Russian and Ukrainian.

In its 50 year history, Radio Canada International has had programs in more than 40 languages; some languages were used for short periods only but in more than 20 languages there were long-term scheduled services. The introduction and disappearance of languages of broadcast and target areas is based on the advice of the Department of External Affairs and the choices are a reflection of Canadian involvement in international affairs. More often than not, languages are introduced because of crisis events: The Hungarian service began during the Hungarian revolution in 1956; the Czech service was introduced during the German occupation in World War II; Armenian broadcasting was introduced for a limited period during the earthquake in 1989. In the 1990s, Creole language broadcasts were beamed to Haiti.

Chinese, one of the "new" languages of RCI broadcasts was introduced spontaneously during the upheavals of the Tiananmen crisis in the Spring of 1989. The broadcasts to China, relayed by powerful transmitters in Japan, was a Canadian radio response aimed at penetrating the Chinese curtain with "true facts", much as Canada's external broadcasting service penetrated the iron curtain in the 1950s.

The introduction of Arabic language programming was yet another Canadian radio response to global turmoil. In the Persian Gulf crisis, following Iraq's occupation of Kuwait in August 1990, Radio Canada International expanded its radio presence in the Middle East where a strong Canadian signal is relayed via transmitters at Wertachtal (Germany), Moosbrunn (Austria) and Sines (Portugal). Newscasts in Arabic, inserted twice a day in the regular French and English broadcasts, were later expanded into full Arabic language shortwave services; including public affairs programming. Furthermore, Radio Canada International makes daily use of a Radio Monte Carlo medium wave transmitter in Cyprus -- providing what is probably the strongest signal into the Middle East -- for a 15 minute Arabic program at prime time.

Radio Canada International contributed in other ways to accommodate Canadian interests in the Gulf crisis: The shortwave facilities were made available to Canadians who wanted to reach family and friends in the region; personal messages were incorporated into the French and English broadcasts to the Middle East. Also, at the request of the Department of External Affairs, RCI transmitted advisory messages telling Canadians in the Gulf area how to arrange a passage home on charter flights.

UN Peacekeeping

In the 1990s, RCI was beaming special programs to Canadians serving with the United Nations peace-keeping forces in the former Yugoslavia and in Somalia. Ever since Lester Pearson helped establish the UN peace-keeping ventures on behalf of the world organization, wherever the Canadian forces went -- in the Middle East, Cyprus, Kashmir, Congo -- RCI provided a radio link. The Canadian radio involvement with the United Nations is especially close and goes back to the earliest days of the world organization.

Transmitters

A continuing problem for Canada's external broadcast service has been adequate shortwave transmitters. The 50 Kilowatt (KW) transmitters, first used at Sackville at the end of World War II, were in service for about 30 years and had been long obsolete by the time they were replaced. In 1996, RCI operated eight transmitters -- three of 100 KW and five of 250 KW. Many countries are using 500 KW transmitters, sometimes two of these in tandem to provide 1,000 KW power output. While Sackville is an ideal site for Canadian shortwave broadcasting to Europe, it is not suitable for Asian transmissions nor is it effective for broadcasting to the Middle East. In order to expand its broadcast horizon and to ensure strong signals to its selected target areas, RCI has agreements for exchanging transmitter time with seven international broadcasters: The British Broadcasting Corporation, Deutsche Welle, Radio Austria, Radio Korea International, China Radio International, Radio Japan and Radio Monte Carlo. The arrangements with the BBC and Deutsche Welle go back to the days of the cold war and helped Canada penetrate the iron curtain, despite heavy jamming. More recently, Deutsche Welle and Radio Austria and Radio Monte Carlo have made it possible for Canada so send powerful signals into the Middle East. Radio South Korea, China Radio International and Radio Japan provided new opportunities in Asia. The transmitter exchanges have revitalized the Canadian radio voice heard abroad. Canada, in return, makes available its Sackville shortwave station to relay radio signals for European and Asian broadcasters to the United States, the Caribbean and Latin America.

The Crisis of the 1990s: RCI Today

Radio Canada International developed into an important voice in the international radio arena. In its broadcasts to Eastern Europe it was much more than an appendage for United States and British broadcast services. Lech Walesa in Poland, Vaclav Havel in the Czech Republic, Boris Yeltsin and Mikhail Gorbachev in the former Soviet Union have all spoken of the effectiveness of western broadcasting in helping to foster democratic practices; RCI contributed much more than is generally realized at home. Before the fall of communism, travellers and refugees from Eastern Europe listed RCI as one of the leading stations that commanded their attention and respect. Listeners from other parts of the world were also impressed. In the 1980s, RCI's audience was estimated at between 12 million and 16 million on a fairly regular basis (at least once a week). Fifty thousand listeners a year -- often from the most unexpected places -- wrote to RCI headquarters in Montreal; nearly all of them praising what they heard on their shortwave radios. The Canadian voice had obvious appeal.

In recent years, however, neither the CBC nor External Affairs attached any priority to the external broadcasting service and when the CBC sought to close it down in the recession of the early 1990s for budgetary reasons, the Department of External Affairs raised no objections. RCI survived more by accident than by intention (discussed later); its funding was cut sharply.

On April 1, 1991, the acting Executive Director of Radio Canada International, Allan Familiant, sent a message to the millions of listeners abroad: "due to reduced budget provided by the Government of Canada, our programming was severely curtailed..." Some listeners were disbelieving; they thought it was an April Fool message. It was not.

Overnight, the once powerful Voice of Canada in international broadcasting was reduced to a whisper. It abandoned services in Polish, Czech, Slovak, Hungarian, German, Japanese and Portuguese. Also discontinued at the same time were the French and English broadcasts prepared for foreign audiences. RCI would now broadcast in five foreign languages; a mere 28 hours of broadcasting a week; an 85 percent cut.

To keep Canada on the airwaves in the tie slots -- totalling 232 hours a week -- where programs in nine languages had been cancelled, RCI began transmitting programs from the French and English networks of its parent organization, the Canadian Broadcasting Corporation/Société Radio-Canada. Carrying these French and English domestic CBC programs on shortwave to audiences in far away countries such as India, Japan, Brazil, Hungary and

Poland, is, in some ways, equivalent to the sort of stand-by messages or test patterns one gets on television when the station is having technical problems. RCI problems, however, are not technical; they are rooted in economics and politics.

The disappearance of RCI appeared almost inevitable but the organization has a remarkable survival instinct. In order to justify its existence, RCI had to do more with less; provide viable broadcasting in the face of drastic financial cuts.

Today, RCI broadcasts, in Russian, Ukrainian, Chinese, Arabic and Spanish. Furthermore, there is French and English programming from the CBC's national network which has special appeal to Canadians abroad but is also drawing audiences in the United States, and the Caribbean and to a lesser extent in Asia and Africa. The signals are strong; giving Canada a crisp and clean voice. Equally important is a relatively new venture -- which was first initiated in China -- to tell the world about Canada through English language lessons. These Canadian inspired language programs are widely rebroadcast by local stations in China, the Ukraine, the successor republics of the Soviet Union and in Southern Africa. Also, RCI's Russian and Ukrainian language programming are rebroadcast by local stations.. New audiences, in the most unexpected places, are learning about Canada and its culture. RCI, abandoned by the CBC and the Canadian government as a sinking boat, refuses to go down.

The involvement of radio in international politics is highly complex but is usually discussed in simplistic terms. Discussions on the future of Radio Canada International have been mostly behind closed doors in Ottawa. Relatively few Canadians are even aware of the existence of Radio Canada International, largely because Canadians have never been significant shortwave listeners and few radios in this country are equipped with shortwave bands. In the absence of strong support from the CBC, from the Government and from the general population the external broadcasting service has been continuously vulnerable and on several occasions was headed for instant eradication.

The devastating cuts in 1991 were followed by further upheavals. In 1995 and again in 1996, there were new moves to close down Radio Canada International. In the atmosphere of budget cuts and fiscal balancing, RCI was seen as expendable by both the Government and the CBC. It appeared that neither wanted to fund external broadcasting. A week before RCI was to turn off its transmitters on April 1, 1996, the Government and the CBC reached a cost sharing agreement for another year. There remains apprehension about the future but the technological infrastructure remains in place and Canada's frequencies are still secured. The challenge facing RCI is laid out in the first words broadcast fifty years ago: "This is Canada Calling the World." In doing so, it has sought to project the meaning of Canada -- its peoples, cultures, the economy and the land. No other broadcaster can do this and RCI is the only significant vehicle for the projection of Canada globally. This is a dimension of foreign policy that is a support structure for our international relations.

International broadcasting organizations are designed to serve national interests in one way or another. These national interests are especially acute in times of war and international tension when, as we will see later, international broadcasting becomes an instrument of psychological warfare. The emphasis in most countries is to use their shortwave service for propaganda with program content coming under direct government control. Some countries, including Canada, have sought to develop an arms-length relationship between the government and the international broadcaster on the principle that the national interest is best served by looking at national and international events through journalistic eyes. Among the matters explored here is the measure of success in the Canadian shortwave experience in insulating the broadcaster from governmental interference.

CHAPTER II

THE INTERNATIONAL ENVIRONMENT

The first voice ever heard on radio was that of a Canadian -- Reginald Aubrey Fessenden-- and the message had a Canadian flavour; it was about snow. Fessenden provided Canada with opportunities to become a world leader in international radio broadcasting but Ottawa's attitude could be described as all ears and tongue-tied; Canada was more interested in receiving messages than sending them. This characteristic of Canadian broadcasting persists to the present day.

Fessenden, born at Bolton in Quebec's Eastern Townships and educated at Bishop's University, was one of the truly great pioneers of radio at the turn of the century. The early 1900's was a time of important experiments based on Guglielmo Marconi's invention of radio which transmitted the dots and dashes of the Morse code. In Fessenden's view, radio waves could also be used to transmit voice. On October 23, 1900, a year before Marconi's first trans-Atlantic Morse code transmission, Fessenden had found a way of sending a voice piggy-back on radio waves. Using the heterodyne system he developed, Fessenden spoke by radio from his laboratory at Cobb Island on the Potomac River to his assistant at a receiving station at Arlington, Virginia, some 50 miles away. Fessenden's message had a very Canadian ring to it: "One, two, three, four. Is it snowing where you are, Mr. Thiessen? If so telegraph back and let me know."

The telegraphy reply from Mr. Thiessen said that it was indeed snowing. Fessenden, understandably excited by his accomplishment, wrote in his log: "This afternoon here at Cobb Island, intelligible speech by electromagnetic waves has for the first time in World's history been transmitted."

Fessenden could not raise money in Canada for his experiments nor could he find an academic position. He was a Canadian nationalist -- his mother led the movement to create Empire Day -- and he reluctantly left for the United States where he taught at Purdue University and the University of Pennsylvania. Furthermore, the U.S. Weather Bureau supported his experiments and the Cobb Island laboratory. Canada, for its part, provided financial backing for the radio experiment of Marconi who had a sense of showmanship and drama.

In the United States Fessenden was instrumental in setting up wireless stations in New York, Philadelphia and Washington. The company he was involved with -- National Electric Signalling Company -- built a transmitter at

Brant Rock, Massachusetts, near Boston, and a receiving station at Machrihonish in Scotland. In 1906, Fessenden was successful in sending Morse code messages to Scotland. Later that year, in November, in a fluke accident, the voice of one of his technical assistants was heard at the Scotland receiving station instead of the dots and dashes. But this event was never followed up; a severe storm a month later wrecked the Scottish station.

Fessenden's most dramatic breakthrough in the invention of "real" radio in contrast to the dots and dashes transmissions, came on the night of December 24, 1906. In a broadcast from Brant Rock, Mass. to the ships at sea of the United Fruit Company,Fessenden hosted a Christmas Eve program featuring Christmas greetings, a recording of Handel's "Largo", and he played "Oh, Holy Night" on the violin. In his closing message he asked listeners to write to him. When letters arrived telling him he had been heard, Fressenden realized he had achieved his goal: he had invented modern radio. The first voice on international radio had a distinct Canadian accent, broadcasting from the United States.

The importance of Fessenden's breakthrough was not immediately realized. There were of course other important inventors experimenting in the radio field; the work of Thomas Edison in the United States and John Ambrose Flemming in England led to the development of the vacuum tube which improved voice and music transmissions. In 1908, a broadcast by Lee de Forest from the Eiffel Tower in Paris could be picked up by radio receivers in London. These ventures were regarded as frivolous, the emphasis in radio was for sending messages to ships at sea, weather information and business transactions. It took another 10 years before voice and music broadcast would be taken seriously.

International Broadcasting

International broadcasting was born of sin, it served as an instrument of war, political intimidation and propaganda long before it found a voice. The first broadcast destined for consumption beyond a country's borders originated in Germany in the first world war, in 1915. Germany transmitted a daily news report in Morse code; it waswidely heard by German agents abroad and made available to newspapers as far away as Mexico.[1]

Russia, after the revolution in 1917, also used Morse code broadcasts to give its account of what the revolution was all about. Lenin inspired these broadcasts which began with a dramatic universal call: "to all, to all, to all." And not long after, the Soviet Union used radio to further its interest in the course of the peace negotiations at Brest-Litovsk when Trotsky insisted on textual radio transmission of the negotiations, thus reaching out to world opinion in a strategy that undermined the German negotiators.[2]

Radio became a medium for information and entertainment in the early 1920's when many countries began broadcasting voice and music. Canada's experimental station XWA (now CFCF in Montreal) -- is the world's oldest radio station; it went on the air in 1918; commercial broadcasting in Canada was introduced in 1922. The first American station, KDKA in Pittsburgh, began its transmission on Presidential election night in November 1920. The British Broadcasting Company, a commercial venture until it was transformed into the publicly-owned British Broadcasting Corporation in 1926, went on the air in 1922. The first Soviet station, Radio Komintern, began broadcasting on November 7, 1922, the fifth anniversary of the Revolution.

For European nations, international broadcasting was largely an extension of their domestic broadcasts across borders; countries were close to each other and within reach of medium wave or standard broadcasting. The conventional view was that the best way to extend the reach of radio was to increase transmitter power and build higher aerials, some reaching 250 metres. The first of these super stations, built in 1925 by the Soviet Union at Chalabrowo, near Moscow, broadcast anti-capitalist messages in English and was also used for intense propaganda in the territorial dispute between the U.S.S.R. and Romania over Bessarabia.[3]

The new medium was perceived as a voice of authority and believability; it could arouse passion more readily than the printed word; it had the characteristics of an ideal propaganda instrument that could penetrate countries and homes without invitation. The Soviet Union attached special importance to the use of radio: at home to reach out to a large population with a high illiteracy rate spread over the world's largest country and abroad to further communist ideology and foreign policy. Lenin, whose writings were instrumental in the revolution, appreciated the potential of radio for political purposes, he described radio as "a newspaper without paper which could not be suppressed or confiscated," he was willing to use the gold reserves for research in radio. His explanation was pragmatic: "I think from the standpoint of propaganda and agitation, especially for those that are illiterate, and also for broadcasting lectures, it is absolutely necessary to carry out this plan."[4]

There was at the same time optimism in the mid 1920s that radio would emerge as a support structure for international harmony. The first issue of the BBC's *Radio Supplement* reflected this optimism:[5]

> We are now definitely entering the era of international broadcasting.... It is a truism to say that nothing is calculated to remove misunderstanding and to re-establish friendships more than a personal exchange of ideas. If this is true of individual relationships it is no less true of inter-national intercourse; and surely when the intercourse is of the informal and recreative character of broadcast programmes the effect -- first socially then politically -- is likely to be far reaching.

There was a lively debate about a universal "radio" language: English, French, German were all considered suitable; a strong case was also made for Chinese, some suggested the revival of Latin. The greatest enthusiasm, however, was for Esperanto-- an artificial language created in 1887 by the Polish occultist and philologist Ludwig Zamenhof. In 1926, 25 European radio stations offered Esperanto lessons.[6]

July 1, 1927: A Milestone Day in International Broadcasting

July 1, 1927 was an especially important day in the evolvement of international broadcasting. It was Canada's 60th birthday as a federal union and the Diamond Jubilee celebrations in Ottawa were broadcast around the world. One of the highlights of the programs from Parliament Hill was the inauguration of the great new carillon with Percival Pines playing "O Canada", "The Maple Leaf Forever" and "God Save the King." A network extending around the world involved the linking of more than a score of Canadian and US radio stations using the facilities of the telephone, telegraph and railway companies. The radio signals were directed towards Europe and Australia by radio beams from which concentration devices had been removed to scatter signals in all directions.[7] It was a primitive radio hook-up but it worked: Thousands of listeners from many countries reported that they had good reception. Canada was being heard globally. The publicity was good but the costs were high and the reception uncertain.

On the same day as the Canadian jubilee broadcast another radio transmission of far greater long-term value was taking place in Holland. The giant electrical engineering firm, Philips, inaugurated the world's first regular shortwave station -- PCJ -- in Eindhoven; the programs were directed to Dutch colonies in the East Indies. It was a low cost operation because shortwave did not require high power to reach the other side of the globe. Queen Wilhelmina made the first shortwave address by a monarch over PCJ and this station was the first to broadcast the chimes of London's Big Ben.

The highly successful Dutch transmission, starting in 1927, and earlier American experimental shortwave broadcasts from Pittsburg, stimulated similar activities in other countries. In 1928, France set up a shortwave transmitter at the Eiffel Tower for broadcasting to French forces in many parts of the world. In 1931, France inaugurated at Pontoise a shortwave transmission station, Radio Colonial, to coincide with the French Colonial Exhibition in Paris. By 1936, Radio Colonial was broadcasting in six languages.[8]

The Soviet Union built two powerful shortwave stations in 1929. The first station at Khabarovsk, on the Manchurian border, broadcast in Chinese, Korean and English. The second Soviet station went on the air six months later, in Moscow, with programs in German; later, French and English transmissions were added.

Germany began shortwave transmissions in 1929 from Zessen, near Berlin, to Germans abroad, many of them living in what had been German colonies until World War I. Italy inaugurated a shortwave station, outside Rome, in 1930, ostensibly to broadcast to Italian colonies. Belgium started its colonial service in 1934.

The Vatican's powerful shortwave station, inaugurated by the Pope on 12 February, 1931, sent out programs in 10 languages, including Latin; on special occasions between 30 and 40 languages were used. The Voice of Australia -- a shortwave initiative of the commercial company Amalgamated Wireless (Australia) which carried in its opening and closing announcements the distinctive laugh of the Kookaburra bird -- went on the air in 1931 and could be heard clearly in Europe for some years. Thailand initiated shortwave broadcasting in 1931, Japan and China in 1935. The first shortwave station in Africa went on air in 1929 in Kenya, then a British colony.

The United States, for its part, left shortwave broadcasting in the hands of the commercial companies such as Westinghouse, General Electric, the Columbia Broadcasting System (CBS) and the National Broadcasting Corporation (NBC). These broadcasters, financed through advertising, had no particular interest in foreign audiences, the American firms were more interested in the manufacture of shortwave transmitters for export purposes.

Of special interest to Canada, were the shortwave intentions of Britain. Canada was among the Empire countries pushing for a BBC overseas service. The BBC, however, was cautious; It was concerned about the reliability of shortwave and, more importantly, it wanted special financing for broadcasting to overseas audiences. These difficulties were overcome and in December 1932, the BBC's Empire Service went on the air in English only. This station attracted enormous attention when, one week after its opening, it broadcast a Christmas Day speech by King George V, the text of the address had been prepared by the renowned author, Rudyard Kipling. The *New York Times*, had a banner headline the next day: "Distant Lands Thrill to his God Bless You." Some 2000 newspapers around the world commented on this first of the Royal Christmas Day addresses that have been broadcast for over 60 years.[9]

Colonial interests, propaganda and counter-propaganda were the driving forces in the spread of international broadcasting. Britain, France, Belgium, Holland, Italy and post-colonial Germany all had special reasons to reach out to their nationals abroad. The most ideologically-oriented programming originated in the Soviet Union, which by 1930 was broadcasting in 50 languages and dialects carrying revolutionary slogans including such proclamations as "A great and holy hatred of capitalism is necessary!" Moscow broadcasts in English to Britain ended with the message: "Workers of the World, Unite." The Soviet broadcasts became less provocative as an increasing number of governments extended diplomatic recognition to Moscow.

The optimism for the peaceful use of radio did not last long. The rise to power of Adolf Hitler as chancellor of the National Socialist Government in January 1933 brought new and bewildering realities: Hitler and Joseph Goebbels, the Minister of Public Enlightments and Propaganda, transformed broadcasting into a "sharp and reliable weapon of government." In *Mein Kampf*, Hitler described radio as "a terrible weapon in the hands of those who know how to make use of it." Hitler wasted no time in putting it to work, in the drive for German expansionism.

In 1934, a massive radio campaign was launched in the German effort to attain sovereignty over the Saarland, a strategic industrial and natural resources region, administered by the League of Nations following World War I. A plebiscite was to be held in 1935 in which the people of the Saarland would vote on their future. To sway the population to rejoin Germany, Goebbel's launched a radio propaganda offensive. The Saarland was flooded with cheap radio sets. In January 1935, ninety-one percent of those who voted in the plebiscite opted for the return of the Saar to Germany. Nazi leaders now felt they could achieve almost anything through the planned use of radio propaganda.

The head of German Radio, Eugen Hadamowsky, considered it foolish to think of radio as a "neutral" medium; he focused his attention on propaganda:[10]

> A miraculous power -- the strongest weapon ever given to the spirit-- that opens hearts and does not stop at the borders of cities and does not turn back before closed doors; that jump rivers, mountains and seas; that is able to force people under the force of one powerful spirit.

Germany broadcast propaganda to harvest "loyalty" from people of German descent in foreign lands. The techniques of propaganda penetration were being refined and agents fanned out abroad to organize and promote listening to the programs from the "Fatherland." For the Berlin Olympics in 1936, Germany built the largest shortwave centre in the world at Zessen; there were broadcasts in 25 languages. After the Olympics, Germany embarked on a highly successful drive to get foreign stations to rebroadcast programs from Zessen. In 1938, as Germany became involved in one crisis after another and threatened war in its drive for territorial expansion, millions of listeners in North America heard rebroadcasts on their local radio of Hitler's speeches at carefully staged Nazi rallies. As one observer of that period put it: "The season of innocence was over."

Italy adopted some of the German innovations in the political use of radio, first focusing on cultural and information programs and then moving heavily into propaganda to promote fascism. Particular attention was given by Italy to transmissions in Arabic -- introduced in 1934 -- to the Middle East. These programs became violently anti-British, especially after Britain's criticism of the Italian invasion of Ethiopia. The Italian hate programs in Arabic were the catalyst for a British response: the introduction of foreign language broadcasting by the BBC; first Arabic in January 1938 and two months later Spanish and Portuguese broadcasting to Latin America. The Munich crisis of 1938 led to BBC broadcasts in German, French and Italian. When World War II broke out in September 1939, the BBC was broadcasting internationally in ten languages. Germany had the most advanced international broadcasting system with transmissions in 26 languages and would soon move into another 13 languages. Italy broadcast in 23 languages, France in 21 and the Soviet Union in 13.[11]

Radio truly went to war in September 1939. It was a potent and proven medium for psychological warfare. Countries already involved in international broadcasting added transmitters and moved into additional languages.

There were 25 countries in international broadcasting at the start of World War II; when the war ended there were 50; including the Voice of America and the Canadian Broadcasting Corporation. The return to peace did not diminish the interest in international broadcasting: newly independent countries wanted their voices to be heard on the international airwaves. The Cold War brought about a return to psychological warfare globally.

The dramatic increase in the number of countries with shortwave facilities resulted in a crowding of the airwaves, where the signals of one country interfere with the signals of another.

In this fiercely competitive situation, countries try to outshout each other through the use of more powerful transmitters. Added to this is the problem of jamming, a form of electronic censorship, widely used during the Cold War to keep out unwanted signals. Furthermore, shortwave signals can be distorted or wiped out by solar storms and other atmospheric disturbances. Despite all these problems, shortwave is largely a reliable medium.

The politics of international broadcasting is complex and unpredictable. There are about 150 countries plus other interested parties -- including the Vatican, Radio Luxembourg, Radio Monte Carlo, All Asia Service, and religious organizations -- utilizing the shortwave frequencies and this requires rationing. Nevertheless, some countries do not respect their frequency allotments.

International competition for frequencies extends also to audiences. A country making a decision on languages of broadcast and target areas has in effect committed itself to projecting its image and viewpoints in areas of special interest. The frequencies can be envisaged as the radio highways for reaching the intended targets and one of the principal measures of success is the size of the audience. The reality is that there is a highly competitive shortwave broadcasting environment which is intimately tied to national interests. Shortwave broadcasters do not usually speak globally, rather they seek out specific audiences to discuss specific issues. The transmission in different languages may project different interpretations and viewpoints on the same issues.

There is, then, a hidden side to international broadcasting; especially in war and periods of international tension when the most sophisticated techniques of propaganda are used to disarm the suspicions of the audience. The link between propaganda and radio goes back to the earliest transmissions.

CHAPTER III

THE CANADIAN BROADCASTING ENVIRONMENT

The link between national and international broadcasting in Canada was symbolically displayed in the inaugural overseas broadcast which was prepared and produced by the CBC national service and transmitted to Europe by shortwave from Sackville, N.B.

Canadians across the country listened in as the International Service of the Canadian Broadcasting Corporation formally launched its overseas transmissions on February 25, 1945. The hour long program that Sunday afternoon had all the trimmings to give it an aura of importance; it went to its intended primary target, Canadian forces serving in Europe, and was also broadcast by the British Broadcasting Corporation and the Allied Expeditionary Forces Program. At home, the Trans-Canada Network of the CBC preempting a scheduled concert by the New York Philharmonic.

The Prime Minister, W.L. Mackenzie King, was the first speaker; he was on-air for three minutes in English from Ottawa. He was followed for two minutes in French by the Minister of Justice (and future Prime Minister) Louis St. Laurent. There was a brief message from London, England by Howard Chase, Chairman of the Board of Governors of the CBC.

Prime Minister King directed his words primarily to the men and women of the armed forces serving abroad. "We are hoping and praying," said King, "for a speedy end to the horrors and sacrifices of war, and above all, for your early and triumphant return." He spoke of the "historic importance" of the establishment of the shortwave service.

> It will serve both a national and international purpose. It will bring the voice of Canada to her own sons and daughters in other lands. It will also bring Canada into closer contact with other countries. In the better world for which you are fighting, Canada will have a large part to play in furthering between nations, the mutual understanding and good will on which the permanence of peace depends.
>
> Through its many-sided contributions in the fight for freedom, Canada has won a place of its own in the world. You, above all others, have shown the world how men of differing backgrounds, origins and

> creeds, can fight side by side in mutual tolerance and mutual respect, in defence of a common nationality.
>
> Into the historic partnership of our two races, we in Canada have admitted thousands who were born of other racial stocks and who speak other tongues. They, one and all, have found in Canada a homeland where nationality means equality and freedom, not domination and slavery. Without the ideal of equality among men, without the vision of human brotherhood, the Canadian nation could never have come into being.
>
> Only by the extension of the ideals of mutual tolerance, of racial cooperation, and of equality among men can nationality serve humanity, can mankind hope to substitute cooperation for conflict in the relations between the nations of the world. International radio broadcasting is a powerful means of helping to extend these ideals throughout the world.
>
> Tonight Canada enters the world radio arena. As we undertake this new service, let us resolve that, in peace as in war, we will be true to the ideals you are so valiantly upholding, ideals which have made our country a nation. The unity of Canada belongs not only to Canada, it belongs to mankind. If we are true to ourselves, Canadian unity may well serve as a model for the wider unity of humanity. In the unity of mankind lies the one sure foundation of enduring peace.[1]

The formal ceremonies took about seven minutes. The rest of the hour long variety program, produced by J. Frank Willis, brought together "the best Canadian talent" from all parts of the country. The first program pickup was from Toronto; it featured the CBC Singers and concert orchestra under the joint direction of Percy Faith and Samuel Horsenhoren. Other contributions came from Vancouver, Winnipeg, Montreal and Charlottetown. Canada's young comedian, Alan Young, contributed to the program from New York.

The official opening program reflected the development of Canadian broadcasting in entertainment and information in the four-and-a-half years since the start of the war. Canadian troops overseas could now regularly receive a 'taste of home' through a service that would also foster closer communication between Canada and other countries of the British Empire, and the rest of the world.

The theme of global understanding, was brought out strongly in Prime Minister King's remarks was also taken up by the Director General of Programs for the CBC, Ernest Bushnell, who said at the conclusion program:

> In the palmy days of Greek civilization it was considered that the size of a state should be so limited that the whole body of citizens assembled could hear the voice of a single herald. That limited audience has been made a world audience by radio.
>
> We can learn to know one another. The songs, the poetry, the music, the drama, the entertainment, and the soul of peoples, can become a common possession. With knowledge comes understanding, and with understanding peace.[2]

There was much to celebrate that last Sunday in February 1945 when the International Service began its formal operations. The Canadian signal was being received loud and clear; better than the shortwave transmissions from the Voice of America. Although beamed to Europe, the signal was also received strongly in other parts of the world. Canada was making her mark in international broadcasting.

The festive air hid, but could not obliterate, the realities of the situation. Canada was scandalously late in entering the international broadcasting arena; the war in Europe would end three months later, all other countries with any significant interest in broadcasting were already crowding the shortwave spectrum, some encroaching on frequencies reserved for Canada. Mr. King's government had been under pressure for some years from the CBC, from Parliament, from the press, from Britain (the British Broadcasting Corporation, the British Government and Prime Minister Winston Churchill personally) to set up a powerful shortwave transmitting service. For three years the appeals fell on deaf ears, Ottawa had its own priorities and concerns.

There were concerns about negative reaction in the United States, especially before Washington became directly involved in the war. In fact, President Roosevelt -- worried about the influential American isolationist movement -- urged Prime Minister King to keep Canada out of propaganda broadcasting to the US. There were two other considerations -- of lesser importance -- for not rushing into shortwave broadcasting: one was the Canadian preoccupation with autonomy and thus holding its distance from broadcast interests sponsored by Britain; the other, was linked to Canadian unity: it was perceived as problematic for external broadcasting to project a national image that would satisfy both French and English Canadians.

The hesitation to enter the shortwave dialogue comes as a surprise; the country's involvement in international radio transmissions goes back to Morse code, the days of dots and dashes. Guglielmo Marconi was in St. John's, Newfoundland, at a spot now called Signal Hill, on December 12, 1901, when he used kites to lift an aerial wire to great heights and receive a clear Morse code signal -- three dots standing for the letter 'S' -- broadcast from a radio transmitter at Poldhu, Cornwall, on the English coast. This first radio message across the Atlantic created excitement, it illustrated experimentally the potential reach of radio. The Ottawa government's enthusiasm for radio was reflected in its investment of $80,000 in 1902 to build a wireless receiving station for Marconi at Glace Bay, Nova Scotia.

The Canadian interest in electronic communications is reflected everywhere in our history. In the 1840's, some 20 years before the establishment of the federal union, Canada became a proving ground for long distance telegraph invented by Samuel Morse in the United States in 1844. In the 1870's, the telephone, which was invented by Alexander Graham Bell at Brantford, Ontario, was quickly adopted in Canada. By the end of the 19th century there was a pressing need for a reliable communication system to link a huge country that had already developed a transcontinental railway system. In the 20th century, "the aeroplane in the physical sphere, and radio and television in the articulate one, are the technological developments that can finally make sense of the country and cross the immense gaps in communication with it."[4]

Canada provides an especially complex setting for the flow of mass communications. Print does not travel well -- at least it did not until communications satellites could be used for facsimile transmissions -- and in Canada newspapers have for this reason, as well as for political, social and economic reasons, developed a local orientation. Electronic communications, with messages, ideas, entertainment programs going piggyback on radio waves created opportunities to develop a mass communications system that could potentially conquer space and distance and domesticate centrifugal pulls by placing them in a national context. Radio was perceived as a key to national understanding.

Canada has to 'think big' when it comes to communications because the problems are formidable. It is a huge country (the second largest in the world), with six time zones and a difficult terrain. Most of the population lives in a narrow ribbon of land parallel to the American border and within easy access of the American communications industry which is the most vigorous that has ever inundated man. Furthermore, Canada, founded by the descendants of the British and French colonizers, has two major languages and cultures that remain preeminent in a multicultural setting. These challenges have provided the dynamics for the evolvement of one of the most advanced communications systems anywhere.

The oldest continuing radio broadcaster in the world is CFCF in Montreal which first went on the air in 1918 as an experimental station, WXA. This station also became the world' first long distance broadcaster when on May 21, 1920 it transmitted a special program from Montreal to the Ottawa meeting of the Royal Society of Canada at the Chateau Laurier Hotel, a distance of about 200 kilometres. Early in 1923, Canadian National Railways -- a crown agency -- pioneered radio on trains, providing an element of public ownership which was one of the models for setting up the BBC's. Later in the century, Canada built the first trans-continental microwave systems, became a pioneer in communications satellites and was the first country to integrate satellites into its domestic television network. It is no accident that Canada produced such noted communications theorists as Harold Innis, Marshall McLuhan and Northrop Fry; their work is grounded in the Canadian communications experience. Despite these and numerous other accomplishments, the history of radio and television has been beset with difficulties.

Commercial radio in Canada was introduced in 1922 and there was a rapid proliferation of stations, all of them owned by vested interests: electronic manufacturers interested in selling radios, department stores interested in advertising; newspaper interested in expanding and protecting their communications holdings; universities interested in a new medium for education, and church institutions promoting their religion beliefs. Owning a radio station was an inexpensive investment for the future: the low powered transmitters were cheap, the licence fee was $50 for a commercial broadcaster.

The growth pattern of radio stations was chaotic with broadcasters generally interested in large audiences in the cities; rural residence did not have much radio. As Al Shea noted in *Broadcasting the Canadian Way*, "Canadians living in smaller communities and rural areas remote from the main centres of the population were beyond the reach of the magic waves" ... at least Canada's magic waves. The American factor which has been a persistent issue in broadcasting over the past 70 years, was already at play; US border stations could be readily picked up. In the cities, several stations would compete over the same frequencies creating poor reception; furthermore, more powerful US border stations were often drowning out the Canadian signals. At night, there was interference from Spanish language stations in Mexico transmitting on frequencies reserved for Canada.

French-speaking Canadians fared especially poorly; there was no French station outside Quebec Province. And even in Quebec Province, where the commercial sector was then dominated by the English-speaking population, there was only one powerful French-language station: CKAC, owned by *La Presse*. Little wonder that radio was far more popular in Ontario where in 1929 there were three radio sets for everyone in Quebec.

The commercial stations sometimes affiliated with US stations, transmitted American programming, including news. This was true even for French stations. On the whole, Canadian programming, when it could be heard, was not of great interest, also it was socially divisive and problematic. Religious broadcasting was disseminating prejudices. There was an incredible amount of advertising, so much so, that politicians were concerned that radio was becoming an atmospheric billboard. It was deemed acceptable that the principal household spenders -- women -- could be mercilessly bombarded with advertising during the daytime, but after 6:00 p.m. when the men were home from work, there were controls on advertising. There was much more political favouritism in granting licences. Radio was operating in a regulatory vacuum and individual initiatives and commercial and politically-motivated interests were shaping the broadcast system.

A bright spot in this bleak picture was the radio network operated by the Canadian National Railways which, through a series of strategically located stations and telephonelinks, was able to provide a limited radio service for train travellers, and for Canadians generally, across the continent. There was a national thrust to the CNR network: it transmitted school broadcasts, radio drama dealing with Canadian history, live classical music programming that included the Toronto Symphony Orchestra and the Hart House Quartet. Sir Henry Thornton, the first CNR president, saw railways as a communication industry that carried goods and people, transmitted messages by telephone and telegraph, and carried ideas and ideals by radio. CNR made a lasting contribution; its facilities provided the nucleus for what was to become public broadcasting in Canada: first the Canadian Radio Broadcasting Commission and later, the Canadian Broadcasting Corporation.

The 1930s: Policy and Regulation

Meaningful regulation of broadcasting in Canada began in 1932 when Parliament passed the first Broadcasting Act. This legislation came three years after the 1929 Report of the Royal Commission on Radio Broadcasting -- headed by Sir John Aird. The impact of this Report is felt to this day; it saw broadcasting as a support structure for building a more meaningful nation. "In a country of the vast geographical dimensions of Canada,'' said the Aird Commission, ''broadcasting will undoubtedly become a force in fostering national spirit and interpreting national consciousness.'' The notion of Canadian presence in broadcasting, was very much in the Commission's mind:

> At present, the majority of programmes heard are from sources outside Canada. It has been emphasized to us that the continued reception of these has a tendency to mold the minds of young people in the homes to ideals and opinions that are not Canadian.

The Aird Commission's recommendations called for setting up of a publicly-owned and operated broadcasting system ''behind which is the national power and prestige of the whole public of the Dominion of Canada.''

The formative years of Canadian radio in the 1920s had been squandered and there was no quick way to move from privately-owned radio to publicly-owned broadcasting. The way the Aird Commission saw it, the private stations would provide a provisional service in the transition stage. Meanwhile, Canada would build a network of superstations -- one in the Maritime Provinces and one in each of the other provinces to provide radio reception across the country.

The major guiding principle in the Aird Report was that Canadian radio listeners wanted Canadian broadcasting. To bring this about, including the building of the superstations, required the spending of large amounts of money; money that was not available in the wake of the Wall Street crash and the Great Depression that followed. Furthermore, the general elections of 1930 brought in a new government. Also, the recommendation for publicly financed broadcasting created controversy because of the strong belief in free enterprise. There was also sensitivity about the Commission's criticisms of the influence of American radio in Canada.

The critically important question of jurisdiction over broadcasting, federal versus provincial, still had to be resolved. The main Canadian constitutional document at the time, the British North America Act of 1867, had been drafted some 50 years before broadcasting became a reality and both the federal and provincial governments -- especially Quebec -- were pressing their jurisdiction rights in this area. It was not until1932 that the Judicial Committee of the Privy Council in Britain, then the highest court of appeal for Canada, ruled in the 'Radio Case' that the federal government in Ottawa had jurisdiction over broadcasting.[6] This ruling has been extended over the years to include television, satellites and Cable TV as new technologies came along. (Nevertheless, the question of jurisdiction in communications remains contentious in the politics of Canadian federalism.)

Acting in the wake of the 'Radio Case' and some three years after the tabling of the Aird Report, Parliament passed the first *Canadian Radio Broadcasting Act*, creating the Canadian Radio Broadcasting Commission, which became the public broadcast network as well as the regulator of broadcasting. The CRBC was modest in its initiatives, it took over the CNR radio facilities and expanded the service. The Commission, however, was not adequately funded and could not cope with administrative and political problems. The private radio sector, for its part, continued to expand.

The big breakthrough for public sector broadcasting came in 1936 when Parliament, recognizing the shortcomings of the Canadian Radio Broadcasting Commission, passed the second *Broadcasting Act*, creating the Canadian Broadcasting Corporation.

CHAPTER IV

THE CANADIAN BROADCASTING CORPORATION

The establishment of the Canadian Broadcasting Corporation in 1936 provided the appropriate conditions to introduce shortwave broadcasting. The public broadcaster had national and international ambitions. Powerful transmitters -- medium wave and short wave -- were seen as complementing each other to stimulate radio to new heights.

The Broadcasting Act establishing the CBC took effect November 2, 1936. The first Board of Governors which had been appointed two months earlier, had support from the public and press. It was a remarkably strong Board and included Alan B. Plaunt, the former President of the Radio League of Canada which played a key lobbying role in steering Canada into public broadcasting. The chairman of the Board was Leonard Brockington, legal counsel for the Northwest Grain Dealers Association in Winnipeg. Brockington was known as a person of great culture, penetrating vision and a marvellous sense of humour, Canada's best after dinner speaker.[1]

On November 4, two days after the formal establishment of the CBC, Brockington gave a radio address in which he outlined the Corporation's main objectives: to make it possible for every Canadian to hear the CBC's programs and to provide the best programs from all available sources. These were mammoth challenges. Under the best of circumstances, less than half the Canadian population -- mostly in large cities -- could receive CBC radio. The first priority for the CBC was new high-powered regional transmitters. Two 50,000 watt transmitters went up (one in Montreal, one in Toronto), increasing national coverage from 49 to 76 percent of the population. A new transmitter was opened at Vancouver. The basic national network expanded to 34 stations and another 26 privately-owned stations also transmitted CBC programming. The network was on the air for 12 hours a day by the end of 1937. Powerful stations were opened at Sackville, New Brunswick and Watrous, Saskatchewan in May 1939. In a period of two-and-a-half years, the CBC had built a powerful network of stations, as had been recommended by the Aird Royal Commission 10 years earlier. When King George and Queen Elizabeth were in Canada for the 1939 Royal Tour, the CBC could reach nearly 90 percent of the Canadian population.

The CBC Board -- all of whose members were unpaid -- took control and of its own affairs and also became the licensing and supervisory body for private broadcasting, a practice which continued for 22 years until it was changed by the Diefenbaker government in 1958. Major challenges facing the CBC included entrenched political and economic interferences. Broadcasts would no longer be sponsored by vested interest. The interests of free speech were to be safeguarded through equitable access to the airwaves for different viewpoints.

Standing in the way of some of the plans of the CBC Board was C.D. Howe, a rising powerhouse in the King cabinet. As minister responsible for broadcasting, Howe steered through parliament the 1936 Broadcasting Act, establishing the CBC. He was the most successful businessman-politician Canada ever had. He was highly efficient, blunt and domineering. His accomplishments in wartime industrialization and postwar reconstruction are monuments to his achievements as are the establishment of Trans-Canada Airlines (now Air Canada) and the building of the Trans-Canada gas pipeline. (He so outraged Canadians in his handling of the pipeline that it undermined the government's position and contributed to the Liberal Government defeat in 1957 as well as the loss of his own seat in the Port Arthur riding.)

Howe's relationship with the CBC generally, and Brockington specifically, soured even before the corporation was formally established.[2] Brockington wanted Major Gladstone Murray as the first general manager. Murray, a Canadian, was the director of public relations at the British Broadcasting Corporation; his insights into radio were well known: in 1932 he had given impressive evidence in Ottawa before the Parliamentary Committee on radio and in 1933 Prime Minister Bennett, sensing that radio was becoming a political minefield, arranged for Murray to become his personal advisor for a few months. At first, Howe favoured the Murray appointment but later shifted his support to Reginald Brophy, manager of station relations at NBC in New York. (Brophy had previously managed the Montreal station CFCF). Both were first rate administrators but Murray was seen as closer to public broadcasting and the British approach while Brophy had the support of the private broadcasting sector which was pushing the American approach. Howe let it be known that Prime Minister King had some concerns about Murray but the reality was that Howe was being successfully lobbied by the private broadcast industry. Rumours were spread about Murray's spendthrift ways and drinking, but the King cabinet decided to back Murray whom the Prime Minister had considered the best qualified in the first place.

Brockington saw the CBC in a far more powerful role than Howe, who as Minister of Transport was the minister through whom the Board reported to Parliament. Howe advised the CBC to concentrate on program development; he wanted the building of broadcast transmitters left to private investment and was not forthcoming with the necessary funding. Brockington was able to reach

King -- directly and through intermediaries -- and have Cabinet back the CBC Board to the embarrassment of Howe. On one occasion, Brockington insisted on Howe's coming before the Board which then threatened to resign on the spot and go public if Howe persisted in his position. Howe gave in, but never forgave the CBC. The Brockington-Howe dispute was a clash of two remarkable people over the principle of government control of broadcasting. Howe never seemed to fully appreciate the autonomy interest of the broadcast sector.

CBC program policy called for the Canadianization of content by producing first rate programs that would attract listeners. The emphasis was on a competitive "home grown" product to serve the special interests of Canadian listeners. The CBC also wanted to bring its listeners "the best available" foreign programming, which would come to Canada as part of a two-way exchange. Canada would thus be a sender and receiver of programming. This exchange required a shortwave station for Canadian programs to go out to the world. International broadcasting via shortwave was envisaged as a core dimension of CBC operations; it would be part of the solution to the programming problem.

In early 1930s, especially after the British Broadcasting Corporation established the Empire Scrvice, Canada sought to diversify the importation of programming. A shortwave receiving station was built on Richmond Road at Britannia Heights, near Ottawa in 1933. The receiving station represented the ultimate in technical design and, as a report at the time noted, "there was no way we can better the reception at this end." The main purpose of the station was the reception of the BBC Empire Service programs for rebroadcasting.

The appetite for BBC programs would grow continuously in the next few years. On July 25, 1939, six weeks before the outbreak of World War II, Brockington and Murray visited London where they negotiated with the Director General of the Empire Service additional time for BBC transmissions to be rebroadcast by the CBC. The recorded shows that Canada, or at least CBC officials, seemed to be especially fond of military band music. (References to band music appeared in numerous documents and there were occasions when the BBC was not happy with the Canadian request. Because of time zone differences, the BBC transmitted its programs to Canada around 4:00 a.m. London time which meant that the bands had to be kept up all night to perform with enthusiasm at what was surely an impossible hour.) Arrangements were also made for various types of other programs, including feature programs, plays and music. The lineup for Wednesday night music offered recitals by Segovia, Myra Hess, Schnabel, Arthur Rubinstein, Smeterlin, Szigeti, Casado, and Magda Tagliafero, among other world renowned artists. In fact, the BBC was offering so many attractive programs that the CBC had to make very difficult choices. The most lasting of the programs from London was the BBC news which has been rebroadcast in Canada for 60 years.

In the 1930s, a period of major growth of shortwave transmissions globally, Canada took only modest steps which, at best, indicated a future interest. Ottawa participated in the International Telecommunications Conference at Madrid in 1932 which provided allocations of shortwave frequencies for distress signals, commercial point-to-point telegraph and voice broadcasting between various countries. As a result of the Madrid meeting, the Berne Bureau was established to register the assigned radio frequencies. Specific wavelengths were allocated to Ottawa for use at such time as Canada entered the field.

In 1934, a preliminary engineering study showed that the Maritime Provinces would be the best location for Canadian shortwave transmitters beaming to Europe, Africa and South America. Transmitter location is especially important in Canada because the North geomagnetic Pole creates a "disturbed area" in which radio waves behave in an erratic manner.[3]

Six months, after the establishment of the CBC, the Board of Governors discussed shortwave broadcasting at its fourth meeting, held in Regina, on May 15, 1937. It found that Canada was becoming a disadvantaged country in international broadcasting.[4] There were seven shortwave transmitters with a combined power of only seven kilowatts. These "kiddie" transmitters were largely experimental; their power was too low for any practical value. The stage was being set to approach the Government for funding to build a powerful shortwave station.

Donald Manson, the Chief Executive Assistant of the CBC, prepared a report which called for Canada to build at least one powerful shortwave station of 50 Kilowatts, to make itself adequately known in other countries. He stressed the urgency of the project:[5]

> Canada should get on the air with a powerful station at an early date otherwise there will be no frequencies available as they are being rapidly preempted by the different countries who realize the advantages of shortwave broadcasting.

The station could be built for about $300,000.

A week later, the Board of Governors held its fifth meeting in Quebec City (August 5-7) and gave its unanimous approval to approach the government.[6] Mr. Brockington went to see Prime Minister King at "Kingsmere" in

September and was encouraged by the response. On October 26, 1937, Mr. Brockington sent the Prime Minister a five-page letter in which he noted that a shortwave station was "a matter in which the state has a particular interest."[7]

Brockington, building on the Manson Report, presented Prime Minister King with foreign policy as well as domestic reasons for building the shortwave station: national prestige, international goodwill, direct communications with European countries, promotion of Canadian culture, national advertising and protecting national radio rights.[8] He told the Prime Minister that Canada, with its seven tiny transmitters, fared poorly in the international shortwave picture, behind Cuba, Bolivia and Colombia.

Brockington's comments about "advertising Canada" covered good sound products and also immigration. While Canada was not encouraging immigration at the time,Brockington thought that in the future Ottawa may be in a position to offer a home and domestic and political security to a number of distressed and harassed people.

Brockington pointed out that shortwave transmitter could be used at night -- when it was early morning in Europe -- to broadcast French programs from Quebec to French speaking Canadians in the contributing "to a better understanding of the two mother races." He also sought to convince the Prime Minister that a shortwave station would lead to a better broadcasting system because Canada, by supplying outstanding programming to other countries, would be in a position to receive the best programming from foreign stations for rebroadcasting in Canada. There was a strong demand for programs from Canada. "The policy of receiving programming cannot be made really effective until we are in a position to reciprocate."[9]

The CBC Board of Governors again discussed the proposed shortwave station in March 1938 and at its 1938 meetings in December. There was support in Parliament where the House of Commons Standing Committee on Radio Broadcasting in its 1938 report urged the building of a powerful station, financed as national project, operated and controlled by the CBC. The Parliamentary Committee noted that Canada was the only major trading nation without shortwave facilities. In 1939, the House of Commons Committee on Radio Broadcasting reiterated its position; it warned that "any further delay" in building the station "may result in Canada losing altogether the short wave channels registered in her name, and as a consequence being shut out of the field entirely." Members from all parties were supportive.

In February 1939, Ernest Bushnell, the General Supervisor of CBC Programs, prepared a memorandum calling for another very determined effort to build a Canadian shortwave station.[10] Bushnell had just returned from

Europe and spoke of the excellent Empire and Foreign Shortwave Service of the BBC. Although the BBC was already putting a lot of its financial resources into the development of television, the shortwave service was constantly being expanded and improved.

Bushnell was enormously impressed by the German use of shortwave. There were seven 40 KW transmitters "disseminating programs of propaganda 24 hours a day." In a six-year period Germany had moved from two hours of shortwave broadcasting to 40 hours a day. Some 60,000 copies of the German shortwave schedule were being distributed around the world. "Next to news and information (of the propaganda type)." Bushnell said, "the Berlin programs offered a cross section of all Germany stands for." The bulk of the programs contained music, ranging from classical, the Bayreuth festivals, Philharmonic concerts, "to the folk songs which are especially liked everywhere."

Bushnell said that Germany offered "as many programs as we could take ... all in English only and containing no word of propaganda." He regretted that Canada had no shortwave stations and therefore could not enter such an exchange.

The memorandum reflects a naive reading by Bushnell of Germany's use of shortwave to promote her foreign policy interests. Bushnell quoted from letters the Germans had received from overseas listeners (e.g., New Zealand) and related in all sincerity an anti-Jewish comment he heard from his German hosts.

One of the issues that was surely on Bushnell's mind was that Canada could be left out from international broadcasting -- As Manson had warned two years earlier -- if it did not make use of the shortwave frequencies that had been reserved with the Union Internationale de Radiodiffusion at Berne. Other countries had already taken over two or three of those frequencies and Germany was the most recent trespasser on Canadian frequencies, taking over one of them at about the same time that Mr. Bushnell was being given his tour of the German radio facilities.

In Italy, Bushnell was again overwhelmed: Five new transmitters of 50kw each and "significant new studios" were being built at Rome which was replacing Turin as the centre of the Italian system. Bushnell also visited shortwave station in France and Belgium. While in Paris, he met several times with the Canadian diplomat, Jean Désy, who was interested in the use of radio in foreign policy. (Twelve years later, Désy would head Canada's International Service.)

Bushnell's main argument for proceeding with the building of shortwave station "at once" was tied to the forthcoming visit to Canada by King George

VI and Queen Elizabeth. Lester Pearson, who was stationed at Canada House in London had arranged a meeting between Bushnell and Captain Lascelles of the Royal Secretariat. Bushnell had been told "in confidence" that the King would be speaking on at least four occasions during the Royal visit. One of the primary purpose of the visit was to acquaint the people of Great Britain with the feelings of the Canadian people towards their Majesties; it was felt that radio transmissions Canada would be most helpful, almost indispensable. The Director General of the BBC, Mr. Ogilvie, took up this matter by letter with the Governor General in Ottawa, Lord Tweedsmuir, and also with the Canadian High Commissioner in London, Vincent Massey.

Bushnell's excitement about the use of shortwave radio for the Royal visit is reflected in a report to Gladstone Murray.[11]

> I do not believe any greater compliment could be paid to their Majesties than that their voices should be the first to be heard over this new station which would undoubtedly have worldwide coverage. I believe we cannot afford to miss such a glorious opportunity.

CHAPTER V

THE BRITISH INTEREST

The Royal Tour in 1939 was a wonderful story for international broadcasting.

The King and Queen were two days late, but it was not their fault. The Canadian Pacific liner, The Empress of Australia, bringing the royal couple for their appointment to meet the Canadian people at Wolfe's Cove had a miserable journey across the Atlantic; icebergs, miles of floating pack ice and fog repeatedly brought the liner to a halt and at one time it was three and a half days behind schedule. At 1:00 a.m. on May 15, 1939 -- the day King George VI and Queen Elizabeth were to arrive in Quebec City -- their liner was off Cape Race, Newfoundland about 835 miles away. After nudging cautiously in the Gulf of St. Lawrence through pack ice as far as the eyes could see, the Empress of Australia sailed at full speed along the St. Lawrence River for that eagerly awaited event, the first ever visit to North America by a reigning British Monarch.

Prime Minister King, who had suggested the tour at the Coronation of King George VI in 1937, was anxious about the arrival. Nothing had been left to chance; the tour was planned to the last detail, now changes would have to be made in the itinerary. The Prime Minister would undoubtedly be blamed -- the political fallout would be on his shoulders -- when the historic city of Kingston would only have a quick royal drive through rather than an extensive visit, as previously planned. In Brockville and Cornwall, on the way to Kingston, the royal train would merely slow down.

The Canadian invitation to George VI was aimed to project the image of this shy and slight man who carried such a heavy title: His Most Excellent Majesty George VI, by the Grace of God, of Great Britain, Ireland and of the British Dominions beyond the Seas, King, Defender of the Faith, Emperor of India. The young King had been brought up in the shadow of his more outgoing brother, the uncrowned Edward VIII, who as Prince of Wales had made a profound impression in Canada and the United States. But Edward VIII did not live up to his title and his abdication, amid scandal at the court, unexpectedly catapulted George VI onto the throne. The royal tour of Canada would be a milestone in the restoration of the prestige of the tarnished Crown.

In the summer of 1938, when Prime Minister King was advised that the Monarch would be coming to Canada, he passed on the word to President Roosevelt. The American leader sent a letter to King George extending his own invitation: "It would be an excellent thing for Anglo-American relations if you could visit the United States." And if the royal couple decided to bring their children -- Elizabeth and Margaret -- he would try to have his grandchildren available to play with them. Mr. Roosevelt saw the American side trip -- three or four days of very simple country life and "no formal entertainment" -- as giving the King and Queen "an opportunity to get a bit of rest and relaxation."

They came without their children for a hectic tour, the likes of which Canada had never seen before and would never see again. As *Macleans* magazine pointed out at the time: "Canadians can't get enough of it ... they opened their hearts to the young and noble King and Queen."

Two Canadian destroyers -- Sheena and Saguenay -- escorted the royal liner; eight Royal Canadian Air Force planes guarded the skies above. On the night of May 17, the King's ship dropped anchor off the island of Orleans with villagers on the island shouting "Vive Le Roi." The eventful trip across the Atlantic had come to an end and the taxing 15,000 miles journey across the continent was about to begin.

When the King and Queen stepped ashore at Wolfe's cove on May 18, Prime Minister King and Premier Maurice Duplessis -- who never cared much for each other -- were thrown together in what had the appearances of a love feast. As the *Globe and Mail* put it in a banner headline: SMILING RULERS TAKE QUEBEC BY STORM: CANADIAN CONQUEST BEGINS IN EARNEST. It was the same everywhere the monarch went. When the King stepped out on the balcony of the royal suite at the Windsor Hotel in Montreal, 100,000 people in floodlit Dominion Square went "wild with joy." More than 2,000,000 joined the ovation in Montreal.

There were three days of celebration in Ottawa. As the newspapers put it: "Canada's King Invokes Peace on Earth." King George assumed the throne of Canada and gave royal assent to eight acts of Parliament in a formal ceremony in the Senate Chamber. The new US envoy, Daniel C. Roper, presented his credentials to the King of Canada. There was a garden party to celebrate the King's birthday. It was also a memorable day for Mrs. Vincent Paquette; she was in the crowd waving at the royal couple when she went into labour. Mrs. Paquette gave birth in a nearby boathouse on the banks of the Rideau Canal.

Toronto did not want to be outdone. The local papers boasted that their city was the heart of their Majesties empire for a day. The crowds -- "a canyon of devotion" -- were everywhere. The Dionne quintuplets, who would be five in another two weeks, were brought to Toronto by special train for a meeting with the King and Queen. There was the King's Plate at Woodbine race track which Archworth won in majestic style by 10 lengths; its owner, George McCullagh, received 50 golden guineas as a personal gift from the King.

The monarch could do no wrong. When the rains stopped and the sun shone in Toronto, it was the King who brought good weather. In Winnipeg, the royal couple endeared themselves to huge crowds, including 100,000 Americans who had come for this occasion, when at the insistence of the Queen, the top of the car was opened up in a downpour and the King and Queen sat in the rear under an umbrella. In Regina, the Monarch was credited with bringing royal rain to end the drought. In Melville, Saskatchewan -- a town of 3,000 -- some 50,000 came from scattered regions to cheer the royal couple, most of them "new Canadians of Ukrainian, German, Scandinavian and Polish backgrounds."

The fabulous tour was, at times, stifling in its formality. The royal couple had the train stopped from time to time for a brisk walk; they needed to get away from it all. As for the Queen, on at least one occasion she sprinted and then jogged for a stretch. These hidden moments were obviously important.

In Victoria, the King presented his colours to the naval forces, as thousands cheered. The Canadian journey was now half over. On the return trip, there was a 24 hour stop at Jasper Park Lodge, where, as the newspapers so quaintly put it, the royal couple did their own housekeeping without servants. In Reditt, Ontario -- a CNR service pointwith a population of 300 -- an additional 12,000 crowded the streets. In Sudbury, the King put on miner's clothes to go ½ mile underground. Then it was on to Niagara Falls where the train went across the suspension bridge to the US side of the border.

Prime Minister King accompanied King George to Washington, to the New York World's Fair and the informal stay at Hyde Park, the Roosevelt's ancestral home. London had thought to have its Ambassador accompany the monarch on the US journey but Mr. King wanted an uninterrupted Canadian dimension to the trip. When Prime Minister King wrote to Roosevelt asking if he would be welcomed in Washington, Roosevelt telephoned him to say he took it for granted that the Canadian Prime Minister was coming. Despite sweltering weather, the American side trip, like the tour of Canada, was spectacularly successful. It was more informal -- the King ate hot dogs at one party -- and US Congressmen taught Canadians a lesson "when they clapped with friendliness and enthusiasm in the Rotunda of the Capitol." The legislative receptions in Canada, *Macleans* pointed out, "were made unnecessarily awkward and tense by the officially imposed injunction to silence which most people (unfortunately) observed far too literally." The monarch may well have been referring to this when he told Mackenzie King that the Canadian Parliament was "extraordinarily well-behaved."

The US trip helped to foster a three way friendship between George VI, Roosevelt and Mackenzie King. Much of the serious talk was about the Nazi threat to world peaceand Roosevelt reassured George VI; "If London is bombed US would come in." Mackenzie King and Roosevelt already had a close working relationship and as Roosevelt once told the Canadian Prime Minister, they understood each other perfectly.

The royal tour ended in Halifax from where George VI and Queen Elizabeth sailed on the Empress of Canada. Some eight million Canadians had seen the monarchs, one million Americans visited Canada for the occasion.

There was much to tell Britain, the Empire and the world about the triumphant royal visit. It was with this in mind that on November 22, 1938 -- some six months before the tour -- that the Director General of the British Broadcasting Corporation, Mr. Ogilvie, had sent a 'Dear Vincent' letter to the Canadian High Commissioner in London, Vincent Massey, telling him that a shortwave broadcasting station in Canada was important from both the broadcasting and imperial points of view.

One of the broadcast highlights of the tour was George VI's Empire day speech from Winnipeg on Victoria Day. The Monarch had a speech defect -- he stuttered -- and the Empire Address of 800 words was the longest he had ever broadcast. He had difficulty with only two words "society" and "inspiration." George VI was in unusually good voice, as he spoke slowly into a gold-plated microphone, in his address to British subjects around the globe.

The CBC did not get its shortwave station for the royal tour and had to make arrangements with commercial US broadcasters to relay the King's speech. There were many missed opportunities in promoting Canada and the King to global audiences. The 1939 Royal Tour was one of the milestones in CBC development; it demonstrated that Canada had achieved a truly national broadcasting system. The daily coverage in both French and English was the world's biggest broadcasting venture until that time.

The Second World War

Many of the plans made in the summer of 1939 fell by the wayside on September 1, 1939, the day Germany invaded Poland. The preparations for war and the madness descending on Europe. Both, were very much in the news during the Royal Tour. The Empress of Australia bringing the monarch to Canada and the Empress of Canada taking him back to Britain crossed paths in the Atlantic with the St. Louis, a liner carrying more than 900 Jewish refugees. The refugees were denied entry in Havana and appeals went out to the King and to a number of countries, including the United States and Canada, to provide a safe haven. No help was forthcoming. The St. Louis took the refugees back to Europe where many were later killed by the Nazis.

Canada, in a symbolic move to reaffirm her autonomy, waited until September 8th to declare war, five days after Britain.

The events leading to World War II put pressure on the radio traffic across the Atlantic. In the absence of a shortwave system of its own, Canada's voice was not heard on the European stage where this country was destined to have such a heavy involvement over the next six years. To send radio programs abroad, Canada could negotiate with NBC or CBS to relay the broadcast, but the American networks -- operating privately -- were themselves hard pressed for broadcast time in the turbulent international situation. Furthermore, the United States was not yet a party to the war, and the American networks did not want to jeopardize their neutral position, and the special broadcast arrangements they made with Germany. The other alternative for getting Canadian broadcasts across the Atlantic was via beam telephone, using the Marconi station at Drummondville, Quebec, but this was expensive and of poor quality.

In Parliament, there were renewed demands to build a shortwave station. Newspapers fully supported the calls to utilize broadcasting for the war effort. An exchange of letters between Gladstone Murray (CBC General Manager) and Kenneth Wilson of *The Financial Post* shows Murray providing information that was used to pressure the government. At the end of October, Prime Minister King began a series of CBC broadcasts on the theme "Canada at War." Murray wrote Wilson that in his opinion it was Wilson's "intervention that decided the Prime Minister to come to the microphone rather earlier than he had planned." Murray was especially enthusiastic about *The Financial Post*'s editorial on October 21 which was headed "Radio Stations vs. Bombing Planes."[1] The paper was promoting the Prime Minister's radio talks which it saw as the start of a "campaign of leadership by inspiration." *The Financial Post* argued that it was essential "to inform and inspire Canadians on the plan and purpose of the war." The editorial declared that such messages were needed not only in Canada but in the United States. "In that country [US], a vicious, inspired campaign of anti-Allied propaganda is being broadcast far and wide."[2] The paper was concerned that Mr. King's message would not penetrate to the US far beyond the border.

> Yet the power, influence, goodwill and cooperation of the United States may be the deciding factor in the war.
>
> Canadians cannot tell this great nation what to do. But we can do our part in offsetting alien and anti-

> British propaganda, now so widespread there. Our American friends will listen to us when they might turn a cold shoulder to similar material from Great Britain.
>
> High-powered radio stations along the border would cost this country about $250,000 each. That is the price of a crack bombing plane.
>
> We spend money on bombers in time of war without question. Why might it not be a good investment to build a few radio stations to supplement our output of instruments of destruction with equipment which would peacefully penetrate the minds of our American cousins?
>
> The benefits from a few well-placed radio stations to carry the story of the Allied war aims and effort into the USA might far outweigh a similar expenditure on bombers, in fact it might hasten the time when such expenditures could be curtailed.

This *Financial Post* editorial led to the important exchange of confidential letters between Wilson and Murray. The CBC General Manager wrote Wilson that he believed "some kind of understanding between Canada and the United States" was behind the Government's reluctance to embark on a shortwave project.

> This, of course, is all very 'hush-hush' ... I have the impression that we have agreed to lay off even the appearance of propaganda, at least for the time being. Of course, such an arrangement, if it exists, need not prevent the short wave station being undertaken.

In an editorial on December 9, *The Financial Post* criticized the Government for not going ahead with the shortwave project. "Ottawa has apparently succumbed to the belief that short wave broadcasting would give US isolationists a 'cry'."[3] The paper returned to the theme that the cost of the shortwave station would be little more than the cost of a bombing plane.

Other papers took up the rallying cry of *The Financial Post*. The *Regina Star* (Dec. 12 and Dec. 22, 1939) failed to see why the US should be concerned about a Canadian station.[4] The *Ottawa Citizen, Montreal Star*, and *The Edmonton Journal* all carried a news story on December 21, 1939 which was really editorial comment, stating that the opening of Australia's new worldwide shortwave broadcasting service emphasized, anew, that Canada continued to lag behind in the establishment of a similar service in this country. On December 27, the *Winnipeg Tribune* asked why Canada should be left defenceless in the field of shortwave radio, saying that already this country has been "attacked" with German broadcasts about the Quebec elections and furthermore there were critical broadcasts from the Soviet Union about the war views of Canadian workers.[5] The *Windsor Tribune* (NS), November 24, 1939, argued that a shortwave station would help to bring in tourists and also pointed out its value in strengthening the goodwill between Canada and the US in time of war.[6] All Canadian newspaper comments on shortwave were supportive.

The British interest in a Canadian shortwave transmission service intensified with the outbreak of the war. British cabinet documents from early 1940 show that the BBC wanted to secure in some British territory overseas a powerful shortwave transmission station in the event that its own facilities were destroyed or seriously damaged by enemy action. Such a station would make it possible for the BBC to carry on its most important round-the-clock programming to Europe and the rest of the world. Quite apart from the concern about the possible damage of the BBC transmitters, the backup station could also be used to make the BBC's overseas service much more effective.

Detailed studies had already been carried out about the proposed transmitting station, and Canada was found to be the best place for reasons of technology and programming.[7] The study indicated that four shortwave transmitters, each of 50kw power, would be needed. The British government knew of the immediate availability of one such transmitter in the United States.

In August 1940, the British High Commissioner in Ottawa, Sir Campbell Stuart, on instructions of the London government, pressed the British case in intimate discussions with a number of Canadian ministers and returned to London to report personally. Shortly afterwards, the British government produced a detailed and somewhat modified proposal for a joint venture involving the two governments -- Canada and Britain -- and the two broadcasters, the BBC and the CBC. Britain offered to pay part of the costs -- capital, maintenance and operational -- but hoped that Canada would agree to put up all the money until the end of the war; London, meanwhile, would pay interest on its share. The proposal had developed far enough that the BBC was ready to send to Canada one of its shortwave engineering specialists, and a nucleus of programming staff experienced in propaganda. The CBC and BBC were to collaborate in the preparation of programs; in the early stages some of the programs would come from Britain.

The British concerns about the danger of the Germans knocking out the BBC transmitters were realistic. In May 1940, Winston Churchill took over as Prime Minister from Neville Chamberlain and formed a National Government. The war situation was bleak. Poland, had been decimated the previous September. British merchant ships were being sunk at a horrifying pace in the Atlantic, and food rationing had been introduced in January 1940. In April, Germany conquered Norway and Denmark. On May 10, three days after Churchill had come to power, Germany began its conquest of the Netherlands, Belgium and Luxembourg. On May 17, Germany invaded France. In ten days, the British forces found themselves in an impossible situation and the evacuation of 300,000 British and Allied soldiers from Dunkirk was initiated. In June, Italy entered the war on the side of the Germans. Before the month was out, France surrendered. In July, the Battle of Britain began; in a 12-day period 90 German bombers were shot down over Britain. The 'blitz' raids on London began with an all-night bombing. On October 2, the liner, the Empress of Britain, bound for Canada with refugees, was sunk. Between October 13 and 21, London was caught up in heavy and continuous air raids.

In Ottawa, on October 10, the Minister of Munitions and Supplies, C.D. Howe, presented the British proposal for the joint-venture shortwave project to the Cabinet War Committee.[8] Mr. Howe was personally opposed and a consensus developed around the position that the responsibility for operating such a broadcasting service should be left to countries more experienced in this area. The bombs were falling in London when the telegram from High Commissioner Sir Campbell Stuart arrived outlining the Canadian rejection.

According to the High Commissioner, Howe, had described the shortwave scheme as a suggestion that had originated with High Commissioner Sir Campbell Stuart as his own initiative. Furthermore, Howe told the High Commissioner that Canada "did not want to be involved in propaganda, especially to the United States, even now."

The Churchill government took the position that Canada -- and certainly Howe -- had the wrong impression about the shortwave project. Firstly, the proposal was not put forward by the British High Commissioner; it had originated with the British government and the BBC. Secondly, the Canadian government was mistaken if it thought the programming would be directed to the United States. If that had been the intention, then the proposal would not have been for a shortwave station.

On November 5, 1940, Howe brought yet another revised British proposal to the meeting of the Cabinet War Committee: Britain was prepared to operate the shortwave station on its own if Canada would build it. Howe also opposed this proposal and the War Committee again agreed with him.[9]

Two months later, in January 1941, the British government made a renewed effort to convince Canada of the need to build shortwave facilities. The strategy of the Churchill government was to bypass Mr. Howe as mush as possible and work through the Minister of National War Service, J.T. Thorson. The latter was more sensitive to the arguments about the contribution radio was making to the war effort and was not nearly as concerned as the American-born Mr. Howe that the United States would be critical of Canadian involvement in shortwave broadcasts. Mr. Thorson told the *Ottawa Journal* that he was in favour of the shortwave station.

With the arrival of the renewed British request, Howe asked the CBC for a feasibility report. The CBC reply on February 1, 1941 said that is would be difficult tosecure four 50 KW transmitters, as suggested by Britain. However, the CBC could envisage an early start of a shortwave facility with two transmitters: one was available in the United States where it had been built for Britain; the second was a 7½KW test transmitter that could possibly be stepped up to 50KW.

Attached to the CBC memorandum to Mr. Howe was an introductory comment from Dr. Augustin Frigon (the CBC Assistant General Manager) which reflected some irritation with Ottawa's procrastination. Frigon stated that the CBC had the capability to build and operate the shortwave station; it was simply a matter of policy and of money which required the decisions of the Ottawa government and the CBC Board of Governors. "The CBC was quite ready and capable of dealing with the shortwave problem in all its phases."

Meanwhile, the War Minister, Mr. Thorson, requested a report of his own from the CBC. In preparation of this report, Mr. Frigon, in an internal memo on July 3, 1941 to the General Manager, Mr. Gladstone Murray, provided technical and financial details: it would cost about $400,000 for building a 50KW shortwave transmitter facility at Sackville, NB, including the cost of two directional aerials.[10] Another $100,000, would be required annually for the operation of the service. Frigon had recently visited the United States and found out that the RCA plant at Camden, NJ was building a 50KW transmitter and if Canada made haste it could buy it; the facility at Sackville would be ready for operation possibly by May 1942 and certainly by September.

In August 1941, the then British High Commissioner in Ottawa, Malcolm Macdonald, went to the Department for External Affairs to press the case.

In September 1941, Prime Minister Mackenzie King visited London. Almost immediately on his return to Ottawa he received a secret telegram from Brendan Bracken, the British Secretary of State for Dominion Affairs, stressing the urgency of the project for the war effort and noting that Australia and India already had shortwave stations in hand. A day or so later, Norman Robertson at External Affairs sent the Prime Minister a memorandum on the subject. And on September 25, 1941 another memorandum from Robertson to Mr. King pointed out that a letter had been received from Mr. Burchell, the Canadian representative in Newfoundland, complaining that he could not get news from Canada because of the lack of adequate shortwave facilities and he was especially disappointed that Newfoundland radio stations could not pick up the Prime Minister's speech which he gave on his return from Britain. Mr. King added a note to this brief memo.[11]

> I favour the shortwave station and intended to recommend the establishment at next meeting of War Committee had principal members been present.

Thorson acted promptly and by early November his Department of National War Services had prepared a draft recommendation to the cabinet to build the shortwave station. The Department of External Affairs wanted to be involved and asked Thorson to modify the recommendation to provide for the joint responsibility of the CBC, National War Services and External Affairs. A letter from Robertson to Thorson, delivered by hand on November 7 to underscore its importance, offered advice and support and called for early consultations between the government and the CBC.

The proposal to cabinet, revised to accommodate the interests of the Department of External Affairs, had the backing of the Prime Minister, the Department of External Affairs and National War Services. It appeared that it would receive easy approval from the cabinet. The record is not too clear as to what new roadblocks appeared. It took nearly another year and a revised proposal -- incredibly detailed -- before the Government acted.

Much had happened in the intervening months since the War Minister had prepared his 1941 proposal. The United States entered the war following the Japanese raid on Pearl Harbour in December 1941. The Soviet Union became an ally in the War when Germany invaded it in June 1941. The theatre of war broadened. Britain did not feel quite as isolated and Canada was using all her might -- industrial and manpower -- in the war effort.

Some initial Canadian steps had been taken to participate in the radio war. In July of 1941, the War Minister, Mr. Thorson, while pushing for the establishment of a Canadian shortwave facility, with cabinet approval entered arrangements for Canadian broadcasts to France. The shortwave transmitters of station WRUL in Boston, owned by the World-Wide Broadcasting Foundation, transmitted six Canadian broadcasts a month to France, one in English, and the remainder in French. The broadcasts were arranged by the CBC in cooperation with Mr. Melacon, the government's Associate Director of Public Information. In this way, the War Minister initiated a Canadian involvement in radio propaganda.

CHAPTER VI

THE WARTIME INFORMATION BOARD AND PSYCHOLOGICAL WARFARE

There was an atmosphere of urgency in the summer of 1942 when Canada suddenly discovered the importance of propaganda and psychological warfare. Ottawa had resisted any significant involvement in propaganda directed at the enemy or at friends, believing such activities could best be undertaken by allies with greater experience. But things were not going well: the allies, now joined by the United States, had suffered serious setbacks and there was an obvious need for an information component to the Canadian war effort. Two events, the referendum on conscription and the Canadian military disaster at Dieppe, became catalysts for major initiatives to establish machinery for information and propaganda.

Prime Minister King's government, in large part an attempt to placate Quebec attitudes, promised not to resort to compulsory enlistment for overseas service in World War II. But the war needs had changed and the government opted to hold a referendum on April 27, 1942, asking Canadians to release it from the anti-conscription pledge. In Quebec province 73 percent voted 'no', while in the rest of the country the vote was 80 percent in favour. The non-binding referendum, and therefore strictly speaking a plebiscite, was essentially a public opinion venture aimed at bringing Canadians together in support of the war effort. As a propaganda event it was a great failure and increased the divisions between French-speaking and English-speaking Canadians. As in the case of all the national referenda held in Canada -- the liquor drinking referendum of 1898 and the referendum on constitutional change in 1992 -- the wartime vote promoted crisis politics; Ottawa ended up with egg on its face.

August 19, 1942 was probably the blackest day for Canada in World War II. Some 5000 Canadian troops took part in the raid across the English Channel on Dieppe, a small French port located between Le Havre and Boulogne. This joint Canadian and British venture was a test operation for a future invasion and was also aimed at showing the vulnerability of Festung Europa; Germany's Fortress Europe. The Canadian forces, previously untested in battle, suffered a major setback; in a raid that lasted nine hours, 900 Canadians were killed and 1874 taken prisoners. In the accompanying air battle, the allies lost 106 aircraft and 81 airmen; 13 of the downed aircraft were from the Royal Canadian Air Force which lost 10 pilots. While every effort was made at the end of the day to put a good image on the Dieppe raid; it was a disaster in both military and propaganda terms.

The government was painfully aware of the need to bolster its information machinery and become involved in propaganda. The government's publicity agency, the Bureau of Public Information, which had been established in December 1939 primarily to keep Canadians and the armed forces informed about the war effort, was in shambles. Made up mostly of government bureaucrats and public relations executives from the private sector, the Bureau of Public Information had failed hopelessly; it had no sense of news and the importance of timing in information flow; its output was 'unimaginative, uninspiring and late'. Charles Vining, the President of the Newsprint Association of Canada, in a Report to Prime Minister King in July 1942, spelled out the horror story in some detail; he urged the government to become serious about information: "This is a war of mind and spirit as well as a war of manpower and weapons." He recommended that the government reorganize totally its approach to information and propaganda. The daily news should be the core of the information flow; not the stress on books, pamphlets and mimeographed releases that had become the almost counter productive operation of the spectacularly unsuccessful Bureau of Public Information.[1] Bureaucrats would have to be replaced by journalists.

Of particular concern was the image Canada was projecting abroad. Publicity about Canada in the United States was especially bad; US newspapers hardly ever mentioned Canada's war effort; on average once in 45 days. The impression in the US was that Canada was not doing anything meaningful, the emphasis tended to be on negative news including rumours of anti-Americanism and that Canada was creating obstacles in the building of the Alaskan highway. A consensus developed that Canada had to improve its information flow to its own population and perhaps even more important, to reach out to audiences in foreign lands. Ottawa needed to project Canadian information and culture to its servicemen abroad, to tell the world about Canada's war effort and to become involved in psychological warfare. To achieve these ambitious tasks, the government established two information agencies within ten days. On September 8, 1942, the Wartime Information Board (WIB) was created and on September 18, 1942, the CBC was instructed to build the shortwave service.[2] It would, of course, take time to set up the shortwave station, but the Wartime Information Board began its work almost immediately. There was an important link between the Wartime Information Board and the CBC International Service that went on the air some thirty months later.

The Wartime Information Board, headed at the start by Vining, had early organizational problems but nothing could now stand in the way of cleaning up the "war information business," as Prime Minister King called it. Journalists and writers replaced officials, well-meaning business executives and their public relations experts. Vining left because of ill health, and the formidable John Grierson -- who had been brought over from Scotland to establish the National Film Board -- was appointed general manager; a job he took without extra pay.

The Wartime Information Board was given a relatively free hand, or as an official report put it, "a rather long leash." It established offices -- looked after by capable journalists and writers -- in New York, Washington, London, Canberra and in Paris (after the liberation of the French capital). A special section was set up under Allan Anderson to channel information flow to Latin America where Axis propaganda had made inroads and a number of countries were adopting unfriendly policies.

The Department of External Affairs had a representative -- for some time Lester Pearson -- on the Wartime Information Board. Pearson saw himself an expert on media and information and the Department of External Affairs frequently relied on this expertise. At one time, Pearson had considered a journalism career. Not long after he went to work for External Affairs he negotiated for a job at the CBC and received an offer in writing. He did not take up the CBC offer but used it to negotiate for a better salary. When he was Minister for External Affairs and PrimeMinister Pearson had close friends in the media world; he did not fully appreciate however the boundaries between the worlds of government and journalism.

When Pearson was Minister-Counsellor at the Canadian Legation in Washington, he had a meeting in New York with the General Manager of the Wartime Information Board, John Grierson. In a personal letter to Under Secretary of State Norman Robertson at External Affairs (June 30, 1943), Pearson complained bitterly about Grierson.[3]

> When in New York yesterday, I spent some time with John Grierson. He immediately reproached me for having criticized his organization at the last meeting of the Board, but was inclined to be charitable when he realized how tired and jaded I was and should not be held responsible for my actions and words!. . . .
>
> Grierson also held forth at some length about grandiose plans he had for this and that, but I must say I found some difficulty in following him. I did gather, however, that his opinion of external affairs is not very high and he doubts its right to be associated with

> him in his plans for the re-discovery of our country. He feels that all worthwhile work in information, Political Warfare, cultural relations with foreign countries, etc., can only be done by W.I.B.[Wartime Information Board], though he graciously agreed that External Affairs might have to be consulted now and again.... Please keep these thoughts of mine very much to yourself, at least keep them away from St. John and his disciples....

(A study by External Affairs some 30 years later suggest that the differences between Mr. Pearson and Mr. Grierson "had more to do with John Grierson's peppery nature than with any more general rivalry or abrasion" between the War Information Board and External Affairs. Later, when E. Davidson Dunton headed the Board, there was an amiable working relationship.)[4]

The Wartime Information Board achieved considerable success, considering Canada's limited facilities. One important accomplishment was its involvement in the allied use of radio for psychological warfare against Germany. This involvement had a low-keyed beginning.

Karl Renner, an Austrian refugee whose grandfather had been Chancellor from 1931-1933 (and would become President of Austria after World War II), had been hired by the Canadian Censorship Board in 1943 to read letters going to German prisoners of war in Canada, and the replies from the prisoners to their relatives in Germany. There were about 32,000 prisoners of war in Canada, including many from the elite Afrika Korps captured by the British during the Allied campaign in North Africa. In going through the prisoners' mail, Renner collected information that was of value to the intelligence community; it also was potentially useful for propaganda.

In Ottawa, the information collected by Renner was channelled to an informal group at External Affairs that would later become the Psychological Warfare Committee, a committee of the Wartime Information Board. External Affairs became involved in psychological warfare early in 1942 in response to British requests for assistance. The Department saw psychological warfare as an extension of foreign policy. In June 1943, External Affairs set up the Psychological Warfare Committee -- an informal interdepartmental committee -- composed of External Affairs, the Wartime Information Board and the three Service Departments. An External Affairs officer was chairperson. Later, a representative of the CBC was added to the Psychological Warfare Committee.[5]

The prisoners-of-war material collected by Renner was shared with the British and American governments. The Political Warfare Executive (PWE) in London was impressed with the Canadian material and shared it with the BBC for possible use in broadcasts to Germany. PWE wanted more, and Ottawa, at the request of London, sent Saul Rae -- a senior External Affairs official -- to Britain in the Spring of 1943. Rae was surprised by the fuss made over him, almost immediately he was received by "various Generals, Air Commodores and the like."[6]

On April 21, 1943 -- only a day or so after his arrival in London -- Rae, accompanied by George Ignatieff, represented Canada at a meeting at Bush House, the headquarters of the BBC. The meeting was chaired by one of the Directors of the Political Warfare Executive, Air Commodore P.R.C. Groves, and was attended also by Mr. R.H.S. Crossman, the Director for Enemy and Satellite Countries, and a group of propaganda experts.[7]

Crossman discussed the valuable intelligence information about conditions in Germany culled from the letter to the prisoners of war in Canada. There was hesitation to use this material for propaganda but there were no qualms about using the return mail from the prisoners to their relatives in Germany for 'listener bait'. Canada was asked to supply a weekly list of twenty-five German Air Force prisoners, together with particulars such as age, service number, unit, home town, date of capture, camp address, state ofhealth, and hobbies. This information was sufficiently important to be forwarded to London by bomber mail each week.

The British authorities were also interested in experimental broadcasts prepared by anti-Nazi prisoners that had been recorded in Hull, Quebec. Crossman wanted more of these; he was especially interested at the time in propaganda to German and Italian merchant seamen. Canada was asked to find soldiers and merchant seaman in prison camps who would be willing to cooperate in anti-Nazi broadcasts. A senior British liaison officer in New York, was in charge of coordinating arrangements with Ottawa.[8]

In Germany, where listening to enemy broadcasts was condemned as "black-listening" and resulted in jail sentences--and the occasional execution of repeat offenders--the BBC had nevertheless developed a considerable audience. Evidence accumulated that the prisoner of war greetings from Canada, broadcast by the BBC, was effective; there were numerous references to them in mail to the prisoners. The German Foreign Office, for its part, was helping the allied initiative, it transcribed the BBC messages for the families of the prisoners. (Also, German prisoners in Canada were receiving radio messages from their relatives at home; broadcast by German shortwave, the messages were recorded at the Ottawa receiving station and sent on to the prison camps.)

The greetings from the prisoners of war in Canada had become a catalyst in drawing German audience interest to BBC broadcasts.

Meanwhile, the Psychological Warfare Committee in Canada divided its work into two parts: the preparation of radio scripts and pamphlet material (for dropping from aeroplanes) directed toward enemy and enemy-occupied countries, and the segregation and reeducation of German prisoners of war in Canada.

Throughout 1944, the Psychological Warfare Committee was preparing for the Wartime Information Board radio recordings--mostly in French and German but also in Dutch, Danish and Czech. Since Canada had no shortwave broadcasting facilities at the time, the recordings were sent to the Office of War Information in New York for transmission by the Voice of America in such programs as "Amerika ruft Europa" and to London for use by the BBC. In all, hundreds of programs were recorded, but there would usually be a delay of about 10 days before they were used by the stations in Britain and the United States; by that time many recordings were outdated. The BBC was not always impressed with the French, Dutch and Czech material; the Voice of America found them somewhat more useful. (One document notes that the BBC considered the Canadian material out of touch with reality and tended to be too sentimental and cultural.)[9] On the other hand, the Psychological Warfare Committee's prisoner-of-war material recorded in German was found most useful by both the BBC and the Office of War Information.

What distinguished the German language material was that it was prepared by very bright persons who understood Germany, could empathize with the German population as well as the prisoners. Karl Renner, the Censorship Board's contribution to psychological warfare, had himself been an internee when he first arrived in this country, although he was a refugee from the Nazis. At the Wartime Information Board, Renner worked with another refugee and former internee, Helmut Blume, who was the chief German-language writer and broadcaster. The standards set by Blume helped to maintain the lustre of Canada's German-language programs for years.

Many of the problems of the recorded program operation were solved when Canada no longer had to rely on British and American transmitters. This happened on Christmas Day, 1944, when the CBC International Service went on the air for the first time with a test broadcast. The shortwave transmitting service became Canada's main instrument for psychological warfare. Canada now had its own shortwave station to conduct psychological warfare.

CHAPTER VII

BUILDING THE STATION

The procrastination in Government came to an end on September 18, 1942 when the Privy Council ordered the CBC to build a shortwave station. The next day, External Affairs dispatched a letter to High Commissioner, Vincent Massey, in London with the good news. After all, it was Massey who had taken so much of the flack from the Churchill government when Canada was not forthcoming with the shortwave project.

Under normal conditions, the station could have been operational in about six months; it took 30 months. Almost everything seemed to go wrong in purchasing the transmitters in the United States, in building the station at Sackville, NB and in setting up the International Service headquarters and studio facilities in Montreal.

In 1941, before the direct American involvement in the war, RCA in Montreal had made an almost irresistible offer to the CBC to provide a powerful shortwave transmitter on short notice and to carry out further development on more advanced equipment that would be reserved for Canada. In September 1942 it was almost impossible to acquire shortwave transmitters.

Washington wanted shortwave broadcasting for its own war effort but had no significant facilities. Such giant American electronics firms as General Electric and Westinghouse conducted important shortwave experiments in the 1920's, designed for developing a potentially lucrative business in equipment. The lack of American interest in shortwave was tied to the financing of broadcasting through advertising; radio was private enterprise operating for profit. Advertisers had little interest in broadcasting to foreign audiences. In the 1930s, when Germany, Italy, the Soviet Union and many other countries -- especially those with colonial interests -- became heavily involved in shortwave, the United States remained largely uninvolved. There were attempts in Congress to legislate shortwave facilities but these were opposed by the broadcasting industry.

The United States had no meaningful plan for international broadcasting when it entered the war in December 1941. It would be another seven months until President Roosevelt established the Office of War Information (OWI) which placed all privately owned shortwave broadcasting stations under governmental control. OWI added additional transmitters, stepped up power, and created foreign language services. It is this collective broadcast service that became known as the Voice of America.[1]

I. Lobbying In The U.S.

Five weeks after the Canadian decision to go shortwave, the CBC distributed the preliminary specifications for the transmitter equipment and sought quotations from three potential American suppliers: Radio Corporation of America (RCA), Federal Electric and General Electric. RCA gave the best delivery promise -- approximately one year -- and the reasonable price of just over $400,000 for each of the transmitters. Furthermore, the CBC Engineering Division was familiar with the RCA equipment; it had installed an RCA shortwave transmitter for the Free French at Brazzaville, then the capital of French Equatorial Africa. On December 4, 1942 the CBC accepted the RCA offer and issued the purchase order almost immediately. There was one catch: RCA delivery promises were tied to priority ratings established by the US government.

In an effort to have the transmitters built at Camden, New Jersey, as soon as possible, the Ottawa government and the CBC, separately and jointly, embarked on powerful lobbying missions. As soon as the ink was dry on the purchase orders, James S. Thompson, who had taken over as general manager at the CBC from Gladstone Murray, visited Washington to make preliminary overtures for a high priority rating. There was acute competition for radio equipment generally and for shortwave transmitters specifically. The situation was bad: "The shortwave broadcasting equipment," Thompson reported to the Prime Minister, "has now become almost part of standard equipment for an army going into battle under modern conditions particularly when it becomes necessary to establish immediate contact with the population of an invaded country."

On the evening of December 26, 1942, Thompson told Prime Minister King at a private meeting that "all the influence that can be used" must be put into play; he asked the Prime Minister to send a personal message to the President of the United States.

> Mr. Thompson was "quite sure that, short of this action, we might very likely be frustrated in our attempts to get ahead with this very important piece of construction."

Prime Minister King promptly agreed to write President Roosevelt and asked for a written statement of the issues they discussed that evening. In his memorandum to the Prime Minister the next day, Thompson provided the reasons why Canada should establish a shortwave station without delay and gave emphasis to one by underlining the following statement:[2]

> Canada being a country that preserves the Spirit of France with its tradition and language, has a specially important contribution to make to the cause of the United Nations.

On his visit to Washington, Mr. Thompson had found much interest in the French-Canada argument; he suggested that the Prime Minister emphasize that "in Canada we have a large French-speaking population and consequently the establishment of communication from a French-speaking people to continental Europe or to French Colonial Africa might be of very considerable political importance at the present time."[3]

The King Letter

The Cabinet War Committee, at its meeting on December 30, 1942, supported the Prime Minister's decision to write President Roosevelt. In the letter, dated January 9, 1943, Mr. King said he was writing "on a matter of urgency and importance to the Canadian war effort, and, I venture to suggest, to the common cause in which we are engaged." Canada wanted to build a shortwave station and it would be "exceedingly difficult" to obtain the equipment "unless the application which had been made by the Canadian Broadcasting Corporation is given a high priority rating, and is strongly supported by the War Production Board in Washington." Mr. King asked President Roosevelt for his active assistance.

In his one-and-a-half page letter, Mr. King covered much territory. He noted the vital importance of shortwave broadcasting as a weapon of political warfare; the need to use shortwave to keep in touch with Canadian force abroad; to provide news to allied countries about Canada's war effort; to utilize shortwave as a means of self-defence and counter attack against the flow of enemy propaganda, and to strengthen resistance movements in occupied countries.

Prime Minister King, following the advice of the CBC general manager, also made the French Canada argument.

> With our large French-speaking population ... a great deal could be done to restore and strengthen the spirit

> of Frenchmen in France and French territories, and to reply to the enemy propaganda emanating from radio stations in Paris and Vichy which they have seized and controlled.

Mr. King's letter was quickly sent to Washington for hand delivery by Lester Pearson; but it never reached the President. At the insistence of C.D. Howe, the Minister of Munitions and Supplies, the War Cabinet reversed itself and forced the Prime Minister to withdraw the letter (See Chapter I). This was a major blow to the joint CBC-government lobbying effort, coordinated by Pearson in Washington.

Under Secretary of State, Norman Robertson, kept Pearson informed of all developments relating to the shortwave project. Pearson, for his part, spent considerable time becoming familiar with the American use of radio in psychological warfare, the role of the Office of War Information (OWI) and the liaison between the British and American governments in this area. In a dispatch to Robertson on November 3, 1942, Pearson said: "It seems clear that we will have to come to someunderstanding with the British and US authorities with regard to the content of programmes."[4]

Pearson was asked to comment on discussions between External Affairs and the CBC on shortwave policy, especially the target area priorities, that is, the countries to which Canada would be broadcasting and in what languages. The suggestions for program content at these talks were strong on propaganda and called for close liaison with the US, Britain and other leading countries of the United Nations.

Pearson became further drawn into the foreign policy dimensions of shortwave in the absence of a strong CBC position. In fact, the CBC was in a state of turmoil as a result of a reorganization imposed by the Board of Governors. The CBC, under its first General Manager Gladstone Murray, had run into trouble -- or at least received the blame -- for the divisive results of the conscription plebiscite in 1942. The CBC Board of Governors in mid-August announced a shakeup of its head office; Gladstone Murray was named "Director General of Broadcasting for Canada" and the Board recommended that the government appoint Dr. James S. Thompson, President of the University of Saskatchewan, as General Manager for one year.[5] Under the new arrangement, Murray, Thompson and Frigon received similar salaries, but Murray was under the control of and responsible to Dr. Thompson. Four months later, it still was not clear who in the CBC was in charge of the shortwave project. Under-Secretary of State, Robertson made this observation in a dispatch to Mr. Pearson:[6]

> Responsibility seems to be divided to a considerable extent within the CBC Frigon and Manson are chiefly concerned with the technical arrangements involved in establishing and maintaining the short-wavefacilities, while Murray will probably do most of the work on the program side. In addition, the new General Manager, Dr. Thompson has shown a great deal of interest in the whole question of short-wave, and in point of fact, has written to the Prime Minister asking him to take up with the President the question of obtaining the necessary priorities on equipment and material.
>
> It is not clear at the present time whether Thompson, Murray or Frigon will emerge as the dominant figure in the CBC on short-wave policy questions and I think you will agree that this is largely a matter to be determined by the CBC itself.

At year end in 1942, the CBC sent officials to Washington to lobby for the transmitters. Assistant General Manager Frigon found the situation difficult. A week later, E.C. Stewart, the head of supplies at CBC Engineering, was in the American capital for a lobbying effort that was designed to coincide with the delivery of Prime Minister King's letter to Mr. Roosevelt. He wrote to the chief CBC Engineer, Mr. Olive, that he was making good progress "even without the help we hoped to obtain from the Prime Minister." The optimistic Stewart described his warm reception at the War Production Board where the Canadian application for priority ranking was being considered. The Chief of the nonmilitary branch of Radio and Radar Division, Mr. McIntosh, seemed to be in favour of the Canadian shortwave station "even to the extent of considering it more valuable" than the stations requested by the Office of War Information which was in charge of the newly-formed Voice of America. Stewart reported that McIntosh mentioned it might be possible for Canada to obtain two transmitters meant for the Office of War Information. Stewart met on January 9 with Elmer Davis, the Director of the Office of War Information, who agreed to support the Canadian project.

Stewart made numerous follow up trips to Washington, mostly on his own, on one or two occasions, with Dr. Frigon. The CBC officials were on an emotional roller coaster. They were received in Washington with enthusiasm and warmth for which Americans are so famous. This American hospitality was at times mistaken as a signal that the requests for high priority would be granted.

At the end of January, Stewart was back in Washington with Frigon who had important contacts in the Federal Communications Commission. The two CBC officials appeared before a sub-committee of the War Productions Board where serious difficulties surfaced. There was strong support for the Canadian project but there were no spare transmitters; American psychological warfare needs and lend-lease commitments to Britain had higher priorities. The American officials said there was small hope in satisfying the Canadian requirements; they suggested that perhaps the US Office of War Information and the Canadian government could agree to share a transmitter, possibly installed in Canada, with particular emphasis on broadcasting to France. Stewart was enthusiastic about such an arrangement which would leave Canada in possession of shortwave facilities at the end of the war. The sharing proposal was pushed aside as Canada stepped up its lobbying. Ottawa learned that six shortwave transmitters of 50KW power were being built for Britain and External Affairs wanted two of these diverted to Canada; Mr. Pearson was asked to contact the Britain Ambassador in Washington, David Bowes-Lyon. This turned out to be a false hope.

The Canadian application was shuffled around Washington. There were letters of support from McIntosh at Radio and Radar and from Elmer Davis at the Office of War Information but nothing meaningful was happening. In mid-February, the Minister of Munitions and Supply, Mr. Howe, who had promised to personally help, reported that there had been no progress. Sensing that the Prime Minister was getting restless and was under pressure for some movement, Howe again urged that Mr. King not communicate directly with President Roosevelt, "as I am sure that a direction from the President would antagonize officers with whom we must deal every day to obtain needed Canadian priorities."

Frigon, accompanied by Mr. Manson (the CBC Chief Executive Assistant), spent the first three days of March in Washington meeting individually with seven US officials involved in ruling on the Canadian application. On this hectic visit, Frigon also met with US Navy Commander Gerald Gross (formerly with the Federal Communications Commission) and C.W. Horn of the Office of Strategic Services (formerly with NBC) who were indirectly connected with the Canadian application. Mr. Pearson, for his part, met with Elmer Davis, the head of the Office of War Information. It was a formidable lobbying effort and as a CBC report put it: "It became evident that obstacles which formerly appeared to exist were being cleared away, with the result that a definite indication, unofficial and off the record, was given to the effect that the application of Canada for the two 50KW transmitters would be granted." It was considered advisable to "discreetly" maintain the lobbying at reasonable intervals "to ensure fulfilment of a favourable decision which we expect will be formally and officially communicated to us at an early date." Canada was concerned now that "its" transmitter might somehow be reassigned.

The teletype machine between External Affairs and the Canadian legation in Washington was kept busy discussing the anticipated approval. Dr. Frigon, according to an official dispatch dated March 4, 1943, had seen a confidential report wherein priority had been granted;[7] it was expected that the shortwave transmitters would be delivered by the end of the year and the broadcasting, station would be in operation around March 1944 (i.e., in one year). But delays were again encountered; more information was requested. It would be another two months until the priority clearance -- AA3 priority -- was issued on 19 May 1943. There was not much to celebrate; Mr. Howe did not believe that the priority rating was high enough.[8]

A year later, Stewart and Dr. Frigon were again visiting Washington to see what could be done to speed matters along. In March 1944 -- about the time Canada had expected to be on the air -- Mr. Pearson was asked by External Affairs to accompany Dr. Frigon to the State Department to again press the Canadian case. Pearson did not believe that much could be done.

Pearson suggested that the Office of War Information be lobbied to give up its priorities in favour of the CBC. Davidson Dunton, the head of the Wartime Information Board, and Pearson wrote to Elmer Davis (Office of War Information) asking for his support. Davis replied that he was unable to help. The Office of War Information, however, offered to put some Canadian programmes on the air until Canada had its own transmitters. Dunton replied that he appreciated the offer, but no thanks.

Canada continued to stand in line, waiting for its turn to purchase shortwave transmitters. The intensive lobbying through External Affairs, the CBC as well as the personal touch promised by C.D. Howe accomplished very little, if anything at all. By the time the first transmitter was in place at Sackville the war in Europe was drawing to an end; by the time the second transmitter was installed, both Germany and Japan had surrendered.

II. The Sackville Project

Canada has always been strong in the technology of broadcasting and building the Sackville shortwave station brought out the best in the CBC. The peculiarities of shortwaves and the effects of magnetic forces on shortwaves meant that the station would have to be located in the Maritimes for transmissions to Europe. This had been established in a series of CBC Engineering studies in 1939, 1940 and 1941 which came up with three sites: Truro, Yarmouth and Sackville. Theoretically, the Yarmouth area -- further away from the magnetic North Pole than Truro or Sackville -- might give slightly better service. But there were other considerations: land with good top soil and good electrical conductivity, easy access by highway, and the availability of electrical power, water and telephone.

The CBC Chief Engineer, Mr. Olive, reported November 21, 1941, that Sackville was "the only location to consider in the Maritime Provinces for a shortwave transmitting centre." The CBC already had a standard broadcasting Station -- CAB -- at Sackville and was impressed with the ground conductivity through the Tantramar marshes. Furthermore, cheap marshland was available. In the direction toward Europe and England there are only a few miles of land and then, open seawater.

There were concerns about the defence of Sackville. The CBC Chief Engineer, Mr. Olive, in a letter to L.W. Hayes, his counterpart at the British Broadcasting Corporation, said that there were worries, that Sackville "is near the Coast and, therefore, more vulnerable to attack." He wanted to know -- as he quaintly put it -- what the experience was "in the old country." Olive personally thought that the transmitter site was a safe place: "Near Sackville there is an RCAF Advanced Training Centre and I believe that arrangements could be made to adequately protect the Sackville location by means of fighter aircraft in the event that the war ever comes to these shores." Furthermore, the Sackville facility would be built with reinforced concrete.

On January 4, 1943, CBC engineers involved in the shortwave project had the first of what were to become regular meetings in Montreal. Chief Engineer Olive spoke about the urgency of their task and announced that Mr. Savignac would leave for Sackville that evening, the Savignac mission was relatively low-keyed: he had been authorized to buy marshland property and arrange for the removal of hay. He was also authorized to spend $300 for the removal of a barn. It was a get-acquainted visit to find out the challenges that would be faced in the construction of the transmitter home. One such challenge was the dikes which keep out the water from the marshlands at high tide; they were leaking. Arrangements for repairs would have to be made with provincial authorities to avoid the potential catastrophe of the high-powered shortwave stationbeing washed out by the Bay of Fundy tides, the highest in the world, which unleash enormous tidal forces twice a day.

Things began to stir at Sackville in the Spring of 1943. Marshland was purchased in April for $4,400 and there were to be additional purchases for a total of about $8,000. (Some of the choice land was valued at $75 an acre but the owners in Quebec wanted more, once they learned that the CBC was the purchaser.) In May, a secondhand car -- a 1941 Chevrolet sedan -- was purchased for $1,200 to provide transportation to the site. The housing situation was difficult, fire had destroyed student residences at Mt. Allison University in Sackville and students were competing with CBC staff for scarce living accommodation. (The CBC rented a tourist camp and built some homes for $6000 which it rented to staff at $40 per month.)

The CBC which, in its formative years, had unhappy experiences with Mr. Howe over money matters, was rightly concerned that the Sackville project could compromise its autonomy. Financing of the CBC at the time was through a one dollar licensing fee paid by Canadian radio listeners and the Crown-owned broadcaster was sensitive about more direct financial dependency on the Government. Special financial arrangements were worked out in the 1942 Privy Council Order because the International Service would broadcast to audiences abroad, and therefore, in good conscience, should not be financed by Canadian listener fees.

The CBC was authorized to build the shortwave station for $800,000, to be paid for by War Appropriations. The annual operation and maintenance costs (e.g., power, telephone circuits, etc.), estimated at $150,000 and the programme costs of $350,000 would also be charged to War Appropriations for the duration of the War. Afterwards Parliament would provide the funding on an annual basis.

An unresolved problem was how the work would be billed. Treasury Board wanted tight control and supervision over construction, including accounting practices similar to other government projects. This would have involved the CBC in unaccustomed procedures including the detailed descriptions and specifications, requirements for tender, publication in the *Canadian Gazette* and hundreds of sets of drawings for contractors. There could be long delays. The biggest CBC worry was 'political interference': "It is possible that the contractor would be restricted in buying materials and employing labour to patronage lists supplied by the Government." The CBC wanted to look after the project on its own and bill the government on a regular basis. There was opposition at Treasury Board but the Government was so committed to the early completion of the project that it agreed to the CBC terms. On April 19, 1943, an amendment to Privy Council Order 8168 established the monthly repayment method. Construction could now begin at Sackville.

Much attention was given at the early engineering meetings to the antennae system. CBC engineers were not impressed with the performance of shortwave stations in the United States which were using rhombic antennae, approximately 100 feet in height. The British Broadcasting Corporation was using a curtain system which delivered a better signal but was far more expensive. The CBC engineers concluded that it would be better to spend moderate amounts on the transmitters and splurge, if necessary, on the antennae.

CBC engineers designed a highly efficient directional system of antennae -- never before used on this continent -- and more sophisticated than those employed by the British. In all, three antennae would be needed to blanket the world, for each antenna could be used in opposite directions. Because of high cost and the fact that some of the antennae components would have to be imported from the United States, the sophisticated curtain antenna would be installed, only for the European beam, which in reverse would also be used to broadcast to Mexico and Central America. The two other antennae, the South American beam (in reverse to be used for Asia) and the African beam (in reverse to be used for Australia), would be of the cheaper rhombic type.

The curtain array antenna for the top priority European broadcasts required four enormous steel towers, 480 feet high and 10 feet square. The towers rested on reinforced concrete bases, which measured 20 feet square and 12 feet high, and weighed 185 tons. The curtain antenna with a total length of 1,220 feet was supported on the towers by counterweights and shaves. The towers and curtain were designed to withstand 120 miles per hour gales and a half-inch coating of ice. An additional $150,00 was required for the antennae. Furthermore, the architects and engineers found other phases of the project would be more costly than expected: labour and material costs had increased since 1941 and worse, competition between contractors had practically ended.

The CBC had established an excellent record of keeping within estimates on previous projects. Dr. Frigon was upset when he was told about the extra costs. "This would be the first time when our estimates were too low." He wanted a re-examination of all projected costs before he asked the government for increased funding; he was worried that repeated requests for additional funding could result in the postponement of the entire project. He met again with the engineering group three days later and it was estimated that if the CBC stayed with the original antennae design and withheld other improvements, the job could be completed for the $800,000 originally provided for. The decision, nevertheless, was to proceed with the advanced antennae.

Actual construction at the shortwave plant began in August 1943. By mid-October, work at the Sackville site was well under way: the basement sub floors were ready; electrical conduits, drain pipes and ducts were being installed and the contractors poured concrete on the main floor on November 1st. In midwinter (February 16, 1944), the CBC reported that the Sackville building would be ready to receive the transmitters by May 1st although they were not expected to arrive until July.[8] Over the next few months, there were further construction delays and cable from the United States for the antennae arrived late. But there was never any doubt about the facility being ready to receive the transmitters.

III. The Montreal Studios

Organizing an external broadcasting service involved in psychological warfare was a major challenge; the British Broadcasting Corporation had offered help for a joint Canada-Britain operation earlier in the war but Ottawa wanted to go it alone. The CBC was working on overload covering the Canadian involvement in the war for the audience at home and had established its own news service in 1942; it could not spare more than one or two persons from its staff. External Affairs, for its part, had taken on so many new tasks in the early 1940's that it too could offer little help. It was suggestedthat Saul Rae head the service but he was needed elsewhere. Besides, there was very little journalistic experience at External.

Peter Aylen was picked in 1943 to organize the International Service; it was not a formal appointment. He slipped into the job gradually. At 33, Aylen was a seasoned veteran of Canadian Broadcasting. He came to the CBC in Ottawa in 1936 when it took over the Canadian Radio Broadcasting Commission facilities which had inherited Aylen from the Canadian National Railways where he was a part-time announcer. The CBC made Aylen station manager in Windsor, acting station manager in Toronto and then manager of the CBC station in Vancouver. In 1939, when war broke out, Aylen was brought back to Ottawa to be a liaison officer for the CBC in its dealing with the government on radio programs relating to the war, he represented the CBC on wartime committees.

Aylen was the Secretary for the joint CBC Government Committee established to advise the International Service and went on to organize the service. The decision had already been made.

Peter Aylen became the principal figure at the CBC in setting up the International Service. It was not a formal appointment, he worked his way into the job gradually. At 33, he was a seasoned veteran of Canadian broadcasting with broad experience as an announcer, programmer and station manager. Aylen's involvement with the International Service had a low-keyed beginning while he was doing CBC liaison with the Government in Ottawa. Gerard Arthur, who went overseas for the CBC French network to cover the early stages of the war, was made Aylen's assistant. Construction at Sackville was well underway and the technical plans were in place before the CBC and the Department of External Affairs came to grips with the problem of programming and production. The decision had already a whole series of questions to be addressed: the location of the production centre, the link with the Government, the languages of broadcast. As Aylen recalled, these basic questions included:[10]

> Would we be an official voice? Should the studio be located in Ottawa, as a convenience to watchdogs in the capital? But Montreal was clearly the better production point. These matters were thoroughly examined. A consensus was reached rooted in good common sense. The choice of languages was made not in the light of just who we might like to broadcast to, but who we thought might be interested enough to listen. This, in turn, was influenced by the availability of talent, and Montreal was chosen, on the grounds that if our programs were not attractive, no one would listen anyway.

Ottawa did not have the kind of talent required by an international broadcaster. Toronto was considered at one time but there was little French speaking talent and it would have been more expensive to send the program by telephone line to the Sackville transmitters. Montreal, Canada's most bilingual and cosmopolitan city at the time, and conveniently close to Ottawa, was seen as the ideal choice. At first, Aylen went to Montreal two days a week and in the spring of 1944 began to work in Montreal full time. His first task was to find a home for the International Service.

There was a fair amount of choice, mostly old big houses. "There was a great old mansion near McGill on the lower slopes of Mount Royal which was very attractive," Aylen recalled 40 years later, "but I felt it should have a businesslike atmosphere"[11] He picked an old garment factory -- 1236 Crescent Street -- right off St. Catherine Street. It turned out a poor choice.

Aylen's assistant, Gerard Arthur, described it as "probably the crummiest building" in all of Montreal. "It was really a traumatic experience to be pushed into that awful building which was a bordello at one time."[12] Mavor Moore, the distinguished Canadian man of letters who was also one of the pioneers of the International Service, remembers 1236 Crescent Street more fondly as "a quiet distinguished old building."[13]

> But soon after I got there, I was puzzled by the appearance of some stray people who looked lost. The reason came to light shortly afterwards. Our offices were just above quarters which had been for some time one of the more distinguished brothels in Montreal. And there were many people who felt that the International Service was a considerable lowering of the purposes of such an establishment. They used to come for several weeks after we moved in, but finally the word must have got around that we were interested in other things.

The Crescent Street studios were not quite ready for the inaugural broadcasts and for some weeks the International Service operated out of the CBC studios in the King's Hall Building at 1231 St. Catherine St. The first broadcasts were on the 19 metre band which is effective in the early hours of the morning. The transmissions were from 6:00 to 9:00 a.m. Most of the staff came in at 4:00 a.m. that first winter and the newsroom was in operation practically all night to prepare the 6:00 a.m. news bulletin.

There was a tremendous spirit of comraderie. The mood of Canada at the time was highly supportive. The idea of the International Service was enormously popular with the CBC and creative people. There was pride in Canada about its forces serving in Europe, the industrialization of which made it possible for the country to make an enormous contribution to the war effort. The CBC had provided coverage of the war. "There was a wholesome good feeling for Canada and people were pleased at the idea of having an International Service" to reflect some of these contributions. At the CBC, Ernie Bushnell, Manson and Frigon gave their full support to Aylen: "they wanted to make it a fine example of Canadian broadcasting ... and persuaded top flight people" to become involved.[14] Aylen recalled that, "it wasn't so much the amount of money, but the quantity of the people it attracted" that propelled the International Service to great achievements in its early years in the world broadcasting arena.

The early staff had little broadcasting experience, except for Aylen, Arthur and one or two others. They were, however, a dynamic group which pioneered international broadcasting for Canada. As Aylen recalled: "They were all people who were much too talented to stay forever but who were marvellous to get something started and set standards that would carry on later." Many of them achieved fame in later careers in diplomacy (René

Garneau), academics (Gordon Skilling, Arthur Phelps), politics (René Lévesque), music (Helmut Blume), television (Eric Koch, Stuart Griffiths, Larry Henderson), poetry (Earl Birney) and other fields. Aylen went on to an illustrious career at the United Nations and helped to establish broadcasting services in many third world countries.

CHAPTER VIII

THE EARLY DAYS: 1945-1948

The booming voice of the CBC on shortwave, directed first to audiences in Europe and later to all parts of the world, was a new adventure in Canadian broadcasting. For the first time, Christmas Day in 1944, Canada was reaching out by radio beyond its borders. For European listeners, the Voice of Canada was the strongest, clearest and steadiest from North America. It was a voice reflecting the youthfulness and visions of Canada as a nation; a voice born of a new Canadian nationalism -- moderate in tone -- and asserting the self-assurance of a country that had burst out of its Imperial encasing and found itself a moderately important actor on the world stage as a result of its military and industrial achievements of World War II. There was much to tell the world about Canada over the airways and there were responsive listeners in the war-shattered countries. The tall towers of the Trantramar marshes in New Brunswick -- the departure point for the radio signals setting out in search for overseas audiences -- were symbols of Canada's determination to enhance her visibility.

It was a clean voice -- almost naive -- in an international radio atmosphere that had been polluted by vicious lies, self-serving propaganda and psychological warfare. When the International Service came on the air, the war in Europe was in its final stages, nearly won. The road to victory had been paved while the shortwave facility at Sackville was under construction. The D-Day allied invasion in June 1944, led to the liberation of Paris eleven weeks later (25 August), Brussels was freed two weeks after Paris. On the Eastern front, Soviet troops were marching through Romania, Hungary, Czechoslovakia, Yugoslavia and Poland on Christmas Day 1944 when the International Service had its first test broadcast. Many difficult battles lay ahead; parts of France, Belgium and Holland were still under Nazi occupation; the great Allied push across the Rhine would not begin for another two months. In early February, 1945, Churchill, Roosevelt and Stalin met at Yalta to discuss the unconditional surrender of Germany. The inauguration of the International Service took place three weeks later, on February 25, 1945. Peter Aylen, entrusted by the CBC and the government to organize the shortwave service, brought together top calibre staff; some with broadcasting experience, others without. "It isn't so much the amount of money", Aylen reminisced four decades later, "but the quality of the people that makes the distinguishing mark of the broadcast service."[1]

The pioneer languages of broadcast were to be English, French, German and Dutch. At the last minute Dutch programming was temporarily shelved and replaced by Czech, mainly because Dr. Walter Schmolka -- a refugee lawyer from Prague and a singer of professional calibre -- was available. Finding the right people took a long time and Aylen started with a small staff -- 41 broadcasters, writers and producers. It was an illustrious group of pioneers. Aylen was a proven broadcaster with a strong background in administration and announcing. His assistant, Gerard Arthur, was a man of culture and had accumulated wartime broadcasting experience with the BBC, headed the French fact in the external broadcasting service.

There was an especially strong team in the newsroom. Patrick Waddington, a brilliant writer and a minor poet, had a thorough understanding of Canada which he used effectively to provide context for international news. Waddington's closest colleague in the newsroom was Edward Dix, a West Indian from the Island of St. Lucia, who had studied in England and had senior journalistic experience on a number of Canadian newspapers. Dix had a special talent for making words talk; his preparation of a newscast was not based on simple adaptation of news agency copy; to him a radio newscast was a story-telling event and he balanced informality and accuracy. Both Waddington and Dix -- later joined by the highly-talent reporter Frank Ward from the *Montreal Herald* -- were the nucleus of the International Service newsroom for over 20 years. It was the premier newsroom in Canada and the training ground for some of the CBC's best talent.

The International Service, at a time of strong public and government support for internationalism, became a powerful magnet for pulling in senior academics: H. Gordon Skilling, a professor of Political Science at the University of Wisconsin and Arthur Phelps, professor of English at the University of Manitoba. One of the biggest catches was Stuart Griffiths who had worked with Waddington at Eaton's Catalogues. They were joined by Charles Delafield who showed talent in avoiding controversies when he headed religious programming at the CBC, a real minefield. The staff increased from 41 to close to 200 in three years.

During the war, there were no doubts about the immediate objectives of the powerful broadcasting voice. There were two principal targets: one was Germany and the occupied countries, the other was the Canadian forces in all theatres of operations. In the broadcasts to Germany, the emphasis was on psychological warfare while the broadcasts to the troops -- many of them in the thick of battle -- sought to provide comfort and entertainment.

Psychological Warfare Broadcasting

The most effective psychological warfare at the time was to provide German listeners a truthful account of what was happening on the battlefields of Europe and Asia; in both theatres of war the enemy was retreating. The German language broadcasters were anti-fascist refugees -- many of them Jewish or half-Jewish -- who had escaped from Germany to England just in time. In England they were classified as enemy aliens and interned. They were shipped to Canada "where they were still considered enemy aliens and placed in internment camps; they were sprung when enough people at the top realized that a blunder had been made."[2] Three of the former internees -- Helmut Blume, Eric Koch and Franz Kramer -- were the start of a small German service, "a very impressive galaxy of first rate people; all very keen and very sharp."

Stuart Griffiths, one of the senior pioneers of the International Service had this to say about the programs in German:[3]

> News bulletins and special programs throwing a new light on Nazi leaders and their aims were important parts of the plan which was designed to weaken the German will to resist. In quality and presentation, the Canadian programs at this state in the war were as well prepared as those sent from any of the allied stations. In the later stages of the war, Canada took part in a stepped-up campaign by all the United Nations to bring about German capitulation. This was during the period when the rapid allied advances, and the continued hammering of allied air-power had virtually destroyed all internal communications within Germany. The German people then, if they wanted news of how the war was going, had to depend in the main on allied shortwave radio broadcasts!

The Czech service, introduced in early February 1945, was designed to bolster the spirit of resistance under the Nazi occupation; it would develop into one of the Crown jewels of Canadian shortwaye broadcasting. The program had to be good because, as the first broadcast put it:

> We are well aware of the fact that listening to foreign short-wave broadcasts in countries occupied by the

> Nazis is not only a very difficult but also a very dangerous undertaking. The realization of this fact burdens us with a great responsibility, we must be convinced ourselves that the danger to which you expose yourselves by listening to our broadcasts in justified to a degree at least.

Most important in these early Czech programmes -- as in the case of the German transmissions -- was the news. An example is the news broadcast on March 26, 1945 -- six weeks before the war ended in Europe. The realities of the fighting spoke for themselves; there was no need to bend the truth. On the western front, the great Allied offensive which had started two days earlier with the crossing of the Rhine by American, Canadian and British forces was gaining momentum.[4]

> German resistance is crumbling all along the front, and all the Allied armies on the east bank of the Rhine are advancing. Four Allied armies have broken the German lines, and are penetrating into the Ruhr Basin. Armoured units of the American Third Army are now 60km. east of the Rhine, and have outflanked Frankfurt on the Main, while the Ninth American Army is engaged in eliminating the Ruhr Basin as an effective factor in the German war effort.
>
> In the north, the First Canadian Army has occupied Spelfort, and the Second British Army, together with some Canadian units, has crossed the Isel River. Allied airborne troops have taken six bridges across the Isel River intact, and have captured more than 4000 Germans.

The newscast went on to describe the activities on the Eastern Front: the Russians had launched a new offensive directed against Austria; capturing or killing 38,000 Germans. In the central sector of the Eastern front Red Army units were massed along the Neisse River, awaiting the signal for the final assault on Berlin.

As the Czech news was about to end, there was a special bulletin:

> Allied troops have entered Frankfurt on the Main; the city which had a population of 550,000 was completely deserted by civilians.

The Central European Section -- made up of German and Czech programming -- that assumed responsibility for psychological warfare from the Wartime Information Board. One of the most successful initiatives of the Wartime Information Board were the radio reports about the German prisoners of war; listeners in Germany were told that the prisoners were safe, well fed and occupied in farming activities and carpentry. This project -- aided by a cooperative German officer by the name of Atwater -- was expanded and developed by the International Service into the famed Barbed Wire Broadcasts.

Blume was in charge of the Prisoners of War programs both at the Wartime Information Board and at the CBC. Certainly, he could empathize with the German soldiers; he had been one himself briefly. His escape from Germany was a remarkable feat.

Blume had been drafted into the German army in 1938 and began acting strangely. His father was a Berlin psychiatrist, his mother was Jewish. At home, Blume had learned from his psychiatrist father about the symptoms of schizophrenia and he effectively mimicked these symptoms in the army.[5] He was discharged on medical grounds and quickly left for England where his sister had already taken refuge. With the outbreak of the war, Blume was interned and later shipped to Canada for further internment.

In April 1945 -- in the final weeks of the war in Europe -- Blume and his assistant Erich Koch began visiting the prisoner-of-war camps. Some 32 thousand prisoners were in Canadian camps and they had been sorted into three main categories: black, white and grey, depending on the kind of Nazis they were. The black camps, such as one located near Gravenhurst, Ontario housed "incorrigible Nazis"; the grey camp at Wainwright, Ontario had prisoners "on the fence," and the white camp at Farnham, Quebec contained self-proclaimed anti-Nazis.

Blume and Koch went first to white camps -- and later also to black and grey camps -- to record messages which would be used as listener bait to attract audiences in Germany for the programs aimed at the "re-education of Germany and her people." For the prisoners, reading the messages scripted by Blume and Koch, the broadcasts were an opportunity to establish contact by radio with family at home; it was the only way, the mail service to Germany had broken down completely. At first the prisoners were reluctant and embarrassed. But after some of the men received word that they had been heard by relatives and friends, the lines began to form to get to the mobile microphones. The early broadcasts came from camps in Quebec and Ontario but within six months the

International Service -- producers, operators and equipment -- went to the prairies where most of the prisoners were located.

The prisoners were encouraged to write short scripts about camp life, their war experiences and politics. The "Barbed Wire" broadcasts were carefully screened or, asBlume put it: the prisoners "did not take over where Goebbels left off.... Our purpose was re-education." Faced with the collapse of their country, their philosophy and the ruin of their homeland, "the prisoners themselves were beginning to analyze the errors of the German past ... to learn something about democracy." Some had been sincere anti-Nazis even before the defeat of Germany. Others were diehard Nazis, one threw away his written script and shouted into the microphone a message calling on Germans to resist forever. The prisoner thought he had accomplished something noble and would be shot for it; he was bitterly disappointed because Blume brought over the recording of the outlandish message and smashed it in front of the prisoner. This incident was an aberration; most of the prisoners became enthusiastic about Canada, especially the prisoners who, under a government labour scheme, were sent out to work on farms and in the bush.

Peter Aylen remembered fondly the experiences with the prisoners who, he recalled, were nearly all from the famed Africa Korps, one of Nazi Germany's elite groups. The prisoners, taken by the British early in the war, displayed pride and arrogance in what Germany stood for and were regarded as activist types. It was only towards the end of the war that there was any sign that they could lend themselves to broadcasting back to Germany. The thrust of the message they sent to their homeland was simple: do you want to live for Germany or die for Hitler. They all said the same thing over and over in one way or another.

One group of prisoners from Sorel, Quebec became involved in a play produced at the International Service Studios on Crescent Street. Aylen recalls the group especially well:[6]

> They were officers. It was indeed a parade because the first time they came in they were all dressed up in the full regalia of the Afrika Korps. This didn't cause a ripple on Crescent Street because everybody thought they were Poles or a Dutch group... a group of some kind or another.

The Canadian officer from International Operation supervising the prisoners was embarrassed about the Nazi uniforms. Aylen wanted to help get new clothes for the prisoners. The next time the German officers came back to

Crescent Street, Aylen took pictures which he sent with a covering note to External Affairs indicating that these pictures would provide good publicity for the International Service; he asked for permission to release the pictures. External Affairs did not appreciate the humour but did come up with its unique solution to the clothing problem.

> The next time the prisoners came they were dressed in Canadian Army uniforms. This caused a serious problem because...at the time conscriptions for overseas services was a big issue in Canada...There was conscription for home defence but then you had to volunteer for overseas service. You volunteered you had GS, (general service) on your sleeve and if you didn't, you were called a Zombie, which was the popular word.
>
> These German officers were very proud soldiers and they didn't want to be mistaken for Zombies so they refused point blank to wear Canadian Army uniforms unless they had GS service on their armbands. So that was finally solved and that is the way they finally appeared for the rest of the war.[7]

Eric Koch, who took over as head of the German Section from Blume when the latter returned to a career in classical music, recalls that the material from the prisoners was interesting; "we gained a loyal audience in Germany for our service and we performed some sort of re-educational task in the camps themselves."[8]

> Around our broadcast sessions, all sorts of discussion groups were formed, and we picked the cream. These were the days of great disillusionment among Germans ... many Germans ... in the Nazi regime. The closer the disaster came, in the last months of the war, the more people we discovered who had never been Nazis, the number of people who had always been decent Democrats assumed gigantic proportions. However, I don't want to make any sardonic comments about this, because no doubt very many of the Germans..and I remember two or three with great

> affection ... were most honestly grappling with their political situation.

The 32 thousand prisoners gradually returned home; it took three to four years. Some later returned to Canada as immigrants.

Broadcasting to the Armed Forces

Despite the importance attached to the European programs as part of the anti-Axis drive, the top priority in the first year of broadcasting was to provide a radio link with home for the armed forces. About half-a-million Canadians in uniform were stationed in Europe and fully 70 percent of the broadcasts in 1945 were directed to them: some in French, but mostly in English.

The broadcasts to the armed forces presented the least problems because the programers understood their audience. The Forces Section was headed by Captain Frank (Budd) Lynch, who gained broadcasting experience with the BBC while recovering from serious war wounds. He was assisted by Harry Henderson, a signal officer. Other military men were released from the service to join the International Service: Mavor Moore of the Intelligence Corps was brought home from Canada House in London to head the English service; the poet Earl Birney, who spoke German, left the army early to head the European service and Major René Garneau was in charge for French language broadcasts to the troops and France. More than half of the initial staff of 41 at the International Service were veterans.

The programs to the forces, sought to foster the link with home, supplied information and entertainment that appealed to those who had been far away too long. This meant a strong touch of nostalgia, including Saturday night hockey games, news about the hometown, dance band music and, of course, Canadian news in English and French.

These broadcasts were made up largely of programs taken from the French and English networks of the CBC. Europe was operating on double summer time (Paris had been on Berlin time until its liberation) and the differences in time meant that most network programs were recorded for later release. The Musicians Union waived its extra payment rules covering recordings.

The English programs from the CBC network included *Neighbourly News* (from the weekly press), the popular *Happy Gang Show* and *John Fisher*

(Mr. Canada), a program of interviews with returned servicemen. An especially successful and innovative program was "From the Front" made up of dispatches from the fighting area in Europe and sent back overseas to the servicemen in battle; the troops heard descriptions of what they were doing.

One such dispatch came from Don Faribairn, a former CBC farm broadcaster, serving with the Royal Canadian Air Force. The broadcast was from Holland where there was hard fighting late in the war:[9]

> Two days of rain and murky weather have rather dampened everything, including our spirits and have certainly hampered operations in the air.
>
> ... However, there is one bright spot these days in the lives of all Canadians on the Western front ... they can listen to the CBC's new overseas broadcasting service. That may not sound like very much of a thrill to you back home but when you have been away from Canada as long as most of the boys over here, well, it is really something. To gather round the radio any time between a quarter to twelve and a quarter after two, that's the time we hear CFTA (the CBC shortwave station) over in Holland and listen to a genuine, loud Canadian voice coming out of our loudspeakers, does something to your insides ... you have no idea how much that means to all the boys here. That's what it seems to do to us: brings home to within shouting distance.
>
> Then the sign-off comes and you play "O Canada." We turn the radio up good and loud so that everybody in the countryside can hear it and we stand up and look at one another sort of sheepishly for a minute until we see that the other guy has tears in his eyes too. Then we know that everything is all right."

The enthusiastic response from the servicemen was reassuring to the International Service staff on Crescent Street. A soldier writing from the front on the river Rhine had this to say:

> I've heard a good deal of Sackville. She really pounds in here and what a treat it is to get some first-hand

> Canadian news and music...When are you going to start a 24 hour schedule?

In the Atlantic, the crew of the HMCS Longueuil wrote: "Your programs are greatly enjoyed by everyone... It's the station we listen to now."

The French language programs to the forces incorporated rich musical and variety offerings from the Radio Canada network. Major René Garneau's talks andcommentaries -- regular features -- were often tailored more to the interests of the audience in France than the Canadian forces. Gerard Aurthur's enthusiasm for cultural programs helped to shape the contents. The news -- supplied in English by the International Service newsroom -- was translated into French by Flaurent Lefebvre, a news editor with extensive French network experience.

At the heart of all broadcasts in all languages -- French, English, German and Czech in the first instance -- was the news which was flowing into the International Service newsroom over a battery of teletypes from United Press International, Associated Press, Reuters and Canadian Press. Five English news bulletins a day were simultaneously translated into other languages including French. While much was to be made in later years about an equal role for French and English newsrooms and equitable time distribution for broadcasts, English was in the early days the dominant language. There were some first rate French language journalists and broadcasters including Gerard Arthur, René Garneau and René Lévesque, but for nearly twenty years French was a language of translation for news.

The relegation of French language broadcasting to a secondary position was a serious error: it contradicted the Ottawa argument when it lobbied for transmitters in the United States that Canada was in a unique position to broadcast in French to France and North Africa. This special Canadian advantage based on the country's linguistic and cultural heritage, however, did not seem to matter when the International Service went on the air.

(Interestingly, it was the Voice of America which developed a remarkable French desk under the leadership of Pierre Lazareff, the former editor of *Paris-Soir*. Lazareff, a wunderkind and exceptional journalist since the age of nineteen, was imaginative and his ideas helped shape a dynamic French service; he hired French speaking refugees including the young actor Yul Brynner, the surrealist writer André Breton and the anthropologist Claude Lévi-Strauss.[10])

After the victory in Europe (VE-DAY) the character of programming changed now that the atmosphere was more relaxing. Increasingly, there was emphasis on matters the forces needed to know, especially discussions on veterans' rights and benefits. On election day in 1945, the transmitters stayed on the air all night to bring the results.

Life was returning to normal in Canada and the forces were being integrated into the peacetime atmosphere. In all, 7,000 special forces programs were broadcast in the first year and an additional 3,000 transcriptions programs were shipped to overseas radio personnel for local broadcast to the forces.

With the troops returning home in large numbers, the forces programs received less attention. The English programs to the troops were integrated into the United Kingdom and Commonwealth Service and the French programs meshed with the service to France. Each of these -- the UK section, and the French section -- developed their own personalities with an emphasis on special programs. This was a period when individual creative talent made itself felt in every area of International Service operations.

There were, of course, interests-in-common to all sections. Special programs were prepared on VE-Day, the death of President Roosevelt, the opening of the first peacetime Parliament, Remembrance Day and other important occasions. On the day the atomic bomb was dropped on Hiroshima, Director Aylen went to the studio to make the momentous announcement.

There was a heavy emphasis on international relations, especially the Canadian involvement. The UK Section -- later called the English Section -- was always on the lookout for interviews with military, political and business visitors from abroad; they were seen as contributing to meaningful international interactions. Music and drama programs were common fare. Perhaps best remembered are the *Canadian Forum* and *Canadian Chronicle* programs which sought to bring to overseas listeners the views of prominent Canadians in the fields of education, science and culture.

The French section, headed by Major Garneau was imaginative in bridging the interests of its audience in France and French-Canadian troops. News, commentaries, book reviews, press reviews, cultural talks and music were always highlighted. An especially important program was *La Voix du Canada*. Three times a week, excerpts from this program were published in Paris in *Bulletin des Ecoutes* (the official French government monitoring bulletin) which was distributed to various ministries and news services. Many French programs were relayed over European radio services.

The Czech programs were generally similar in content -- an emphasis on news, commentaries and cultural talks -- as the offerings to France and Britain. It was however, not a duplication of material, rather an adaptation placing the programs in a context familiar to the audience; there was always a unique personalized touch.

Dr. Schmolka's Czech section featured an enormously successful personal message service. In co-operation with the Canadian Red Cross, thousands of messages in Czech were collected across Canada for the *Czech Bulletin Board*. The program provided a link between Canada and Czechoslovakia before postal service was resumed; it played an important role in helping refugees find their relatives and friends. One Czech postmaster transcribed the messages and passed them on to 'lost relatives'. A Czech composer who sent a song to the CBC heard it broadcast before mail could get through with the news that it would be aired.

Canadian programs were often rebroadcast on Czech radio, reflecting the superb quality and the popular appeal. There was a memorial service on the life and work of Thomas Masaryk, President-liberator. The opening program in the series features the Little Symphony of Montreal in a half hour of Czech music, Dr. Schmolka himself was soloist.

1945-1948

The first three years, 1945 - 1948, were boom years for the International Service. Many of the hidden problems -- especially technical -- had been resolved. There was a realignment of staff, which expanded from 41 to 185. Many of the university people went back to their academic posts. The journalistic approach in policy was gaining dominance. The armed forces section was phased out. Psychological warfare against Germany, largely focused on de-Nazification and re-education, was rapidly losing its significance as friendship policies emerged. Most important was theinauguration of services in new languages and target areas in quick succession. Just as the last rounds of ammunition were fired in Europe, Dutch-language broadcasts were started on May 1, 1945. There was a large audience in Holland reflecting a true interest in and goodwill towards Canada: Queen Wilhelmina had found a safe haven in Ottawa during the war. Canadian troops played an important role in the liberation of Holland and spent much time billeted in that country. One of the happy side effects of this Canadian-Dutch interaction was the movement of war brides to Canada. An obvious interest in Canada developed. Special programs, many involving war brides sending home their observations about their new country, contributed to the wide appeal.

Canada's broadcasts in Czech were going out to only one part of the country's population and this was corrected on July 1, 1945, when Slovak broadcasts were added. On that same day, the English -language service to the

Caribbean was started. Much like the programing transmitted to European countries, there was a personal touch to the Caribbean transmission.

The International Service hit a responsive chord in the West Indies where Canadian National Railways ships -- the Lady Boats, as they were called -- were an integral part of the transportation system in the 1940s. West Indian students had been coming for many years to Canadian colleges and universities, especially McGill and Loyola in Montreal. Trade in foodstuffs between Canada and the West Indies dates back to long before Confederation, Canadian pharmaceutical, furniture, industrial goods are as commonplace in the islands as Canadian apples. International Service broadcasts were an indicator of Canadian interest in the West Indian people and they reciprocated. Almost immediately radio stations in six islands began rebroadcasting the Canadian programs, including news bulletins.

The Voice of Canada could be heard across the Caribbean region from Jamaica to Trinidad. That voice had a strong Caribbean accent. Calypso music had become popular during the war years and the programs to the West Indies regularly featured the famous Calypsonian, Lord Caresser. Since Lord Caresser had no back-up music, International Service staff members were organized by Mavor Moore to provide rhythm and chorus. Reminiscing about the pioneering days four decades later, Moore said "The International Service did serious things but it also knew how to have fun and this was projected in its broadcasts."[11]

The expansion drive in languages and target areas continued in 1946. On April 23, programming was inaugurated to Scandinavia in Danish, Swedish and Norwegian. Spanish-language programs to Latin America began on June 1, 1946. In March of 1948, Canadian broadcasting in English to the South Pacific -- specifically Australia and New Zealand -- was inaugurated. Two months later, the Latin American Service was expanded with programs in Portuguese to Brazil. This was followed in the fall of 1948 by broadcasts in French to the Caribbean and broadcasts in Italian to Southern Europe. The Canadian shortwave broadcasting horizon had expanded in many directions. The International Service was on the air for 12 hours a day, broadcasting in a dozen languages. At the same time, there were huge gaps in the broadcasting map; conspicuously absent were three of the Great Powers: the United States, the Soviet Union and China.

An internal CBC report commented about this period of expansion:

> The world saw itself as a brotherhood of nations and many nations entered the shortwave broadcasting field with the intent of friendship. The language services

> inaugurated were those spoken in countries espousing a liberal democratic intent similar to ours. Propaganda was unthinkable in broadcasts to friends, and one of the main foci for programming was the emergence of the United Nations, and Canada's role in that organization.

The International Service interest in and support for the United Nations began with the founding conference at San Francisco on April 25, 1945, when Canada's shortwave broadcaster was in its infancy. In the two-month period of the conference, 54 items in French and English were broadcast to Europe plus many German and Czech translations. Also, the precedent was set to make the broadcast facility available to foreign officials.

A sampling of the broadcasts in the formative years, some in External Affairs archives and others in CBC files, provide a footprint of the Canadian march into international broadcasting. There are flashes of individual genius in the Czech and German broadcasts, there are many marvellously nostalgic programs addressed to the forces, there are insightful discussions in the French and English language services, there is a solid flow of news in all languages of broadcasting. The International Service was telling the world about Canada.

In the news, the International service adopted the tradition of CBC integrity that had developed, sometimes painfully, in the nationally-owned broadcast system. One of the lessons of World War II that we learned from the BBC was the need to develop the confidence of the listeners in the reliability of the news. The Canadian Press NewsAgency, Reuters and Associated Press provided the International Service with the same basic news service that went to Canada's newspapers. The International Service developed a reputation for being the CBC's premier newsroom and public affairs service.

The two major reasons for establishing the International Service -- broadcasting to the forces and psychological warfare -- were no longer valid. The main objective had become to make friends for Canada and advertise the country. Trade considerations were always important. The stereotype image of Canada -- trap lines, deep snow, the RCMP on horses, the Nelson Eddy/ Jeanette MacDonald projection of the land -- needed adjustments to reflect the industrial capacity. The ultimate consumer abroad needed to identify Canada not just as a source of raw materials but as an important manufacturing nation. The indirect advertising of Canada was seen as an adjunct to the Canadian foreign trade drive. It may have been envisaged as a soft sell but one that was expected to reap profits.

More importantly, the sampling of programs reflect a strong picture of the country, especially its cultural stamp. The many scripts prepared by historians, political scientists, geographers, agricultural experts, scientists and educators, among others, provide the Canadian dimension of each topic. The scripts, dealing with sophisticated themes, had to be written in a simple style to be understood by foreign audiences and they had to be clear so that they lent themselves to translation. Some of the most insightful material ever written about Canada came from distinguished scholars who perceived a special challenge in explaining Canada to the world. Leading journalists, artists, musicians and composers helped to shape the image of Canada; they created textbooks in scripts and recorded in words and sounds things which until then had often been intangible.

Stuart Griffiths, one of the true geniuses of the International Service and later of Canadian and British television, noted that he was constantly amazed how much of Canadianism exists in the minds only, and how much of it needed to be written down and talked about.[12] The International Service projected an inclusive picture of the contribution of the Englissh, French and Native peoples which were placed in the context of the broad Canadian cultural setting which, among other things, was producing worthwhile orchestral and instrumental music for films, radio and for the concert-hall. The International Service, through its broadcasts in six languages in 1946 and in 16 languages a decade later had become a catalyst in Canadian cultural affairs. As Griffiths put it: "Within Canada, radio is said to be an entertainment medium with educational possibilities. The reverse could almost be said of Canadian shortwave programs."[13]

CHAPTER IX

INTERNATIONAL SERVICE - EXTERNAL AFFAIRS: THE EARLY RELATIONSHIP

The International Service, though part of the CBC, was very much a child of government. The Department of External Affairs had, and continued to have, a special interest in the shortwave broadcasting organization which it regarded as an instrument of foreign policy. Furthermore, External Affairs felt that the International Service would be perceived abroad as the Voice of Canada and this voice had to be carefully modulated to reflect the official Canadian position. The thinking of External Affairs was not easily translated into practice; the International Service was not easily tamed and it did not take long before dynamic tensions developed.

The relationship between Ottawa and the International Service began smoothly; it was wartime and everyone had pulled together to get the service launched. The camaraderie that developed in the joint effort to obtain the transmitters in the United States soon soured in peacetime; the CBC and External Affairs had different priorities and eyed each other suspiciously. In this section, we will focus on this relationship in the planning stage and the first three years of broadcasting.

Organized and financed by the government, there was an umbilical cord linking Ottawa and the International Service. This linkage was given official recognition in the 1942 Order-in-Council establishing the service.[1]

> In view of the fact that such short wave broadcasts would constitute a factor affecting Canada's relations with the other countries of theCommonwealth and with foreign countries, the work of the Canadian Broadcasting Corporation in this field should be carried on in consultation with the Department of External Affairs.

The word "consultation" lends itself to different interpretations and, indeed, it took on different meanings over the years. Even before construction began at Sackville, there was little doubt as to who was in charge. In 1942, the CBC, which had itself been in existence for only six years, had its hands full with covering the war, and in the first instance it wanted the shortwave service utilized for winning the war; plans would be made later about the role of shortwave in peacetime. The assistant general manager of the CBC, Dr. Frigon, who was a driving force in building the shortwave facility, had recommended that External Affairs appoint one of its own, preferably Saul Rae, as first head (Supervisor) of the International Service. Rae was not available and the job went to a veteran CBC employee, Peter Aylen, who was known and liked in government circles.

In the spirit of the cooperative venture between government and CBC, the Short Wave Committee, later called the CBC-International Service Advisory Committee, was established to make policy decisions and provide guidance. There was an immediate recognition that the Psychological Warfare Committee would provide very specific guidance for broadcasting to Germany and the occupied countries. External Affairs "exerted primary leadership" in both the Short Wave Committee and the Psychological Warfare Committee and, as the Department historian points out, "this was generally acceptable."[2]

On June 22, 1944, six months before the start of broadcasting, the most senior officials of the CBC and External Affairs attended the Short Wave Committee meetingin the East Block office of the Under-Secretary, Norman Robertson. The minutes of the meeting state: "It was agreed ... that External Affairs was the final authority in all policy decisions."[3] This supremacy position of External Affairs applied to the International Service, the Wartime Information Board and the Psychological Warfare committee.

The ties were cemented in a number of ways. Officials of the CBC shortwave service would become members of various Political Warfare Committees. A liaison arrangement was also worked out: the CBC would have a shortwave representative in Ottawa for close contact with government officials and External Affairs, for its part, would designate an officer through whom shortwave problems would be cleared.

External Affairs exerted its authority gently in the early days; it was not challenged; certainly not in wartime. If the International Service was to be a meaningful instrument of foreign policy and psychological warfare, it would have to be taken into the confidence of the Department of External Affairs. The International Service was integrated into the External's information loop. As a memorandum (January 18, 1945) observed, External Affairs regarded the shortwave broadcasting service as "virtually a new Wartime Information Office abroad" it would receive the same information that is sent by Ottawa to WIB offices in New York and Washington.[4] The boundaries between the International Service and External Affairs -- between journalism and diplomacy -- had become blurred at the organizational level.

The January 18 memorandum notes "the wartime partnership interest" and speaks of the marvellous things that can be expected from the International

Service which will have a ''superb'' news operation in that it will be served by the major news agencies: Canadian Press, Associated Press and Reuters. The International Service will be immensely enriched in that it will have access to the full text of official documents for government announcements. The memorandum also discusses the news selection process:[5]

> In its wartime role at least, CBC International Service in its official news will have to maintain the same degree of accuracy as WIB (Wartime Information Board). In other words, it cannot afford quite the same leeway on selection and perspective that the commercial news agencies enjoy. Prompt access through WIB to texts of documents, etc., will enable it to check the news stories against the documents. Another factor is that the emphasis in the news stories it will be receiving from the commercial agencies will be conditioned by Canadian or American news interest, whereas complete texts may include European angles of interest that have been dropped from the news stories.

A teletype connection was installed to link the International Service on Crescent Street in Montreal with the Wartime Information Board's Ottawa -- New York -- Washington circuit. Also a courier bag service was initiated for confidential and secret documents. For highly secret and urgent information, the messages appropriately marked as to category of secrecy, were dispatched to the External Affairs Code Room from where they were sent scrambled over the Ottawa-Montreal teletype. External Affairs was concerned about security. All messages and documents ranging from ''confidential'' to ''secret'' and beyond, were addressed to Supervisor, Aylen personally. Aylen was cautioned that Canadian reporters were ''continuously on the lookout for Canadian news, and special attention should be given to protect the security of the information.''[6] The security concerns were about Canadian journalists, not enemy spies.

The record shows that Aylen adopted a subservient role in relation to External Affairs; he did everything possible to please Terry MacDermot, the officer who kept an eye on the service. MacDermot, in a document reporting on a meeting with Aylen, notes with obvious satisfaction that ''Mr. Aylen again asked for as much general advice as could be supplied by the Department on current topics. He said that the comments and observations now being received on particular and general points had been of the greatest value to him and his staff.''[7]

Aylen told MacDermot that one of his first challenges was to train a group of broadcasters to handle international news; special comment from External Affairs would be helpful. "In this process," Aylen told MacDermot, "the quick and confidential means of communication provided by the teletype is most useful."

Reminiscing about this arrangement some 40 years later, Aylen gave a very different picture of the value of the teletype and the advice from External Affairs:[8]

> To reassure External Affairs what a responsible group we were, we put in a teletype with a decoder and a coding machine on it so we could always send a coded message to Ottawa to get any advice. This thing gathered dust over the years. But I thought we should try it out and this was after Holland had been liberated and we were getting quite a lot of letters from young women in Holland saying how much the Canadians had been admired, how popular they were and how everybody liked them.

Aylen sent a coded message to External Affairs noting that he was getting a lot of mail from Holland asking about immigration to Canada. "How should we deal with these letters?"[9]

> A couple of days went by and the only directive I think I ever received from External Affairs said you shall do nothing that will either encourage or discourage immigration.

Aylen recalled that people at the CBC were worried about the governmental role in news and information; they believed that "External Affairs would want to watch over us like a hawk." Instead he found ambivalence at External Affairs "they would prefer to be able to disown us ... if we had done something silly." The files at External Affairs, however, show no such ambivalence and in fact the Department was monitoring closely the output of the shortwave service. External affairs had detailed views on policy aspects of broadcasts but at the same time had no meaningful machinery for translating the policy into practice, except in the case of German-language programs which were closely tied to the Psychological Warfare Committee.

Aylen had a pragmatic approach to policy issues, in part based on his observations at the British Broadcasting Corporation in London in the fall of 1944. He had gone to Britain to learn about the BBC's external broadcast service and his experience was almost humorous. As an example he cited a controversy involving the BBC and the British Foreign Office as to whether General Charles de Gaulle was to be allowed to claim that he had liberated Paris. Aylen was in the office of J.B. Clarke, the head of the BBC's European Service, and a newsman, came rushing in with a dispatch saying that De Gaulle was in Paris. The phone was ringing and Clarke picked it up to speak to the Foreign Office. "He looked at his dispatch and said into the phone, 'I am sorry, it is too late; we have just broadcast it.'"[10]

Aylen was impressed with the specific details that had been worked out at the BBC as to what the news should feature on a given day, and which personalities should be highlighted. But when he went to subsequent editorial policy meetings, much of the discussion was taken up with explanations why senior regional language advisers had not followed the precise details of policy. He concluded at the time that laying down policy in detail was not suitable for a small organization: "If you try to put people in a strait jacket, they are going to try and wiggle out; it will become a challenge to them to get around it."[11]

Aylen's approach was different from what he found at the BBC. He gave responsibility to area supervisors and it was up to them to know if there was a problem in the text and if it should be referred to someone. There was much uncertainty as to what the policy was and Aylen said he felt the International Service had to be thoughtful and careful because it did not want to give a misleading impression to listeners overseas who had no Canadian context against which to interpret the news that was flowing from Canada.[12]

Aylen, for his part, was less personally involved in policy than Ottawa had hoped. In theory, the responsibility for policy control was vested in the General Supervisor (Aylen) and the Policy Editor, but in practice it was being handled almost exclusively by the Policy Editor. In part, this was a reflection of the Aylen style not to become involved in details and, in part, it reflected his confidence in Sally Solomon, the first Policy Editor, who was admirably qualified for the job.

Sally Solomon was incredibly knowledgeable, and despite all the efforts by External Affairs to discredit her as a security risk during the cold war, she made an enormous contribution to the orderly development of the International Service. Aylen appointed Solomon as Policy Editor because she spoke most of the languages that were being broadcast and she had, largely on her own, become a specialist in international affairs. More than anyone else in Canada, she knew the sound of shortwave radio; before going to the International

Service her CBC job was to monitor shortwave broadcasts from abroad at the Stittsville receiving station near Ottawa.

As Policy Editor, Solomon "kept an eye" on the material being broadcast. If the heads of target areas had any concerns about their scripts, they were to address them to Solomon. "She wasn't exactly a censor but she was there to consult with if they were troubled by something." If the target area supervisors wondered whether or not to broadcast a story or if they needed some clarification to put an issue in a Canadian context, they were supposed to go to Solomon. She did not edit the scripts but she made suggestions. If the target area heads had a problem and did not consult with Solomon and it turned out that they were broadcasting something that was regarded as giving a misleading or invalid perspective of Canada or its policy, "then they were in trouble."[13]

Looking back 40 years later, Aylen said the Policy Editor approach was good, "it kept the place fairly free-wheeling but there was some consciousness that we were supposed to be responsible." Aylen added that the system worked well; while Solomon was regarded as a bit of a nuisance by the broadcasters they certainly made use of her. "She relieved me of a great deal of time spent on ... detailed problems and languages that I really didn't know."

Solomon was Policy Editor for seven years until she was abruptly ousted at the insistence of External Affairs, a matter that will be discussed later.

The Changing Relationship

On the surface, External Affairs and the International Service developed a smooth-working relationship in 1946 and 1947 -- years of expansion for the broadcasting service. Almost by default External Affairs had loosened its ties to the broadcaster, reflecting the peace-time atmosphere in Ottawa. Occasionally, there was guidance along general lines. The International Service focused largely on providing a news service -- national and international -- and general information about Canada, it did not find much need to consult closely. In the background, however, tensions were building up, almost inevitably.

Early indications of External Affairs' displeasure with International Service broadcasts appear in a memorandum prepared for F.H. Soward, a senior official, in July, 1946.[14] A departmental official who had been scrutinizing scripts broadcast to Germany and other European countries observed: "I must say I am far from impressed." He described the Germans as "an exceptionally serious minded people'' who would be interested in talks on the Canadian economy, Canadian federalism and other serious problems; instead he found talks on Eskimos and Indians which he described as ''Boys' Own Papers'' material. The External Affairs official was specific in criticisms of some scripts (e.g., ''Austria and the Paris Conference'') and called the content woolly. He went on to describe the news review -- a highlight of the broadcasts -- as very mediocre. He questioned the value of CBC broadcasts to Europe: ''If it cannot be done better than this, it seems to me it had better not be done at all.'' External Affairs notified Stuart Griffiths, a senior manager at the International Service, of its displeasure.

The criticisms appear to have had little merit. By mid 1946, the International Service had superb newsroom responsible and much admired. The Austrian and German scripts by Helmut Blume, Eric Koch, Charles Wassermann and others were held in the highest regard by the British and Americans. The BBC worked out an arrangement with the International Service to rebroadcast the German language commentaries.

The memorandum calls for a change in the make up of the Shortwave Committee with External Affairs representation increased from two to five members. The committee was stacked to help External Affairs exercise the final authority on all policy decisions. The new committee would meet more frequently and work out a clear policy to guide the International Service. Also, more External Affairs officials would have to become familiar with the broadcast service so they could play a lager role in policy and operations.[16]

The memorandum served its purpose and the CBC government Shortwave Committee was transformed into the ''Advisory Committee on the CBC International Service'' with more External Affairs representation and of a higher rank. At the June 1947 meeting of the Committee, Pearson called for monthly meetings, which was readily agreed on. External Affairs, thus, through structural change of the Advisory Committee and its intended ''more hands on'' relationship with the International Service, was giving new meaning to ''consultations.''

CHAPTER X

THE COLD WAR: THE EARLY DAYS

The building blocks of the cold war include a dramatic incident in Canada: the defection of Igor Gouzenko, a cypher clerk at the Soviet embassy in Ottawa. Mr. Gouzenko walked out of the embassy on September 5, 1945 -- just three weeks after Japan's surrender and the end of World War II -- with incriminating evidence about Soviet spy rings and infiltrations in Canada and other western countries. Official Ottawa did not want to believe Gouzenko and he sought shelter at the *Ottawa Journal*. When Soviet embassy staff tried to retrieve Gouzenko, he and his family were finally provided protective custody on September 7. The incident led to the arrest of a dozen suspects who later appeared before a Royal Commission of Inquiry which confirmed the seriousness of the Soviet espionage activities in July, 1946. By that time, the Soviet intentions against western countries had been projected into the limelight by Winston Churchill who, in a speech at the University of Missouri in Fulton, warned western countries to beware of the USSR, referring to an 'Iron Curtain' descending across Europe.

Whatever the root causes of the cold war -- including Western suspicions of the USSR and Soviet paranoia of Western intent, Canada was bound to be a party to it. Certainly, External Affairs attempted in the early days to show restraint; the files indicate much enthusiasm about maintaining the allied relationship with the Soviet Union that developed during the common war effort against the Nazis.

In 1947, during the extensive expansion of languages of broadcast, the CBC and External affairs were consulting frequently on introducing broadcasts to the Soviet Union. The strong Canadian signal from Sackville had proven its ability to reach the Soviet Union in a number of programs beamed to the USSR, with the approval and cooperation of the Soviet embassy in Ottawa. About half a dozen of these special programs, beginning in 1945, had been transmitted to the Soviet Union commemorating Canadian and Soviet national holidays (e.g., Canada Day, Soviet Army Day). Through these special programs Canada became the first allied country to broadcast in Russian. The BBC wanted to introduce a Russian service during the war but Moscow advised that this would be considered a 'most unfriendly' act. (The Soviet government had confiscated shortwave sets from the general public at the beginning of hostilities; consequently that broadcasting in Russian would be heard only by government officials who were not considered an appropriate audience). The United

Nations, using the Sackville transmitters made available by Canada, was broadcasting Russian material regularly and this was received clearly enough in Moscow for recording and rebroadcasting. Canada knew, then, that its signals were audible in the Soviet Union. But in 1947 alone, daily programs in four new languages were inaugurated -- Spanish, Danish, Norwegian and Swedish -- and a weekly service was established to Australia and New Zealand. There were problems of space; although the original Crescent street facility had expanded to include offices near Bishop Street, but this was not enough. Finding staff to meet foreign language needs was always difficult; there was no one around to test the language skills of the new announcers. When Italian was introduced, the International Service sent scripts and recorded programs to the BBC for language evaluations. Most problematic was transmitter time, both CBC shortwave transmitters were working at full capacity.

The International Service had not yet developed to the point where it -- and External Affairs -- considered it advisable to begin regular broadcasts in Russian. A memorandum prepared by the assistant Supervisor of the International Service, Charles Delafield, on January 5, 1948, noted that there was no especially high priority attached to Russian broadcasts: "In other words, the Russian language broadcasts are awaiting their turn in our schedule of detailed planning."[1] It would be another two years before Canada began broadcasting in Russian.

Among the many CBC listeners in Europe, the programs to Czechoslovakia were especially successful. As soon as mail services in post-war Europe were restored, letters began arriving from many appreciative listeners saying how much they enjoyed the Czech and Slovak programs; they requested program information, including transmission times and the transmission frequencies. In 1947, there was a flood of letters from Czechoslovakia -- more than 1000 a month -- and a reply went out to every writer. The Canadian Chargé d'Affaires in Prague, R.M. McDonnell, in a dispatch (January 1948) declared that the International Service was the most effective and successful instrument for the distribution of Canadian information in Czechoslovakia, "while the owners of shortwave receiving sets did not constitute a mass audience, the CBC was reaching thousands."[2]

The Coup in Czechoslovakia

On February 25, 1948, the very day that the CBC was marking its third anniversary of service to Czechoslovakia, a Communist takeover resulted in the proclamation of a Socialist Republic in Prague. The cooling relations between East and West was now turning into a cold war. The new situation had major implications for Canadian foreign policy and for the International Service.

The CBC worried immediately about its listeners in Czechoslovakia, especially those who had been writing letters; the recipients of program schedules and other information. The Chargé d'Affaires in Prague, MacDonnell, telegraphed Stuart Griffiths, the head of the European Service, to stop all mailings; no further replies to Czech mail or sending of schedules; he was receiving letters and phone calls in Prague from worried listeners.

McDonnell had an appreciation of the predicament of the Czechoslovak listeners and in a letter (March 5, 1948) to Dr. Schmolka, the head of the Czechoslovak Section, he observed:[3]

> From what we know of the way of life in iron curtain countries, we can be confident that before long, if not already, any sort of contact between a Czech and Western influences will be a source of danger for the individual. We can expect that the mail will be watched closely, and that those who are found to be sending or receiving mail from the West will be investigated unpleasantly by the police.

The Chargé d'Affaires thought the International Service could take in its stride the disappearance of letters. Czechs and Slovaks would spread the word quietly from one to another about the program schedule and indications were that they were still listening. The Czechoslovak press, now under the control of the Communist authorities, was already "complaining bitterly that people are treacherously listening to foreign news broadcasts instead of being content with the home grown product."[4]

Political Warfare

External Affairs was troubled about the Czechoslovak situation specifically and had wider concerns about the dissemination of information behind the iron curtain. The Department thought it might be useful to reconstitute the Psychological Warfare Committee which, during the war, had been closely tied to Canada's involvement in international broadcasting. Marcel Cadieux circulated a memorandum on March 11, 1948 calling for a study for reactivating

Psychological Warfare. One of the positive responses came from Saul Rae who called for a well-staffed Psychological Warfare working unit rather than a Departmental Committee as was previously the case.[5] On April 2, 1948, a blue ribbon group at External Affairs -- Cadieux, Rae, Watkins, Crean and Southam -- met to discuss psychological warfare and the setting up of machinery for this task.

On April 16, 1948 -- six weeks after the Czechoslovak coup -- Lester Pearson, who was then Undersecretary, called a special meeting late Friday afternoon in the East bloc. The memorandum on the meeting is entitled "Political Warfare." Ten persons attended: nine of the most senior people at External Affairs and the Chairman of the CBC, Davidson Dunton.

The meeting focussed on how Canada could disseminate information in communist-dominated countries and how to ensure that such information was presented in a "suitable form, e.g., in line with the general objectives of our external policy."[6] Mr. Pearson was concerned that the CBC should not give the impression, through their broadcasts to Czechoslovakia, that Canada "is prepared to continue normal trade relations with that country under their present regime."[7]

For all practical purposes, the International Service was the only means through which Canada could penetrate the iron curtain; there were negligible, if any, facilities for film and print distribution. But External Affairs had doubts about the size of the political audience in communist countries and was concerned that jamming might prevent Canadian programs from reaching their target audience. It was suggested that if the number of listeners in communist countries was too small to make the broadcast worthwhile, it would be preferable for Canada to concentrate its broadcasting efforts "for friendly or marginal countries like Italy or Sweden."[8]

There was agreement at the External Affair meeting that if Canadian broadcasts were to be directed systematically to communist-controlled countries, close arrangements would have to be worked out with the CBC to ensure that the broadcasts were properly related to Canadian policy objectives. CBC Chairman Dunton appreciated the need to have liaison but was also seeking limits to the government's role. It was agreed that External Affairs could not write the broadcast scripts; it would, however, prepare for the International Service guidance notes on policy and the interpretation of current questions of interest. Three principles were adopted for the guidance notes:[9]

1. Nothing should be said or done that suggest Canadian approval of communist-controlled governments.

2. Use every opportunity to encourage democratic elements.

3. Avoid situations that could lead to diplomatic protests, as technically Canada is on friendly terms with the communist countries.

In preparation for the April 16 meeting, Pearson conferred with Frank Nemec, the former Czechoslovak ambassador in Ottawa, who left his diplomatic post in protest against the takeover and was given sanctuary in Canada. Nemec was a man of principle, he had served the Czechoslovak government in exile and negotiated with Churchill. Members of his family were wiped out by the Nazis in retaliation for his London wartime broadcast over the BBC. Nemec told Pearson that the Soviet Union, in its propaganda, depicted itself as the protector of Czechs and Slovaks against the Germans. This was a highly effective propaganda line; the Czechs and Slovaks were concerned about future German aggression. Mr. Pearson thought that Nemec could explain very usefully that no one in Canada or the western democracies intended to allow Germany to threaten her neighbours again.[10] Nemec was invited to prepare talks for the International Service. (This marked the beginning of an association which led to Nemec becoming a full-time employee of the International Service until his death in the early 1970s.)

The April 16 meeting in the East Bloc took place in an atmosphere of suspicion, a feeling that Canada had been duped and that the worst fears of the Gouzenko affair were being confirmed. The question of loyalties of Czechs in Canada surfaced. There was at the time only one Czech language newspaper in Canada and it was according to reports received by External Affairs, communist controlled. (Another Czech newspaper suspended publication shortly before the February takeover.) have to be revived or,better yet, a new Czech paper with the appropriate ideological perspective would have to be established. The Canadian Chamber of Commerce, "through appropriate channels," would be requested to establish "a truly democratic newspaper." Such a newspaper could serve an additional role in providing useful material for broadcasts to Czechoslovakia.[11]

The atmosphere of suspicion extended to the Czechoslovak programs of the International Service. The External Affairs' officials noted that the Czech editor (Dr. Schmolka) wrote his scripts in Czech; while there was no question about his loyalty, it would be advisable to have English translations of Czech scripts to ensure that the programs conformed to Canadian external policy.[12]

At the end of the meeting, it appeared that the International Service which was then broadcasting to only one communist country -- Czechoslovakia -- would extend its iron curtain service with broadcasts to the USSR, Poland

and Yugoslavia. The Canadian missions in these countries were asked to advise on the policy lines for the broadcasts.

Within a week, the Advisory Committee for the International Service set up a sub-committee to examine the new interest in broadcasting to communist countries, the liaison between the broadcasting service and the CBC, and the security aspects of this liaison. The sub-committee's report of July 3, 1948, -- adopted by the Advisory Committee at its July 15th meeting -- called for a much closer relationship between the International Service and Ottawa. The close liaison had two main aims: (a) providing the International Service with detailed information about conditions in communist-controlled countries, and (b) providing the International service with background notes on government policy. The background notes were actually envisaged as the policy guidance notes to which the International Service would be expected to adhere. The International Service would become, in External's view, the Voice of Canada.

The close interaction was facilitated with tri-weekly diplomatic bag service and a scrambler telephone. The International Service liaison officer -- Arthur Pidgeon, at the time -- was provided with an office at External Affairs where he was treated pretty much like an External Affairs officer; he collected material and advice for broadcasts. Special attention was given to the security of secret documents. Furthermore, hiring practices would be changed to ensure that security standards at the International Service were equivalent to those at External Affairs. This included clearance by the RCMP, a practice that would be in effect for more than 20 years.

External Affairs wanted a better grasp of what was going out on the air in foreign languages and translation into English of scripts (on a selective basis) was organized. The recommendations also called for new language broadcasts to Italy, Yugoslavia and Poland; a limited service -- news and news reviews only -- to the Soviet Union, and daily programming in French and Flemish to Belgium.

External Affairs felt somewhat uncertain as to how to deal with difficult international broadcasting issues, and the diplomatic missions in London and Washington were asked to find out how Britain and the United States approached similar problems. The detailed dispatch from Washington about the Voice of America operations and the linkage to the State Department were particularly revealing, but this system was more applicable to a huge broadcast enterprise compared to the small Canadian shortwave operation. In contrast to the Washington approach -- regarded as somewhat heavy-handed -- the BBC external broadcasting operation was seen as closer to Canadian thinking, especially since the CBC was modelled after the BBC.

On June 21, 1948, a small group of senior External Affairs officials met in the Undersecretary's office with Sir Ian Jacob, the Director-General of the BBC's Overseas Broadcasts about the British experience.[13] (CBC Chairman Davidson Dunton and the BBC's Canadian representative, Michael Barkway, also attended.) In reply to a question from Saul Rae about the BBC link with the Foreign Office, Sir Ian described Europe as the battleground at that time and he said that it was always necessary for the BBC to consider political factors. At the same time, the BBC maintained a long view, their purpose was not to try to influence people to do something at any particular moment. The aim was a positive rather than negative job: rather than trying to counter communism, emphasis was palced on expounding Western civilization in all its forms.

Sir Ian allowed that while the BBC tried to keep out of the immediate battle, an exception was made in the Italian elections because, as he put it, the prevention of a communist victory in Italy was clearly in the interest of Italy as well as the United Kingdom. Even in that case, the BBC tried to influence the Italians indirectly, by expounding the British view of events in Europe and by showing clearly what had happened in Czechoslovakia.[14]

Sir Ian thought that broadcasting to Soviet satellite countries was analogous to Britain's broadcasts to occupied countries during the war. No amount of broadcasting will make up for hard facts. The aim was to let listeners know what Western civilization stands for, and to build goodwill which will pay dividends in the future. He had some other points of advice about broadcasts:

- Be positive -- do not denigrate and lambaste our enemies, but present our case as favourably as possible.

- Balance cultural and political broadcasting; more friendly links are built up by cultural broadcasts than by political ones.

- In a critical situation, political emphasis is necessary lest listeners get the impression of indifference. The aim in Czechoslovakia and Finland (both crisis spots at the time) is not to advise people what to do, but to show an interest in their affairs and keep hope alive.

- Do not respond directly to lies; in attacking another broadcast directly, one merely advertises its existence.

- Do not become a mouthpiece for emigré interests. (The BBC uses emigrés on air only if there is something to be gained from the British point of view.)

- Teaching English by radio builds up an audience.

- The Russians have started jamming foreign broadcasts (American and Spanish) and it is probable that they are developing a jamming organization.

- American broadcasts were sometimes too obviously propaganda.

- Some critics of overseas broadcasting have an exaggerated idea of what propaganda can do; it cannot drive out an occupying army by itself.

Escott Reid asked Sir Ian a curious question; he wanted to know if it was useful for Canada to broadcast news in view of the fact that the BBC was providing such thorough coverage in its newscasts. In response, the BBC official presented a strong argument for Canadian news: Canada is of interest to European listeners as a country standing away from Europe and yet extremely interested, a detached observer with no axe to grind except to maintain peace and friendship.

Lester Pearson directed Escott Reid to arrange the Departmental flow of guidance notes on current international developments. Reid sent memoranda to the various divisions at External Affairs in which he sought to clarify what he wanted:[15]

> 'Guidance' notes is a polite term for what in wartime was called 'directives' -- that is to say, they should set forth the general attitude of the Canadian Government to a question and suggest the way in which a question should be approached in the international broadcasts of the CBC.

The guidance notes prepared by the European and UN Division were to be sent to Saul Rae of the Information Division for editing. It would be six months before the first of these guidance notes -- on broadcasts to Germany -- were sent to the International Service.

As External Affairs, in response to the takeover in Czechoslovakia, was contemplating the reactivation of political warfare machinery and examining language for accommodation of this in the Cabinet War Book, there were a number of other developments that further complicated the international situation. On May 14, 1948, the State of Israel was established and this in turn set off an invasion from neighbouring Arab countries. In Ottawa, there was much internal debate in view of different pulls from Washington and London on the recognition of Israel. (While the Israel-Arab disputes and subsequent wars would become major issues of contention in the Cold War, Washington and Moscow were the first to extend diplomatic recognition to Israel.)

A major contributing factor to East-West tension came on June 24, 1948 -- four months after the coup in Prague -- with the Berlin blockade; the Soviet Union stopped road and rail communication between Berlin and the western zones (British, US and French) of Germany. This led to the Berlin Airlift. Ottawa declared full support of the airlift but decided not to take part.

The Berlin blockade and the airlift provide examples of difficult international situations that required coverage by the sensitive International Service. It would be another six months until External Affairs sent policy guidance to the International Service for German broadcasts to explain Ottawa's complex and contradictory position.

"The time had come," External Affairs said in a five page letter to Dilworth, "for Canada to take a more active part in the war ideas that is now being waged between the democracies on the one side, and the Soviet Union and its satellites, on the other." These introductory remarks set the tone of the detailed letter which declares that in the broadcasts to Germany "you should loose no opportunity to stress the dangers to peace that are inherent in the Soviet Government's policy, particularly in Germany." There was also advice on how to wage psychological warfare:

> It is, of course, desirable that you should be as subtle as possible: wherever possible, we should like you in your commentaries, to relate Soviet actions to the Soviet grand strategy which is derived from the teachings of Marx, Lenin and Stalin. The Germans see for themselves what the Russians are doing in Germany. Our object should be to make them understand that they are being used to promote the long-term objectives of Soviet Government's activities. It would be desirable to concentrate on activities since the conclusion of the war and avoid derogatory reference to Soviet war-time behaviour.

The External Affairs letter discusses many dimensions of Canada's views on Germany which should shape the broadcasts:

On Democracy

- The German people are confused about the exact meaning of democracy.
- It would be bad policy to attempt to define democracy in the abstract.
- Distinguish between "popular" and "democratic" and on every possible occasion point out that communist methods fail to measure up to democratic standards.

On Berlin

- Canada regards the Soviet Union as being responsible for the Berlin situation which had become a threat to international peace and security.
- Canada's non participation in the airlift is not an indication that it is not sympathetic with either the Western Powers or the inhabitants of Berlin.
- Canada never rejected the principle of participation in the airlift but there are practical, legal and possibly, domestic difficulties.

The letter declares that Canada is sympathetic towards the German people who were in an "inevitable position." In line with this, the International Service was told to avoid whenever possible, without evading an obvious issue, the discussion of past events. At the same time, External Affairs cautioned that on no account should there be "any support whatever to the reviving belief in Germany that the Nazis were fundamentally right but their tactics were wrong."

The External Affairs guidance letter stated that the prospects for a peace treaty were "difficult at this time" and while immigration was "presently prohibited", Canada was admitting displaced persons. Also, Ottawa had extended most-favoured nation status to enhance trade relations.

The enhanced liason between External Affairs and the International Service was essentially an exercise by Ottawa to tell the International Service what to do and how to do it. It did not resolve the problems; it was an open secret that Lester Pearson was troubled by the shortwave operation. A memorandum of September 8, 1948 from Allan Anderson to Saul Rae refers to Pearson's views:[16]

> Mr. Pearson said ... that he is now anxious to have a proper discussion on the whole question of our liaison with CBC-International Service. He mentioned par-

> ticularly that he understood they had picked up, and used 'erroneous reports.'
>
> Mr. Pearson thought that we needed a more positive role in this whole contact. It was not merely the negative matter of stopping errors, but the positive one of keeping these people informed of our policy. Up to now we had not succeeded in devising a really satisfactory means of communication.

There was also unhappiness at the other end. At the beginning of 1948, some three weeks before the coup in Czechoslovakia, the Supervisor at the International Service, Ira Dilworth, discussed with his program committee the extent to which the service was dependent on External Affairs, "an issue which had raised its head in a recent incident." (The minutes of the February 13, 1948 meeting provide no clues about the specific incident.) Dilworth stated that in discussions with officials in Ottawa the understanding reached was that External Affairs did not want to be put in the position of giving permission to the International Service for the contents of broadcasts. External Affairs, however, would always be glad to cooperate when referred to for information. Dilworth stated that the International Service's future approach to External Affairs would be made in the framework of this understanding. He requested all Supervisors to refer to Sally Solomon, the Policy Editor, the subjects which they assign when these subjects impinge in any way upon the field of political or economic policy.

In the next six months with the unfolding of the Czechoslovak takeover and the Berlin blockade, the relationship moved in the reverse direction: there would be greater dependence on External Affairs. At the same time, External Affairs wanted its role to be invisible. In the Advisory Committee Report of July 15, there was a "laundering recommendation"; it stated that directives affecting the actual content of programs should be issued by the General Supervisor or his Assistant, i.e., External Affairs would not be put in a position of giving permission to the International Service.

In the fall and winter of 1948, progress at External Affairs was painstakingly slow in developing guidelines on policy on complex international issues. For one thing, the journalists and news analysts need to simplify and use words sparingly in the short period their scripts are on air. The need to be clear and precise is especially important for translation purposes; being vague in English can result in outlandish interpretations in Czech, or German or Spanish, as the case might be.

The trauma created by the coup in Czechoslovakia brought controversy to the Czech programming. Emigré Czechs in Canada complained that the programs gave comfort to the communists. The Canadian Chargé d'Affaires in Prague, McDonnell, had been asked by Ottawa to listen to the CBC broadcasts and give an evaluation, although he had only a rudimentary knowledge of Czech. In a dispatch dated May 25, 1949 he dismissed the émigré complaints by saying that, "such people would like ... to take over, and are not likely to be satisfied with any shortwave service that does not lash out at the Czechoslovak Government"

At the same time, McDonnell allowed that the CBC failed to recognize the special problems presented to the foreign broadcaster: "not only is there no fight in the CBC programmes, as there sometimes is in the BBC and Voice of America, but there is even an implied suggestion that the cold war and dictatorship in Czechoslovakia are indelicate topics to be avoided."

The dispatch from Prague said that the Czech broadcasts seemed to be saying the same things as the Canadian programs in French and Dutch; in fact, McDonnell thought the Czech service was soft. He was especially critical of the news commentaries which, he said, "had been lacking in vigour and too much inclined to passive on-the-one-hand - and-on-the-other position. Fence-sitting is seldom a dignified posture."

McDonnell was sensitive to the fact that "broadcasters and information people generally are apt to raise the issue of propaganda over programmes of opinion, " but he was prepared to live with this: "they are also apt to ascribe to foreign offices a devilish desire to engage in propaganda which can only be held in check by the pure and blameless information experts."

The Chargé d'Affaires' three-page dispatch provided very specific advice: more news of special interests to eastern Europe; more commentaries on world news, giving opinion as well as facts; fewer run-of-the-mill Canadian programs relying on statistics and details. He wanted less projection of Canada and more emphasis on what he thought the Czechoslovak listener wanted above all: news about Czechoslovakia and its exiles. He wanted Canada to do its share in "that part of the cold war that is fought in the information field."

Throughout 1948, the relationship of trust between External Affairs and the CBC which had developed in the war years when there was close cooperation to set up the shortwave service was floundering. External Affairs had become suspicious of the political reliability of two key personalities in the International Service: Sally Solomon (Policy Editor) and Stuart Griffiths (Supervisor, European Section).

At the February 17, 1949, meeting of the Advisory Committee, Dilworth raised the question of policy control at the International Service. He was worried by the existing situation which in effect gave the Policy Editor in Montreal, Sally Solomon, the power to require the deletion or amendment of material contained in the news and commentaries. Dilworth proposed establishing a three-member policy group: Sally Solomon, an additional editor "close to External Affairs", and the head of the news section. The head of news would have the power to appeal a decision of the policy editor.

E. Benjamin Rogers, in a memo to Pearson the next day, said the discussion was inconclusive and that at External Affairs "the enthusiasm for the proposal was nil." He added:[17]

> The fact that the political reliability of the present policy editor, Miss Solomon, has been questioned was not brought out in the open. It is obvious, however, that the CBC is failing to live up to the real problem.

Rogers suggested that at the next meeting of the Advisory Committee, External Affairs raise the question of Solomon and Griffiths and state that "the Department cannot have confidence in the service until these two people are removed." He also felt it might be useful for External Affairs to place one of its own men at the International Service as a member of the policy group, but first they would have to get rid of Solomon and Griffiths.

Two months later, External Affairs was still pressing the CBC to clean its house. A memorandum for Pearson said that Davidson Dunton (Chairman of the CBC) had advised the Department that "efforts were being made to obtain satisfactory evidence that would justify" the dismissals; the CBC did not want to take action until it had 'a fool proof case." It was suggested that Pearson and Dunton discuss the matter. In the end, the CBC was not able to find satisfactory evidence against the suspects and External Affairs certainly was not producing any. The External Affairs' historian writing about this nearly 30 years later suggests that "the security situation needs to be seen in the light of the atmosphere generated by the Gouzenko revelations, the Spy Trials, the communist coup-de-main in Czechoslovakia, the spate of Communist front organizations, etc."

Tom Benson, who had been a principal CBC announcer and was brought into the International Service by Dilworth to serve in Ottawa as liaison officer at External Affairs was close to the hushed-up controversy. Recalling the events in 1981, some 32 years later, Benson says those were "bad times.[18] There was a communist scare and people were seeing communists behind every door, under every desk, under the carpets."

According to Benson, Dilworth was called in for a meeting in Ottawa with the Under Secretary of State (Pearson) and told that Griffiths and Solomon had to go, that he had no choice.

> He was a very good man, Ira Dilworth, and he looked after his people ... he did not believe in removing somebody merely because of rumours or alleged communist leaning if he did not have any proof ... they finally insisted that they be removed.

Both Solomon and Griffiths were forced out of their positions. Solomon was shunted to a job translating foreign language scripts into English for scrutinizing by External Affairs. Stuart Griffiths went on to fame in television, first at the CBC in Toronto and then in commercial television in Britain; he was regarded as a genius in the information field.

The day that Dilworth was told by Pearson he had to get rid of Solomon and Griffiths was an extremely difficult one for the General Supervisor. That night he had a heart attack. Benson recalls that SDilworth phoned him from the Chateau Laurier Hotel at 3 a.m. and asked him to come down. Benson called the doctor. He also phoned CBC Chairman, Davidson Dunton, who joined them in the hotel room. The doctors took Dilworth to hospital in Ottawa where he stayed for three months.

CHAPTER XI

BEHIND THE IRON CURTAIN

When Newfoundland joined Canada as the 10th province of the Dominion on March 31, 1949, the country could hardly take time out for celebrations. There were ominous developments that year on the international scene. In January, Comecon, aimed at unifying the economic ties of the communist countries, was established in Moscow and, on April 4, Canada was a signatory in Washington to the treaty setting up the North Atlantic Treaty Organization (NATO). That year two Germanies came into existence: on May 23 the Federal Republic of Germany in Bonn and on October 7, the German Democratic Republic in East Berlin. The division of West and East Germany would last for 40 years.

In China, the Communist armies drove the Chinese Nationalists off the mainland and Chang Kai Shek's government moved to Taiwan; on October 1, a Communist government was set up in Peking (Beijing) under Mao Tse Tung setting off shock waves in the United States and recriminations that China had been lost to the Reds.

Before 1949 was out, the Soviet Union exploded test atomic bombs, setting off new concerns in western countries about global security. In another six months or so, some of the worst fears about world peace were realized on June 25, 1950, when North Korean forces invaded South Korea.

By the time the Korean War broke out, the Soviet and communist threat had become a focal point of foreign policy concerns in Ottawa, reflecting the view in Washington where the decision had been taken to discard all niceties in criticisms of Moscow and communism. The United States had its "Campaign of Truth," launched by President Harry Truman on April 19, 1950, in which he called on the American information media to promote the truth about the United States and to counter communist propaganda and criticism. Later in the year (in September), Mr. Truman sent a classified message to the State Department and all American diplomatic missions to take the offensive against communism by exposing its lies - subjecting it to ridicule. This has been called the beginning of the era of the 'hard line' which was a suitable label for the harsh and dramatic language used on specific criticisms of Soviet ideology.

Canada was under intense pressure at home and abroad to take a similar line; this had major implications for the International Service. An External Affairs memorandum discussing the Department's relationship with the International Service noted that "the average foreign listener regards the CBC-

International Service as the Voice of Canada and would doubtless be astonished to learn that opinions expressed by commentators have not always reflected official policy''.[1] In formulating new objectives, External Affairs said that the International Service should participate actively in the cold war; it should promote Canadian trade and attract desirable immigrants from certain countries but carefully refrain from encouraging immigration from certain other countries.

External Affairs wanted the Voice of Canada -- speaking in 13 languages in 1950 -- fine-tuned to carry different messages, depending on the political ideology of the target audience. This policy approach was critical as Canada prepared to broadcast to the Soviet Union.

The increasing international tensions and the Canadian experience in the Gouzenko Affair heightened the concerns about security risks in the International Service. This in turn set off misgivings about the value of the shortwave service. There were other irritating matters: recurring questions about factual errors -- some real, others not -- in programming were brought out in public as a result of press stories and questions by members of Parliament. Then, there was the unsolvable problem of some political significance: ethnic spokespersons in Canada who listened in on the shortwave broadcasts in their native language were critical of what they heard in the transmissions to Eastern European countries. Canada, they said, was not sufficiently critical of the Eastern European and Central European regimes. As refugees from Communist-dominated countries, ethnic groups had their own agenda that was not necessarily in tune with Ottawa's policies.

The criticisms of the International Service were closely followed at External Affairs and reached the ear of Prime Minister Louis St. Laurent. The Prime Minister told Jules Léger, then the Assistant Under-Secretary of State, at a meeting on July 6, 1950, that he was concerned about the International Service and he wanted Pearson to know that he ''did not feel too happy about this situation.'' In fact, the Prime Minister indicated indirectly that he wanted the departure of the Director of the International Service, Ira Dilworth, although he himself had pressed for Dilworth's appointment three years earlier. The way Mr. Leger put it in his memo was: ''The Prime Minister brought up the question of the reorganization of the staff of the International Service following the eventual retirement of Mr. Dilworth.''[2]

Léger explained to the Prime Minister that Pearson was already looking into the problems of the International Service and an officer was preparing a report for the minister.

> ... The Prime Minister's view is that as close and permanent a liaison as possible should be established between the Department of External Affairs and the International Service of the CBC.... It might be necessary to find a way whereby a senior officer of the Department could be appointed on their staff or at least take some responsibility in supervising their programme....[3]

The Prime Minister also referred to the eventual possibility of having External Affairs take full control for the International Service, "financial and otherwise." This suggestion and the possible appointment of a senior External Affairs officer to supervise the shortwave service touched off long-term planning. In more immediate terms, an External Affairs officer with Eastern European experience, John A. McCordick, was seconded to the International Service as a coordinator of policy; he was to become the principal instrument of liaison.[4]

McCordick, a middle rank officer who later held a number of ambassadorial posts, went to the International Service in Montreal in February 1950 and stayed there for six months to give policy guidance, especially as it related to psychological warfare. He was at the time the key person at External Affairs dealing with psychological warfare. The guidance link with the International Service was the principal activity in the psychological warfare field in 1950. There were however, other objectives that included a largely unsuccessful attempt to plant articles in the media by sending out 'leaks' to journalists in unmarked brown envelopes.

McCordick was officially well received at the International Service; it could hardly be otherwise. But he was viewed with great suspicion by the broadcasts and journalists in the foreign-language sections. It was taken for granted that McCordick was spying and would be making a full report on any security suspicions or other misgivings about the staff and programs at the International Service. His report, which does not appear to exist in External Affairs files, was probably a factor in the 'house cleaning' that took place under the next director of the International Service, Jean Désy.

McCordick, commenting some 30 years later on his secondment to the International Service, said that despite the concerns about communism, he felt there were no subversive elements in the service.[5] His job was "not to look for unreliable people, but rather to tighten the link between the shortwave service and External Affairs." The service had grown up originally by itself for lack of supervision from External Affairs and he had concerns about a lack of coordination within the International Service where the various sections wrote their material independently of each other. There was a looseness and a lack of supervision and External Affairs did not know what the Voice of Canada was broadcasting to foreign countries.

McCordick kept two apartments: one in Montreal and one in Ottawa and spent several days a week in each city. He read hundreds of scripts to discover the general patterns of approach to Canadian and international events. When Charles Ritchie, the Deputy Under-Secretary of State visited the International Service on March 17, 1950, McCordick told him that his general impression was that the many scripts he had examined in the six weeks since his posting to Montreal "contain little or nothing which is objectionable from the point of view of this Department [External Affairs] or which reveals a divergence from Government policy ... they seemed very 'objective' in character and they struck him as rather colourless." McCordick also told Ritchie that since he was advising the International Service on policy matters, he felt the need for written policy guidelines from External Affairs.[6]

Ritchie's visit to Montreal provided him an opportunity to meet the staff and to talk over some of the problems between External Affairs and the International Service. In the evening he met socially with staff members at Dilworth's apartment. His notes on the visit indicate that liaison challenges were formidable; he was concerned about the 'guesswork' of the broadcasters in interpreting Canadian foreign policy.

The Assistant Under-Secretary was pleased that Dilworth was now enthusiastic about receiving written notice of general guidance or policy. The International Service head had previously felt that there should not be too much interference from the Department but the "present international situation" had helped change his mind.

Ritchie, nevertheless, was not fully convinced that the International Service was enthusiastic about policy guidance: "I formed the personal impression that the staff was for the most part inclined to favour their present 'objective' treatment of news and might prefer it to a more actively 'cold war' approach."[6] Ritchie's impression was astute: the International Service had attracted "the best minds of the CBC and Canadian journalism" and was not easily intimidated.

Some 14 months later, Ritchie made a return visit to Montreal and reported that there had certainly been an improvement. The machinery for cooperation included background papers from External Affairs, and also comments and suggestions from diplomatic posts abroad.

The International Service was attacked for not being more violently anticommunist; its response was that in broadcasting to Czechoslovakia and the Soviet Union, it would be bad practice to swamp the material with diatribes against the communist regime in power. Though basically sympathetic with this answer and attitude, Ritchie noted his misgivings:[7]

> ... I said that I could quite see the effectiveness of this 'objective' point of view as a matter of technique in attracting and holding audiences. On the other hand, I pointed out as forcefully as I could that no one could pretend at this stage in the world struggle to perfect objectivity of intellectual judgment and that even if in theory such objectivity could be obtained, our shortwave broadcasting organization was no place in which to air it. I think this was necessary because there is, I believe, among some people at CBC-International Service a slightly 'holier-than-thou' point of view and a misplaced scrupulosity which should be discouraged.

Broadcasting in Russian

On January 18, 1950, Mr. Shannon of the United Kingdom High Commissioner's Office in Ottawa, called at External Affairs and left a memorandum that indicated that Washington and London assumed that the CBC was already broadcasting to the Soviet Union in Russian and would like the International Service, to coordinate its time schedules with those of the BBC and Voice of America. The memorandum was vague. It lent itself to other interpretations, but its intent was clear. External Affairs was dumbfounded by the British memorandum and sought clarification in a secret letter to Dilworth. The head of the International Service, for his part, already knew about Shannon, the British official had also visited CBC Chairman Davidson Dunton and left copies of the BBC and Voice of America broadcast schedules to the Soviet Union.

Canada had attached no special urgency in broadcasting to the Soviet Union. In the summer of 1949, when Sir Ian Jacob of the BBC was in Ottawa and met with officials of External Affairs and the International Service he was asked for his views on Canada beginning programming in the Russian and Ukrainian languages. The head of the BBC's Overseas Service was not enthusiastic about Ukrainian broadcasting; there were problems in playing the ethnic card against the Soviet Union. The Russian language programs, however, could be valuable, particularly if they came at the same time as the BBC and Voice of America transmissions. The Canadian transmitters would thus be additional help in the "barrage" being laid down to penetrate the Soviet Union.

The initiative by the British High Commissioner's Office was an effective catalyst in getting Canada to put greater emphasis on broadcasting to communist countries. Jack McCordick, who was in charge of psychological warfare at the time, recalls that both the BBC and the Voice of America were investing heavily in shortwave programming to break through the Soviet jamming system. London and Washington continually encouraged Canada to join in this effort. McCordick explained the Canadian decision to begin broadcasting to the Soviet Union this way:

> I felt that if it means that much to them, we should not turn a deaf ear. I likened it to membership in an important club. The Canadians have a special relationship -- we certainly did at that time -- with both the United States and the United Kingdom. We were privy to their most secret councils in matters of intelligence and planning. They value our input but we are junior members of the club and we mustn't fall behind in our dues....

McCordick had no great expectations as to what the Canadian shortwave broadcasts would accomplish. He supported Russian language broadcasting for political reasons: to maintain Canada's right to sit at certain high councils in both Washington and London.

Broadcasting to the Soviet Union in Russian was a conscientious decision by Canada to broadcast to communist countries; it was also a difficult decision in that Ottawa felt its broadcast policy -- especially in relation to psychological warfare -- had not matured sufficiently. The broadcasts to Czechoslovakia -- in Czech and Slovak -- were the only International Service experiences in Iron Curtain programming.

Broadcasting to Czechoslovakia had begun when the country was under Nazi occupation and flourished after liberation. Following the coup in 1948, the International Service was broadcasting to these same Czech and Slovak listeners who now lived in a Communist-controlled country. This was not a deliberate attempt to penetrate the Iron Curtain.

A second population group behind the Iron Curtain was East Germany. The International Service did not make any distinctions in its German-language broadcasts between its audience in West and East Germany. It was not until 1953, when arrangements were made to supplement German language shortwave programs with recordings and transcriptions made by the International Service to be retransmitted from (German) radio stations, that External Affairs gave serious thought to this matter. Some of the retransmitting stations were closed to the boundary-line between the Federal Republic and East Germany and would therefore be penetrating into the "Soviet zone." An External Affairs memorandum said that "there may be substantial advantage in stressing the idea that we make no distinction between Germany living on either side of the demarcation line." The International Service was told to continue to treat Germans living east of the Elbe as Europeans temporarily separated from the Western world, and "to give the impression that we consider Germany as a whole, despite the present political division." In fact, the German language section at the International Service was considered a western European section.

Canadian broadcasting to Eastern Europe, then, was limited to Czechoslovakia -- in Czech and Slovak -- until February 1951 when a Russian-language service was inaugurated. There was much preparation for this service; R.A.D. Ford of External Affairs, an authority on Russian poetry, who later became Ambassador in Moscow, came to the International Service to give a lecture on the Russian audience and Russia's socio-cultural structure; External Affairs prepared policy guidelines. For a whole month before the service went on the air, there was a dry run -- preparation of programs that were recorded and analysed but not broadcast. The inaugural broadcast carried a message in Russian by Dana Wilgress, a former Canadian Ambassador in Moscow, reflecting the difficult international situation and professing Canada's desire for friendly relations, if not with the government of the Soviet Union, then with the people of that country.[8]

> In these days of international tension, ignorance and misunderstanding of other countries and peoples are exploited by the propaganda of the ruling circles of the USSR to create fear and suspicion. We believe that one of the surest ways to mutual understanding and peace is through the free exchange of information. The Canadian people earnestly desire this exchange....

Broadcasting in Ukrainian

Before the decision had been taken to go ahead in Russian, consideration was given to the use of other languages, chiefly Ukrainian, Serbo-Croat, and Polish.[9] But there was neither the money nor the technical facilities, in January

1951 to expand beyond one new language -- Russian. All the same, the question of broadcasting in Ukrainian was not entirely shelved, "partly because of the constant pressure exerted by Ukrainian groups in Canada."[10]

On January 22, 1951 -- shortly after the inauguration of the Russian Service -- External Affairs asked its diplomats in London and Washington to provide some opinions from the British and Americans about Ukrainian nationalism and "the advantages of a Ukrainian shortwave programme in the present 'cold war'."[11] This memo, signed by Ritchie for the Secretary of State, noted that Ottawa found the whole Ukrainian issue perplexing and felt that "the greatest caution must be exercised in exploiting Ukrainian nationalism either now or in wartime."[12]

> First of all there are in Canada important political aspects to the question arising from the existence of various rival Ukrainian organizations embracing the large numbers of Canadian citizens. Furthermore, the experience of two Great Wars has left a legacy of the greatest reluctance to make promises or even mild hints of support for the future independence for national minorities. Finally, we feel that the risk of losing more than it is hoped to gain must be weighed very carefully. It is arguable that by appealing to and possibly pleasing one Ukrainian we may antagonize two and a half Russians. The Russians remain the largest national group in the Soviet Union and the mainspring of Soviet imperialism. It is their drive which we wish to slacken and their will and morals which we wish to undermine. Any campaign which might possibly defeat this purpose must be approached with the greatest reserve.

The memorandum lists the pros and cons of broadcasting in Ukrainian to exploit Ukrainian nationalism which it describes as a phenomenon difficult to analyse and assess. It noted that the protagonists for exploitation argue that the Ukraine was the weakest and most vulnerable part of the Soviet Union through which the greatest damage could be done to the Soviet Union's fighting capacity without having to "await the beginning of war." These protagonists, according to the External Affairs document, stressed that from their point of view the Germans made a great mistake in 1941 and after "by not realizing their intelligent exploitation of Ukrainian nationalism (which was made plain to them through the defection of whole Ukrainian divisions and the warm welcome tendered them in Ukrainian towns and villages) would have carried them triumphantly into Moscow and might have led to the ultimate defeat of the Soviet Union...."

External Affairs, however, was not convinced of the merits of supporting Ukrainian nationalism through shortwave programs as part of the "cold war". "In the event of war, the document declared, "consideration would naturally be given to exploiting the nationalism of the Soviet Union and the centrifugal tendencies to which it gives rise."[13]

The British and American replies to the Canadian inquiries confirmed the views at External Affairs. The United Kingdom advised Canada against becoming involved in Ukrainian broadcasting. The United States, for its part, had some Ukrainian broadcasting -- within the context of its programming to the Soviet Union -- but exercised great care in avoiding any commentaries which might be termed nationalistic or separatist in character.[13]

The question of broadcasting in Ukrainian was not, however, decided solely on the basis of Canadian foreign policy interests or the advice of the United States (the State Department and the Voice of America) and Britain (the Foreign Office and the BBC). Other factors came into play, specifically Canadian internal politics.

External Affairs was cautious in watching the developing pressures for a Ukrainian service. In May 1951, the Liberal member of Parliament for Vegreville, John Decore, in a letter to Pearson, urged broadcasting services in Ukrainian and Polish. In an effort to avoid public controversy, the Minister for External Affairs arranged for Decore to meet with Jack McCordick, the External Affairs' official most involved with the Eastern European broadcasts. McCordick wrote a six-page report following the meeting at which he had explained to the Member of Parliament that "the prominence of Czech in the broadcasts was an historical development and not the result of a decision that it was far more important than Ukrainian, Polish, etc." Decore left the meeting empty handed, he was told that there was no free transmitter time at Sackville, nor the financial resources for additional transmitters and editorial staff to allow further expansion of language services. All the same, the External Affairs' official felt that the conversation had gone well, although Decore did not change his opinions about the need for Canadian broadcasts in Ukrainian. A week later, Pearson sent a letter (drafted by McCordick) to Decore reiterating the points made at the Decore-McCordick meeting and adding his views that he was well aware of the importance of the Ukrainian language in Europe and of the distinctions between Russians and Ukrainians.

At about the same time that Ottawa was trying to contain the political pressures of adding Ukrainian to its Eastern European broadcasts, the Voice of America on May 26, 1951 inaugurated a daily 15 minute broadcast in the Georgian language. Over the summer, broadcasts were added by the Voice of America in Tartar, Turkestani, Azerbaijani, Armenian, Latvian and Estonian. These new broadcasts were in addition to the Lithuanian and Ukrainian and, of course, Russian programs beamed to the Soviet Union. The United States, however, kept tight control of these various language programs to the Soviet Union in that they were seen as cultural bridges not a support structure for secessionists.

The Canadian Chargé d'Affaires in Moscow, Mr. Hart, was visiting the US Minister, Mr. Barbour, at the embassy when a telegram arrived from the Voice of America to announce the expansion of language services to the Soviet Union. This telegram contained an amusing message: "It is solemnly suggested that the (US) embassy might wish to notify prominent citizens of Georgian extraction in their locality of the new programmes; the names of J. Djugashvili (Stalin) and L. Beriya (the head of the KGB) had been mentioned in that connection."[14] The official who prepared the list did not seem to know who was who in the Soviet Union.

Meanwhile, the United States made it clear to Canada again that it was Washington's policy not to support Ukrainian separatism in any broadcasts, and that the Voice of America was under strict instructions from the State Department to avoid this issue in their programs. Ottawa was told that the United States and its allies were seeking to preserve peace through building up their collective strengths and taking limited military measures to deter aggression such as in Korea and it would be premature for Washington "to define its attitude to the political future of Russia." Over the next few weeks a series of External Affairs memoranda addressed the question of Ukrainian broadcasts; an increasingly firm position had developed opposing such broadcasts. On June 23, 1951, the Ukrainian-language newspaper, *Homin Ukrainy* (*Ukrainian Echo*), published in Toronto, carried an editorial appealing to its readers to send petitions and letters to External Affairs Minister Lester Pearson, and the CBC (Chairperson Davidson Dunton and International Service Supervisor Ira Dilworth) in favour of Ukrainian broadcasts. On its front page, the Ukrainian-language paper carried a letter in English, addressed to Pearson with a blank space at the bottom for signature. The newspaper also called for the formation of regional committees to help in the lobbying process.

Ottawa braced itself for a flow of letters from some of the 350,000 Canadians of Ukrainian origin, by far the largest Ukrainian émigré group in the world. External Affairs was heartened by what it viewed as an indifferent response to the appeal, only four or five petitions were addressed to the Minister. This evaluation was obviously faulty. On October 19th, External Affairs Minister Pearson received a letter from the Secretary-General of the "Canadian League for Ukraine's Liberation," calling for the inclusion of the Ukrainian language in broadcasts of the "Voice of Canada" now going out in 13 languages. With the letter came a binding case containing sheets with 11,741 signatures. The petition carried an important political reminder, if one were needed: In Canada the Ukrainian language was spoken by over 350,000; the largest racial group and one of the fundamental ethnic elements of which the Canadian nation is composed.

Within a day or two, a memorandum was prepared which suggested that External Affairs should not be over impressed by the large number of signatures; it must have been "relatively easy" in that "Ukrainian organizations are active and enterprising and since no Ukrainian-Canadian, except the Communist minority, is likely to oppose an appeal of this kind."

The name of the organizations-Canadian League for Ukraine's Liberation-suggested to External Affairs that its "earlier fears" were real:[15]

> ... much of the Ukrainian-Canadian reasoning submitted in support of their plea for Ukrainian broadcasts was sophistry behind which lurked the desire to forward the cause of Ukrainian independence, that is dismemberment of the USSR. Perhaps the foregoing may be thought to impute an overly Byzantine plot to the Ukrainians ... to appear after CBC-International Service has started broadcasting in Ukrainian and the criticisms have begun to roll in.

Whatever the thinking of External Affairs officials, Pearson had already taken matters into his own hands. A day or two after receiving the petition from the Ukrainian Canadians, Under Secretary Rathke made an urgent phone call to Dilworth, informing him that the Minister wanted broadcasts in the Ukrainian language to begin as soon as possible. The head of the International Service was unprepared for the call and replied that it might not be possible to get anything started for a month or six weeks.

In a letter (dated October 23, 1951) to confirm the telephone conversation with Rathke, Dilworth made it a point to state that the way he understood it, the Ukrainian broadcasts "would not represent a sort of 'separatist movement'."[16] "In otherwords," Dilworth wrote, "Canada would be broadcasting to the Soviet Union in Ukrainian and not broadcasting to the Ukraine as a separate part of USSR." This, of course, had major policy implications and the way Dilworth saw it, broadcasts in Ukrainian "would be subject to the same policy as our broadcast in the Russian language."[17]

Dilworth reported that he had already had discussions with members of the Russian service; they understood Ukrainian but thought it would be a mistake for them to broadcast in Ukrainian. New staff would have to be hired. It took another eight months until the Ukrainian Service was inaugurated on Canada Day, July 1, 1952 by Jean Désy, the next director of the International Service.

Broadcasting in Polish

The pressures for a Polish Service were less dramatic but equally fruitful. There were representations by Members of Parliament who had significant Polish-Canadian constituencies, from Polish-Canadian organizations, and by the Leader of the Opposition, George Drew. While Polish-language broadcasting was not as controversial and sensitive in international relations as the Ukrainian-language issue, nevertheless Pearson had his misgivings. The Ukrainian experience (discussed later) confirmed his concerns but he seemed to have lost his fighting spirit. In a "Dear Colleague" letter to Walter Harris, the Minister of Citizenhip and Immigration on March 21, 1953, Pearson said that the only valid arguments that could be presented in public against establishing a Polish service were limitation of funds and technical facilities, but he doubted that these arguments would satisfy the Canadian Polish Congress. In his rather remarkable letter, lacking the political niceties associated with the External Affairs' Minister, Pearson declared that funds were not the paramount reason for eliminating a Polish Service and there was indeed a "more important consideration ... one which could not be publicly stated."[18]

> ... establishment of such a service would be a perpetual thorn in the flesh of the CBC and the Government. You know of the problem for the Czechoslovak Service of the CBC-International Service caused by the conflicting claims of Czechs and Slovaks and of numerous subdivisions within those nationalities in Canada. Each of these small and mutually antagonistic groups keeps a close watch on the broadcasts of the Czechoslovak Service and strongly criticizes what does

> not suit its own particular 'line'. The same is true with regard to the Ukrainian Service. It can reasonably be assumed that establishment of a Polish-language service would merely provide further opportunities for unwelcome criticism from various highly partisan Polish groups in this country.

The External Affairs Minister was, at the same time, sensitive to the "sound psychological warfare reasons" for having a Canadian shortwave service directed at Poland. He thought it might be equally embarrassing for the CBC and the Government if the Polish Service were not created or if it were created. Furthermore, Pearson thought that the Government may very well have to reconsider its position in that he expected the House Committee on External Affairs would submit a recommendation favouring the inauguration of Polish broadcasts.

The International Service began broadcasting in Polish on July 11, 1953. This brought to five the number of foreign-language broadcasts directed to Eastern Europe: Russian, Ukrainian, Czech, Slovak and Polish.

Hungarian was introduced during the Hungarian uprising in the autumn of 1956, first on an emergency basis when a 10-minute Hungarian-language newscast was inserted into the Polish program. Within weeks a full-fledged Hungarian Service was inaugurated. The emphasis on broadcasting to Eastern Europe with the very specific goal of piercing the Iron Curtain, had become, after overcoming considerable doubts, the top priority of the International Service.

CHAPTER XII

THE DÉSY ERA

Ambassador Jean Désy succeeded Ira Dilworth on January 1, 1952 as head of the International Service. The atmosphere changed totally. Dilworth, who overcame his parochialism, was a benevolent and open-minded leader; he was "like a mother hen and wanted to protect [his employees] against evil people."[1] Désy, for his part, was "hard nosed, violently anti-Soviet" and made his career as a diplomat who thrived on international affairs; his style was to instill fear in his subordinates.

The Désy appointment had been arranged in secret by Prime Minister St. Laurent and External Affairs Minister Pearson while Dilworth was still at the International Service. When Dilworth called a special meeting of all the staff in the first week of November, 1951 to announce his departure, he assured them of continuity; his close associates Charles Delafield and Arthur Pidgeon, would move into the top positions. But that was not in the offing. A few days later, Prime Minister St. Laurent announced that Ambassador Désy would become the Director-General -- a newly created title -- reflecting the awesome powers sought by the diplomat turned broadcaster.

Désy had a most impressive Curriculum Vitae. He was a pioneer at External Affairs, joining in the days when the Prime Minister also served as Secretary of State for External Affairs. Canada was still searching for full independence from Britain in the 1920s and Ottawa's involvement in foreign affairs was a principal avenue for achieving this goal.

The Department of External Affairs, established by legislation in 1909, was a small operation until the early 1920s when Ottawa became more active and visible internationally as a result of Canadian participation in the Paris Peace Conference after World War I, and Ottawa's representation at the League of Nations. Prime Minister Mackenzie King brought in Oscar Douglas Skelton, the Dean of Arts at Queen's University, as an adviser on foreign policy. Skelton became the first Under-Secretary of State for External Affairs and was the chief architect and builder of the Department.

Prime Minister King had made it a point to have French Canadian representation in the delegation to the League of Nations and the groundwork was being laid for a francophone presence in the developing Canadian machinery for foreign policy. It could hardly be otherwise, for Ernest Lapointe, Mr. King's Quebec lieutenant, was, at his own request, kept fully informed of

Departmental promotions and appointments with particular attention to the progress of Francophones. Philippe Roy, the Commissioner General in Paris, and Lucien Pacand -- who resigned his seat in Parliament to serve at External -- were the first French Canadian officials in the foreign relations field. Pierre Dupuy was brought in shortly afterwards. One problem was that the Francophones were serving abroad and therefore were not involved in Skelton's machinery-building venture.

Prime Minister King insisted on Skelton making himself available for imperial and international conferences. To free up the Under-Secretary, a senior position was created. It called for very specific credentials: a lawyer with practical legalexperience, a good knowledge of both French and English, and two year of post graduate studies in international relations. Skelton, a strong supporter of the merit principle, had expected there would be much competition for the position but only one man (women were not eligible) applied: Jean Désy.

Désy was bilingual, a professor at the University of Montreal where he taught international law, constitutional law and political history. He had previously taught history for a year at the University of Paris. On his arrival at External Affairs, he was given responsibilities for treaties, the League of Nations, protocol and legal matters; all handled until then by Skelton himself. But Désy did not stay long in Ottawa, for in 1927 he was appointed as counsellor of the legation in Paris where he remained for 11 years until he was named Canada's first Minister to Belgium and the Netherlands in 1938.

Désy's stay in Brussels was cut short by the German invasion and he followed the Belgian Government in exile to Poitiers, France, staying on the way at abandoned houses and farms, very different from the luxury he had become accustomed to. Ottawa did not want Désy involved with the Poitiers group and he left for Portugal. At the time Canada was establishing a legation in Rio de Janeiro and Désy was happy to become its first head in October, 1940, with the title of Minister which was changed to Ambassador in 1941. In 1947, he went from Rio to Rome as Minister and assumed the rank of Ambassador to Italy the following year. Désy stayed in Rome until he became Director-General of the CBC International Service in 1952.

Désy thrived in post-war Italy. It was the third Canadian diplomatic mission he had pioneered -- Brussels in 1938, Rio in 1940, now Rome in 1947. As was the case in all hisprevious diplomatic postings, Désy was interested in the cultural and economic dimensions and had little enthusiasm or involvement in the matters of foreign policy. He never lost sight of his own personal interests which defined for him the limits of his involvement.

As Ambassador in Rome, Désy had responsibilities relating to the Vatican. A staunch Catholic, he enjoyed the intricacies of Vatican diplomacy: "he was in his element with priests and cardinals''[2] and was appreciative of the pomp tied to the symbolic activities of the Church.

Désy was, despite his impressive credentials, a problem for External Affairs. No one knew him well for he had not served in Canada since his first posting in Paris in 1927. He continuously refused to return to Ottawa which would have given him insight into Canadian foreign policy. Désy's principal protector was Louis St. Laurent. There were close ties between St. Laurent and the Boucherville family of Désy's wife. Désy was treated with caution by his colleagues but was considered a lightweight. As retired Ambassador Geoffrey Pearson put it; ``He had no clue of what was going on and he did not really care.''[3]

The profile of Désy that emerges from External Affairs files and interviews with some of his colleagues and associates show that he was an incredibly complex person; often despised, much feared, brilliant, extraordinary, with views on everything. The noted Montreal literary critic, Jean Éthier Blais, who as a young Canadian diplomat worked closely with Désy for three years at the Paris embassy in the mid-1950s, paints perhaps the most appreciative picture of Désy:[4]

> He was a snob: liked high circles which he naturally considered his circles. He had a tremendous personality and while he was extremely short -- practically a dwarf -- he had a dynamic presence; all eyes were on him when he entered a room. He had a big head, huge protruding eyes; he judged you immediately and he was harsh in his judgements. He enjoyed luxury and the company of flashy, high level European intellectuals and moneyed people. He saw money as a great source of power.

Désy, who was difficult and condescending, could also be rude: for two years he made life almost unbearable for Éthier Blais. (According to another staff member at Paris, Éthier Blais was being used as a valet and briefcase carrier.) Éthier Blais' sense of humour helped him survive those two difficult years for he could look at events in broader terms and laughed at his difficulties in sharing details of them with fellow diplomat René Garneau (formerly of the International Service). But Désy, who was very impatient -- not only with fools but with everybody -- came to appreciate Éthier Blais, ``for no one else at the embassy ever stood up to him and his wife Corinne, and a friendship developed''; although the word friendship can hardly be used to describe the unequal relationship between a rank-conscious ambassador and a third secretary. "Certainly, as I began to know him better," says Ethier Blais, "he gained very much in stature in my eyes."[5]

> As a diplomat, Désy was second rate: he could not take orders; he would not obey; never obeyed anybody. But he would have been a first rate foreign minister; he was a man to give orders, command and demand obeyance.

As an ambassador, Désy was a big spender and, as will be seen below, this was a characteristic he brought with him to the CBC International Service. His wife Corinne was tall, beautiful, blonde and came from the wealthy and prominent de Boucherville family. She had a 'tremendous personality of her own' and had a strong influence on him. They were an incongruous-looking couple but together, they sparkled.

Désy had an appreciation of literature and found pleasure in ideas. One of the reasons he never wanted to work in Ottawa was that he could not express himself in the Canadian context as exemplified by English-speaking External Affairs diplomats.

Geoffrey Pearson, who had his first assignment abroad in Paris under Désy, found him a pompous man who felt senior and stood on his dignity. And, like Ethier Blais, Geoffrey Pearson respects the cultural accomplishments of Désy: "A patron of the arts, he made it possible for Canadian painters, playwrights and musicians to visit Paris and find some recognition there." According to Pearson, Désy was not interested in French politics, "did not regard it as important and rarely went to the Foreign Ministry." He usually came to the Embassy Office around noon, never wrote much and only signed dispatches. He was more interested in projecting a Canadian cultural profile, including "our French heritage" but he did not discriminate against English Canadians. He wanted to change the Canadian image of "lumbermen, coureurs de bois" that prevailed in France. He made his personal mark in Parisian society and at the same time promoted effectively Canada's cultural interests.[6]

There is a hint of Désy's idiosyncrasies in John Hilliker's historical account, *Canada's Department of External Affairs: The Early Years, 1909-1946.*[7] Désy's activities in Rio de Janeiro are cited as the prime example of Ottawa's loose surveillance of its diplomatic representatives. Désy, in 1943, launched initiatives to promote Canadian-Brazilian cultural relations which led to an exchange of notes and the making of costly commitments. Ottawa had far higher priorities relating to the war and was not enthusiastic about cultural matters, "but by the time it [External Affairs] became aware of Désy's activities the negotiations had proceeded too far to be turned back."[8]

The criticisms of Désy abound, although he died long ago -- in 1960 -- shortly after retiring from the Paris ambassadorship. Ethier Blais agrees with many of the broad criticisms but also thinks that some of Désy's critics have aged badly. There are, nevertheless, rumours -- some appear realistic and are in character, others not -- that are of some importance in analysing Désy's 18 months at the helm of the International Service. Two rumours came from highly regarded sources although no direct evidence can be found in External Affairs files.

One relates to Désy's Ambassadorship in Rome. Reference has already been made to Désy's close ties to the Vatican and his interest in the intricacies of Vatican politics in which he may have become personally involved. It is reported that the Vatican found Désy a responsive supporter when it sought to find safe havens in Brazil and Canada for a number of important and controversial Europeans with problematic wartime records.

The second matter of controversy relates to Désy's role in handling information. Ambassadors are privy to secret documents and this access to documents stayed with him when he was seconded to the CBC. Désy also had his private channels of information; for example, there is correspondence from Robert Keyserlingk -- editor of *The Ensign*, informing him about alleged intrigues in Ottawa and the CBC (not real) -- against Désy. According to one extremely well-connected person, with ties to the CBC and External Affairs, Désy was one of the indirect sources of information in the US Congressional hearings that publicized the communist past and questioned the loyalty of E. Herbert Norman, the Canadian Ambassador in Cairo. Norman, who had close ties to Lester Pearson going back to their student days at Oxford, died in a suicide leap from the roof of the Canadian Embassy in the Egyptian capital.

At first glance, Désy's appointment at the CBC International Service is baffling. He had no previous broadcasting experience although his name comes up in connection with Canadian shortwave broadcasting in the archival files. As Minister to Brussels, he was enthusiastic about shortwave when the CBC explored the feasibility of setting up an international service; in 1948 he was in San Francisco with Louis St. Laurent at the founding conference of the United Nations and they were both featured in French Service broadcasts of the International Service.

In 1950, Prime Minister St. Laurent told Assistant Under-Secretary of State Jules Léger that it might be necessary to find a way whereby a senior officer of External Affairs could be appointed on the International Service staff.[9]

In mid-1951, an exasperated Charles Ritchie (Deputy Under-Secretary) did not think that the Department had a suitable person with the required qualifications whom it could make available to head the International Service. But he came up with another alternative: put "a more active general manager" as head of the whole CBC to succeed Frigon, "with special responsibility with regard to CBC International Service." He thought Mr. Désy could fill this position, if he were available. "I think it would do CBC International Service no harm and some good," said Ritchie, "to be under the continuous supervision in Montreal of a forceful and experienced personality, well acquainted with the objectives of our foreign policy."[10]

It was thought unlikely that Ambassador Désy would consider a long-term appointment at the CBC which would undoubtedly have meant an end to his External Affairs career and his dream of becoming ambassador to Paris. He was, however, not needed by the Department in the short term. After Rome, his next obvious assignment would be Ambassador to Paris but the post was held by General George Vanier and it was unthinkable to move Vanier to make room for Désy. Vanier expected to remain in Paris until mid-1953 and that meant Désy could be spared for 18 months. It would, however, require a selling job.

The negotiations to bring Désy to the International Service were delicate and involved Prime Minister St. Laurent, his special Assistant, J.W. Pickersgill, and Secretary of State for External Affairs, Pearson. The files indicate that the Prime Minister and Pearson had a series of conversations about the appointment. In a letter to the Prime Minister (September 21, 1951), Pearson spelled out the details of the offer he made to Désy the previous day. The terms were attractive: Désy would go to the CBC on a temporary basis -- seconded from External Affairs -- for 18 months: he would retain his position and status in the Foreign Service and would continue to be paid his $10,000 yearly salary. He also received assurances from Pearson that he would receive full consideration for a future diplomatic appointment in line with his seniority and experience. Two weeks later, Jack Pickersgill sent a letter to Désy in Rome by diplomatic air bag, at the direction of the Prime Minister. Although the terms of appointment still required approval from the Treasury Board, Désy was told he should nevertheless regard the offer as firm. The terms include the following: the regular $10,000 a year salary from External Affairs; an additional $5,000 a year from the CBC; a drawing account of $2,000 a year for hospitality, apart from the travelling expenses.

Ambassador Désy made another demand and Pickersgill wrote him that the Prime Minister agreed to this: the announcement that Désy would take the CBC post would be made by St. Laurent himself and not by the CBC, as would normally be the case. Also, the Prime Minister agreed to Désy's request to withhold the announcement until after a NATO meeting that was to be held later that fall. St. Laurent assured Désy that if through inadvertent circumstances news of his forthcoming appointment as Director-General of the International Service should be leaked, then Mr. St. Laurent would advise Désy immediately and would make the formal announcement within two or three days. It is significant that Désy insisted on the title of Director-General, with sweeping powers, rather than the usual title of Supervisor.

The Prime Minister made his announcement as arranged. The Director-General arrived in January, 1952 to take up his post and so began the Désy era -- a mere 18 months -- that was to have repercussions over the next 20 years. He insisted immediately on being addressed as 'Your Excellency', whether in person or by memo. (There is at least one instance where Désy turned back a memo because he was not addressed asYour Excellency.) His shortness was obviously a problem for him and he had a platform built behind his desk that would raise him to higher levels. The door to his office was lowered so that he would look less small when he stood in the doorway, or so he thought. It was clear almost from the day he arrived -- and his arrival was awaited with justified apprehension -- that dramatic changes were in the offing.

One of Désy's first moves was to send a cable to Yvon Beaulne at the Canadian embassy in Rome asking the Foreign Service officer to join him at the CBC. Beaulne was seconded by External Affairs to the CBC and, as he puts it himself, he was "a sort of chéf de cabinét to Mr. Désy ... "I was secretary and executive assistant ... "a sort of ménagère de Curé of Jean Désy."

Unlike Désy, Beaulne had broadcasting experience. He was, as he himself puts it, "sort of Jack-of-all-trades" and his first task was to find out whether the Voice of Canada was "representative and authentic." He scrutinized the scripts of the various sections and says that he found that generally the Voice of Canada lived up to its title, but "there were some imperfections that had to be corrected." Over a period of time, he says, he could very easily find where the problems existed: furthermore, there were letters from listeners and criticisms sent by some of the Canadian diplomats abroad.

Beaulne thought that some of the International Service broadcasters did not understand what they were doing. He points specifically to the Italian section, probably because he understood the language. There was a critical election campaign underway in Italy and, according to Beaulne, the head of the Italian section in his broadcasts would urge voters in a rather aggressive way to vote for De Gasperi and his Christian Democrats, otherwise all sorts of dire things might happen. Beaulne considered De Gasperi the greatest political leader in Italy since the beginning of the century but thought the Canadian broadcasts amounted to "direct intervention in the affairs of other countries and this could not be tolerated."[12]

In an interview in 1986, Beaulne noted that the Ukrainian broadcasts, which were inaugurated under Désy's stewardship, "were rather unruly.... Every broadcast for about three months ... ended with 'Long Live a Free Ukraine' and we had to explain to the Soviet Ambassador, apologize...."[13]

In more general terms, he thought that the broadcasters, in English, as well as in other languages, did not appreciate that foreign audiences did not understand the 'fine subtleties' of Canadian politics; they could get the wrong impression about Canada, especially if opposition leaders were given as much prominence as the Prime Minister. The record, however, indicates that explaining Canada in realistic terms was not a real problem for the International Service: in fact this was its greatest strength.

The challenge was for Désy to change things and Beaulne was his principal instrument for change; he relied on Beaulne to advise him, to write his reports for him and to keep him out of trouble. The Désy-Beaulne team may have been a good one as far as Désy was concerned but its operations were bizarre. Beaulne describes his activities this way:[14]

> I would spend three days a week in Montreal doing that kind of job [liaison] and three days in Ottawa trying to get support for the CBC International Service. But I was alone doing that so I would travel backand forth. Mr. Désy was the Director-General of the CBC International Service and there were certain things that he did not want to do and that he objected to and so I would write some harsh letters to the Under-Secretary of State ... Charles Ritchie. Then I would take the letters back to Ottawa.
>
> I would show the letters to Charles Ritchie who would jump in his seat and say 'preposterous, who does Mr. Désy think he is? Well, please write him along these lines.' So I would write to Mr. Désy and give him hell for trying to run an independent show.... I would bring that letter, after having it signed by Charles Ritchie, to Jean Désy.... I was engaged in a great dialogue with myself.

The exchange of letters between Désy and Ritchie which in practice were letters from Beaulne to himself, were handled with top security: only Beaulne was allowed to carry them and no one else at the International Service was allowed to see them. Beaulne also brought with him background notes on Canadian foreign policy for Désy and directives for the heads of sections, invariably critical. Beaulne had concerns about the foreigners of the foreign sections and about security. He said the members of the sections knew the country to which they were broadcasting and they spoke the language, but they were problematic. "Many of them had been in exile, had axes to grind, they were not necessarily the most reliable." He noted that the head of one section had been arrested in connection with the Gouzenko case but "had not been convicted for insufficient evidence." He recounted that the head of another section had been making numerous trips to New York where "his brother was a spy, a Soviet spy that had been allowed to stay there so that the CIA and the FBI could follow his movements."

There appeared to be much doubt about the Beaulne version on security matters, certainly at CBC headquarters where Davidson Dunton was in charge. Beaulne took hisconcerns to Dunton -- asking for dismissals -- but was rebuffed; he was asked if his evidence would stand up in a court of law. He found the CBC attitude unfortunate and presented his own view that even if it did not stand up in a court of law, where there was doubt about a person's integrity, i.e., guilty by suspicion, the Government should have the benefit of the doubt. "Well, that argument did not carry much weight with ... the President of the CBC."

Nearly 40 years later, Beaulne thought his security concerns were real. It is more meaningful to examine the Désy-Beaulne views in the context of the times. Guilty by suspicion was very much in vogue and while not as acute a problem in Canada as in the United States, careers were made and broken on the basis of an unfortunate word, the attendance of a political meeting as a student, or sometimes, outright lies and gossip.

Lester Pearson, who was Minister of External Affairs at the time, was circumspect in his relations with Désy. Correspondence from Pearson to Désy reflects a laid-back attitude and Pearson seemed to try to have as little as possible to do with Désy. In fact, Pearson was himself under considerable pressure.

In March 1952, Pearson was at UN headquarters in New York attending a Committee meeting. Sidney Freifeld, junior Foreign Service Officer at the UN at the time was told by Tad Schulz, then working for United Press, that Elizabeth Bentley was going to give testimony the following day in Washington to a Congressional Committee, stating that Pearson was in a Communist apparatus. Freifeld went to the UN Committee meeting and "whispered this information in Mike's ear."[15] Pearson asked Freifeld to take his seat and left immediately for Washington where he met with Secretary-of-State Dean Acheson. Bently never gave testimony against Pearson.

The Désy Reforms

Désy was frightened of people he did not understand; people who he thought might indeed be communist agents. His cold war views were out of place at the International Service, no one shared his perspective of the world. Most of the Canadian-born staff had liberal views; that was the kind of world they grew up in. The recent immigrants in the foreign sections were anti-fascist and some of them were Jewish or partly Jewish. Désy was strongly anti-Semitic and his suspicions about Jews and foreigners made itself felt in his house cleaning, or reorganization, as it was called.

Jean Désy was a diplomat and interested in a highly controlled situation. He sought to translate this thinking through administrative reorganization which strengthened the central direction and left no doubt about the Director-General's control over all matters. He created an Executive Committee -- acting under his guidance and authority -- made up of senior officials, each with clearly defined duties.

The senior officials assisting the Director-General, whose own powers and functions were defined, were as follows:

Assistant Director-General
Supervisor of Sections
Head of Policy coordination and his assistant
Head of Program Operations
Senior Engineer
International Service Administrative Officer
Press and Information Representative.

Mr. Désy was especially concerned with curtailing the independence of the foreign language sections. As he put it, "the relative autonomy of the various language sections made it difficult to exercise close and immediate control on news and commentaries." Furthermore, he was not comfortable with what he called an "undue reliance on outsider contributors" -- the commentaries and news backgrounders that came from journalists, academics, scientists and other specialists. He felt this problem could be resolved by developing specialized writers within the International Service.

Control over the language sections came from two directions: the Supervisor of Sections and the Head of Policy Coordination. The Supervisor of Sections was responsible to the Director-General for implementation of policy and supervision of operations throughout the sections and also acted as an intermediary between the Director-General and the Sections. The Head of Policy Coordination was responsible for the news from the central news section and the commentaries from the central writing section.

The reorganization of the service -- with particular emphasis on policy control -- was accompanied by strengthening the liaison machinery with External Affairs. This was, as he put it, "my first concern." In addition to having the Foreign Service officer, Yvon Beaulne, bring him classified documents from External Affairs each week, Désy himself made frequent trips to Ottawa. Also, Robert Reford, was stationed in Ottawa as a permanent International Service correspondent to provide news on government and diplomatic activities.

All these steps, Désy said in a report to CBC Chairman Davidson Dunton at the end of his tenure, were helpful but not sufficient. Partly as a result of his intervention and partly as a result of planning at External Affairs, a Political Coordination Section was established in the Department in February 1953, headed by Lyn Stephens, with its main function to give guidance and information on international events to the International Service. Désy wanted to make the link between the International Service and External Affairs even closer; he recommended that the International Service be moved to Ottawa "at the earliest possible moment."

The Cold War was, of course, the main reason that the Government (and especially External Affairs) was paying so much attention to policy and administration control at the International Service. Much time and thought was devoted in Ottawa to the policies that were to be pursued in carrying Canada's views to the Soviet Union and the people of communist controlled countries of Eastern and Central Europe.

In a report to Lester Pearson on May 26, 1953, Désy painted a dismal picture of what he found when he came to Montreal:[16]

- a lack of purpose and direction throughout
- various language sections operating as autonomous units
- haphazard treatment of political questions
- some politically unreliable persons

- many of the persons in key positions were foreign nationals or recently naturalized immigrants.

The way Mr. Désy saw it, until he changed things around, "the International Service seemed to be coasting [and] was generally rendering poor service and sometimes disservice to Canadian interests."

Lyn Stephens, writing some 35 years later about Mr. Désy's views, suggested that the Director-General had painted perhaps a bleaker picture than others saw it, although "there were faults of system and performance to be corrected."[17]

> Mr. Désy proceeded to sweep the Augean stables with his own renowned vigour and ... something less than compassion for human circumstances. In the eighteen months of Désy's leadership there was a great shake-up of personnel, largely of persons who needed to go but also including first-class people who could not well tolerate the autocratic regime.

Désy had created a storm with his house-cleaning at the International Service but his actions were warmly welcomed in some media circles. *The Ensign*, the Catholic weekly which strongly supported Désy, noted that "no less than 19 responsible editors and policy-makers were 'moved', re-allocated, or in a very few cases dismissed for various reasons." The dismissals came in the form of resignations rather than formal actions by the CBC.

Robert Keyserlingk, in an *Ensign* editorial after Désy's departure for the ambassadorship in Paris, heaped great praise on Désy "for straightening out the International Service which was once full of the friends of communists."

> The service was popular in Red quarters.... Then a change of management and organization came. The pro-Soviet, pro-Red China, anti-US, and anti-anti-communist policy was replaced by a straight Canadian policy.

But Mr. Keyserlingk was concerned that those who had been squeezed out of the International Services may still be in a position to threaten Canada specifically and western society generally. "No less than 14 have been absorbed by the CBC Toronto operations, some in high posts of television, of domestic talks or other programs."

At External Affairs, where neither Keyserlingk nor Désy were heros, the head of the Political Coordination Section, Lyn Stephens, wrote a brief comment to Charles Ritchie which was sent on to Lester Pearson.

> Had you seen this recent sally of Mr. Keyserlingk? Having freed the International Service from the trammels of Communism, St. George is riding forth to slay the Red Dragon which threatened the Domestic Service. Where will he look next?

Ritchie, in a memorandum to Pearson the same day said, "Mr. Keyserlingk seems to be attacking Canadian foreign policy." In fact, it had been reported for some time that Keyserlingk's allegations in *The Ensign* and in radio talks over Montreal station CJAD were always in large part attacks on the Pearson foreign policy but *The Ensign* editor did not feel sufficiently secure to attack the Minister of External Affairs directly. Pearson, for his part, was developing a strong international profile at this time. In 1952 he had been considered a leading candidate for Secretary-General of the United Nations until the Soviet Union indicated it would veto such an appointment. In the fall of the same year, Pearson was elected President of the UN General Assembly by a vote of 51-4 (five abstentions).

The files show that the External Affairs Minister was not particularly impressed with the "improved" International Service. At about the same time that Désy was drafting his self-congratulatory report to the Minister, recommending that the International Service should be maintained in the form that he had devised, Pearson was thinking of doing away with the Service. On May 2, 1953, Dana Wilgress, then the Under-Secretary, sent Pearson a memorandum dealing with the future of the International Service as Mr. Désy was preparing to leave.

It can be anticipated with some certainty that when Mr. Désy's departure is announced this Department will once again be attacked, rightly or (more probably) wrongly, for whatever the CBC-International Service may be charged with having done or left undone.... In looking towards the future of the International Service, a number of possible alternatives present themselves:

a) To carry on with the present operation, and guidance for the International Service and urging the International Service to complete its own organization to the desired level;

b) To abolish the International Service. This is the line Walter Lippmann has recently taken with regard to the Voice of America;

c) To restrict the CBC-International Services' activities to a much smaller volume of shortwave broadcasting and to have the International Service concentrate on making recordings for medium-wave broadcasts in foreign countries. (The International Service already does a good deal of this, of course.) The time of the CBC shortwave facilities and transmitters could then be made available to the Voice of America, BBC and UN radio;

d) To have this Department take over full operations as well as policy responsibility for CBC-International Service. Mr. Graydon seems to favour this course but I cannot recommend it.

What is remarkable about this memorandum is not so much the options it presents but the handwritten comments by Pearson in the margin. Next to option b) -- abolishing the International Service -- he pencilled "I am coming to this view re CBC-International Service." Next to section c) calling for massive cuts to the activities of the International Service, Pearson wrote: "This might be tried -- and afterwards we would see whether we should then recommend b)." In effect, the Minister for External Affairs was in favour of either the immediate abolition or an intermediate step leading to abolition. Under the fourth option d) which called for External Affairs to take over the International Service, Pearson simply wrote "no." He did not want more of the International Service, if he had to have one at all.

As Mr. Désy was leaving International Service with a great sense of accomplishment and the changes he had brought were receiving praise in the media, the reality of the situation was quite different.

About six months later, in February 1953, Prime Minister St. Laurent would discover for himself traits of the Désy personality and his extravagant ways. The Prime Minister was visiting Europe for talks with political leaders and in Paris stayed at the Canadian Embassy, along with his daughter Madelaine and Charles Ritchie (serving as his External Affairs adviser). Writing 30 years later in his memoirs *Diplomatic Passport*, Ritchie recalls the unhappy stay at the Embassy, "a magnificent house in the rue du Faubourg Saint-Honoré.[18]

> The visit got off on the wrong foot from the start. From the moment that we entered the panelled salon with its chandeliers and elegant eighteenth-century furniture, with a footman bringing glasses of champagne

on a silver salver, I could see that the Prime Minister, who was tired anyway, did not at all appreciate this style of "gracious living" (which I know he thinks is "un-Canadian). The Ambassadress, the beautiful Madame Désy, did not help matters. Encased in satin, she seemed frozen into a formal attitude like an ambassadress in a play. Jean Désy talked with nervous intensity. He is a highly intelligent man but should have sensed that the Prime Minister was not in a responsive mood.

Dinner was even worse. We filed into the beautiful but chilly Louis Seize dining-room and were spaced at wide intervals round a marble table. The food was elaborate, the wines varied, the conversation stilted in the extreme. At times there were pools of silence of several moments' duration. For some reason, and although I was not in any way responsible for the social freeze, I began myself to feel both nervous and embarrassed.

CHAPTER XIII

THE GREAT CONTROVERSIES: THE LOBSTER FESTIVAL

Charles Delafield, the Assistant Director General, became the head of the International Service when Désy left to take up the Ambassadorship in Paris in July 1953. Delafield was unique among International Service leaders in that he stayed at the helm for nearly two decades until his retirement in 1972. Gossip in the hallways had it that it took Delafield 19 years to repair the damage caused by Désy in 18 months.

Delafield's longevity as director was no mean feat in that he headed the shortwave service during some of the most difficult years of the Cold War, the period of détente, and the years of the great thaw. One of his great strengths was that he projected a reasonable position and came across as a fair person, even when he was carrying out some of the most controversial orders of Jean Désy. There is no evidence in the files of any apparent friction between Delafield and Désy or, in fact, between Delafield and senior officials either at the CBC or External Affairs. This quest for harmony carried with it a price tag: he was a leader without providing much leadership, and under him the International Service became almost invisible on the Canadian political and media scene. He was, for a time, just what was needed after Désy's overbearing leadership. But, in the long term, the lowprofile of the International Service made it vulnerable to near fatal thrusts on several occasions.

External Affairs Minister Lester Pearson, in a statement to the House of Commons Committee on External Affairs in 1951, spoke of three periods in the International Service: first, the wartime effort to keep in touch with Canadians abroad (the armed forces) and psychological warfare; second, the post war years when the thrust was on the projection of Canada, a period that did not last very long; and third, the cold war years where the thrust was on "participation in the war of ideas" which became the raison d'être for the Canadian involvement in international broadcasting.

It was, thus, in the difficult years of the Cold War that Eastern Europe became the major target for Canada's international broadcasts and remained so for 40 years. There was a sense of mission in penetrating the Iron Curtain.

The International Service became entangled in the 'behind the scenes' pulls at External Affairs on how psychological warfare should be conducted. Furthermore, Delafield could not begin rebuilding the service after Désy's departure; budget cuts were introduced in 1954. There had been staff departure under pressure during the Désy period and now more would have to go.

Delafield himself was in a precarious position, he was the Acting Director. External Affairs, realizing the low morale and uncertainties at the International Service, announced the formal appointment of Delafield about a year after Désy's departure.

External Affairs found itself in the difficult predicament of preparing policy guidelines for the International Service on issues on which it had not yet made up its mind, and more often than not, preferred not to make up its mind. The files reveal contradictions, fragmentation of views and internal differences, augmented sometimes by ideological outlooks on what was at the time politically safe. They show the many directions of thinking that became part of the decision-making process. The focus on controversial issues was global -- the entire spectrum of Canada's involvement in international relations -- and how these issues were reported and commented on in broadcasts beamed to penetrate the Iron Curtain.

Our Man in Prague and Other Controversies

One of the earliest of the great controversies relates to the broadcasts to Czechoslovakia. The Chargé d'Affaires in Prague in 1951, Benjamin Rogers, who earlier had played a major role in developing psychological warfare thinking in Ottawa, was asked to comment on the Canadian broadcasts to Czechoslovakia. He did not think much of them; they dealt too much with things Canadian and he felt that Czechoslovaks who were risking fines and imprisonment, and possibly their lives, to listen to these broadcasts were not receiving the programs they wanted or deserved. External Affairs passed on this information to the International Service which could then use the feedback for future program decisions. But the dispatches from Rogers contained more than External Affairs had bargained for and they created concern in Ottawa on what was a "delicate issue" in the days of the red scare. No one wanted to be accused of being soft on communism, but the committee structures of External Affairs were used to contain the dangers of extremism in the war of ideas.

In a dispatch of November 30, 1951, Rogers wrote approvingly of stirring up the situation in Czechoslovakia and other satellites through the adoption of a policy of arming underground movements.[1] The dispatch caused concern. The European Division at External Affairs advised Ritchie that the idea of arming underground movements was sufficiently dangerous to warrant asking Rogers to give it no further consideration and not to discuss it with his colleagues.[2] Ritchie gave his approval. Six weeks after Rogers first sent his despatch he was told in a message from A.D.P. Heeney that his plan had no place in Canadian policy.[3]

Rogers sent back a detailed dispatch expressing his distress that External Affairs was disturbed by his suggestions and quickly returned to the charge.[4] He said that Ottawa must decide whether its policy should include liberation of some or all of the satellite peoples as a long term objective. In presenting his argument, Rogers referred to a statement by President Truman (October 1951) to the effect that the American leader looked forward to the time when freedom would be restored in the satellites. External Affairs interpreted Rogers'understanding to be that President Truman supported a policy of liberation. The Department took special note of a sentence in the dispatch from Prague which suggested that while a final decision need not be made now, preparation was necessary: "When we achieve the position of strength towards which we are striving ... to exploit any favourable situation that might arise to effect a restoration of freedom in the satellite countries."

External Affairs took the position that it certainly hoped that some day the satellites would free themselves from Soviet domination and from domestic totalitarian rule, but it did not intend at the time "to take any practical steps towards liberating the satellites by force," nor did it wish to give the satellite peoples "false hopes for liberation by force." A dispatch from the Canadian embassy in Washington showed that US policy seemed to be similar to Canada's. External Affairs inserted a copy of President Truman's October 1951 statement in the file to back up its contention.[5]

Rogers' dispatch spoke of the "positive aim" of the restoration of freedom in the satellites, and he compared the inherent risk in arming an underground resistance movement similar to the risk of rearming the West Germans.

External Affairs decided not to answer specifically the many points raised by Rogers. A short dispatch was sent to him stating that there was no intention whatsoever to liberate satellites by force or to give serious consideration to the arming of underground movements.

The broadcasts to Czechoslovakia (Czech and Slovak) were the first to become embroiled in controversy because they were, for nearly three years, the only ones directed to a Communist country. The controversy involved different factions of Czechoslovakia's émigré community in Canada, officials at External Affairs, the Canadian media and the International Service staff. While no one at External Affairs questioned the loyalty of Dr. Walter Schmolka, who was instrumental in getting Canada involved in broadcasting to Czechoslovakia, the Department was concerned about the principle of "foreignness" and steps were taken almost immediately after the coup in Prague in 1948 to keep a close watch. Dr. Nemec, the distinguished Czech political leader who was Prague's ambassador in Ottawa and defected after the coup, was highly regarded by Lester Pearson, and at Pearson's suggestion was invited to prepare talks at the International Service. Nemec probably knew more about Czechoslovakia and the difficulties it faced after 1948 than anyone else in North America and, indeed, he wrote memorable scripts which undoubtedly provided insights for policy shapers at External. Nemec became part of the full-time staff of the International Service but it was not long before medium and junior rank officials at External found fault with his views. Their evaluation suggested that Nemec was not privy to the secret information they themselves had and which had been passed on to Désy and Delafield but not to Nemec because he did not have the security clearance. In effect External Affairs and the International Service had put Nemec into a 'catch-22' situation.

Of all the bright lights that moved through the corridors of the shortwave service, none was brighter than Dr. Schmolka who became a victim of vicious attacks by the Catholic weekly, *The Ensign,* and was promptly demoted when Désy took over as Director-General. One of Schmolka's memos to the Director-General reads like a letter of confession of sins, hardly likely to appear in the files of the CBC. Schmolka had a Jewish background and that complicated Désy's perception of his "foreignness." In later years Dr. Schmolka was promoted (by Delafield) and was shown the respect he deserved. Memoranda from the BBC and Voice of America and internal documents of External Affairs speak with great praise of Schmolka's insights into propaganda, reliable news reporting and cultural programming. In fact, the two sections that were showered with praise were the German and the Czechoslovak for the quality and effectiveness of their programming; both of these sections were initiated by refugees from German persecution. And even in the case of the German scripts, there were wide swings in the tone of the evaluations. At the same time that External Affairs was praising the German Service which attracted a wide following in West Germany and had many of its programs rebroadcast on local radio stations, the Canadian Foreign Service Officer in Bonn, Mr. Davis, was not impressed. He criticized the scripts on four points: little information about Canada; inadequate in strengthening the moraleof the East German people; dull and shallow; lacking Canadian "flavour" and viewpoint. External Affairs generally dismissed the criticism although it found some merit in the labelling of the scripts as dull and shallow. But it noted that this was the result of the "necessary" restraints placed by External on the German Section to prevent possible misinterpretations of Canadian policies.

In May 14, 1952, R.A.D. Ford, the Canadian Chargé d'Affaires in Moscow, wrote to External Affairs that he was "rather disturbed by the highly polemical tone of many of these (Russian Service) broadcasts and the language and assumptions which would be ... offensive to most Russians." He had been sent a series of scripts for his evaluation and thought that many of them were good, some excellent (e.g., "Cobalt Bomb," "Canadian Trade Unions") and others very interesting ("The Anniversary of the Death of Patriarch Tikhan"). But Ford vented much anger on a commentary that portrayed Maxim Gorky in "very poor light," although "Gorky is a great writer, and the Russians are proud of him." Ford's comments were generally restrained and offered reasoned advice. He was concerned, however, that some of the Russian-language scripts were getting away from Ottawa's proclaimed policy, and the danger in this was that "a few misrepresentations of facts or badly presented broadcasts can do as much harm as fifty good ones." Both Charles Ritchie and Escot Reid wrote brief comments on Mr. Ford's dispatch.

Comment by Mr. Ritchie

> I am disturbed by the trend reported by Mr. Ford.... If we broadcast insulting diatribes we might as well close up the service (International Service) entirely.

Comment by Mr. Reid

> I agree with Mr. Ritchie. If CBC- International Service cannot be brought into line, we must take it up with the minister.

There was virtually no politically viable way to discontinue the Russian Service in 1952, without closing down the entire shortwave operation. In fact, preparations were well underway at the time to inaugurate the Ukrainian Service on Dominion Day, July 1.

The Ukrainian Controversy

External Affairs Minister Lester Pearson opened the Ukrainian transmission with a statement that did not reflect his private apprehensions.[6] He noted that Canadians of Ukrainian origin formed "one of the larger of the national groups which, added to the basic British and French elements of the population, make up the Canadian people...." One of the purposes of the program, the Minister said, was to tell listeners about the Canadians who came from the Ukraine. Another purpose was "to bring ... truthful, unbiased information about the world and world events." Pearson added that Canada sought to penetrate the artificial wall which the Soviet authorities had erected and the broadcasts would seek to establish contact between the Canadian people and the Ukrainian people.

It was not long after the July 1 inauguration of the Ukrainian Service that External Affairs started having misgivings about what it had created. The Department sent frequent letters to Jean Désy, bringing to his attention "serious defects" in the Ukrainian scripts which "compared unfavourably to the scripts prepared by other sections." On June 18, 1953, Dana Wilgress reported that the Ukrainian scripts were getting worse.[7] They were criticized for their strong underlying nationalist sentiment, factual errors, poor style and lack of clarity and continuity.

Wilgress' harsh letter to Désy urged him to find a way to solve the problem. A memorandum was drawn up by External Affairs to discuss the specific "shortcomings" of scripts in some detail. Furthermore, the Department prepared a memorandum entitled *CBC (International Service) Ukrainian Scripts* which provided policy lines and pinpointed danger areas relating to Ukrainian broadcasts. The International Service was cautioned to be particularly careful not to let it appear that Ukrainian Canadians were Ukrainians first, and Canadians only incidentally or temporarily. External Affairs noted that this generally was not the case, but allowed there were some Ukrainian Canadians whose Canadianism was a minor part of their makeup; great care had to be taken to ensure that these individuals did not speak for the whole group. The other major danger was rooted in the existence of "militant, nationalist, separatist, Ukrainian émigré groups which had been promoting an independent, national Ukraine" and working for the overthrow of the Soviet system.

External Affairs made it clear that the Ukrainian Service was operated purely in Canada's interests:

> The CBC (International Service) is at all times the voice of Canada, no matter what individual may be at the microphone or what language he may be using.

One of the best examples of the concern at External Affairs over Ukrainian-language scripts relates to a broadcast of March 28, 1953. The script referred to the song, "Vkraino Maty, Kat Skonav" and questions were also raised about using such phrases as "Red hangmen and oppressors." The handwritten evaluation stated the script was "pretty bad." The song was, "O Mother Ukraine, the Hangman is Dead." While the External Affairs evaluation did not know the historical origins and significance, he thought the song's "application in this case was obvious, and in extremely bad taste."

> The script puts over pretty clearly the idea that Russians are always oppressors--which is not in line with official policy--and is another example of the tendency to give undue prominence to the brief period of Ukrainian independence. This, of course, is the case for Ukrainian separation, which we're not supposed to be plugging.

The Ukrainian scripts which caused problems for External Affairs were those that dealt with Ukrainian nationalism; there were of course many other scripts that were deemed to be good. The Ukrainian section was headed by Mr. Panchuk who had a remarkable ability to disregard the orders from Director-General Désy. Normally, Désy did not deal directly with section heads and left this chore to Delafield, but the Panchuk situation required his personal intervention. Désy forwarded to Panchuk comments by External Affairs on Ukrainian broadcasts (on June 23rd, 1953) and promptly received back a 12-page argumentative memorandum.[8] Désy responded with a one paragraph statement that he was not seeking a lengthy justification of the scripts or a rebuttal; he called on Panchuk to conduct the Ukrainian Service along the lines laid down and to pay special attention to the comments of External Affairs. The "unabashed Mr. Panchuk" came back with a further 11-page memorandum of argument and justification. An External Affairs' memo on the matter noted it was all "a bit discouraging" and "it may be that a new man will have to be found to head the Ukrainian Service."

A handwritten notation by a senior official (signed W, probably Dana Wilgress) said the affair was a good illustration of Mr. Désy's difficulties. "It shows the imperative necessity of having Canadians head the language sections. Otherwise objectivity is lacking."

Panchuk was a Canadian with impeccable credentials. He had indicated an interest in the Ukrainian Service in a letter from London, England, at the time that the International Service was having difficulty in finding a suitable person to head the Ukrainian Section. He was born and educated in Western Canada, had been a high school teacher there and had served in the Royal Canadian Air Force during World War II. After the war he had been a representative of Canadian Ukrainian groups, acting on their behalf to settle displaced Ukrainians. He was hired before the Ukrainian transmissions began.

The pattern of the Ukrainian broadcasts was expected to be similar to those going out to other Eastern European audiences. At the same time, the International Service wanted to devote a portion of the program to reflect the lives and accomplishments of Canadians of Ukrainian origin. Almost from the beginning, External Affairs officials and International Service management considered the Ukrainian broadcasts problematic; they seemed to be designed "more for the Ukrainian listening public in Canada and in the United States than for ... listeners in the Ukraine." International Service management tried to constrain the "secessionist tendencies" of the Ukrainian section and was disturbed that Panchuk had developed a practice of distributing copies of his section's broadcast material to organizations, groups and individuals in Canada, the United States and other countries. Panchuk outlasted the short tenure of Jean Désy and appeared to be in a much stronger position vis-à-vis Désy's successor, Charles Delafield. At one time Delafield became so exasperated with Panchuk that he wanted to cut him off from any confidential material to which Section heads had access. Delafield announced that henceforth only Canadian born members of the International Service could see such documents. "Panchuk had fun with that because he was Canadian born and Delafield was not. Mr. Delafield had forgotten that."[9]

In the Spring of 1956, Panchuk was fired. Delafield said there were "irregularities in his [Panchuk's] administration which, in the view of CBC Management, warranted such a step." External Affairs, which for some time had suggested that Panchuk had to go, took the position that his dismissal was strictly an internal CBC matter.

Carol Chipman, the son of one of Canada's foremost diplomats, who had been hired by Désy in 1952, was named as head of the Ukrainian Section. Chipman did not speak Ukrainian but undertook to learn. He had proven language skills (English, French, Spanish) and was considered perhaps the best script writer in the Policy Coordination section. For the Ukrainian community, appointing Chipman to replace the fired Panchuk, was adding insult to injury. The files show enormous pressure being put on the CBC and External Affairs to rectify the situation. There were letters from the President of the Ukrainian-Canadian Committee; from A.P. Stepovy, President of the Ukrainian Association of Victims of Russian Communist Terror, from Fedorenko of the Ukrainian Democratic Youth Association of Canada who wrote for Ukrainian-language journals in the United States and Germany, among others. Delafield had a series of meetings with Senator W.M. Wall, conducted detailed inquiries into the practices of the International Service. There was representation by Mrs.

Dyma, who represented the Ukrainian Canadian Committee at the International Council of Women Conference in Montreal in June 1956. The Head of the Ukrainian Orthodox Church in Montreal, Father Sluzar, intervened. Letters of protest about the Ukrainian Section sent to the Prime Minister were referred to External Affairs. Under Secretary of State, Jules Léger, in a reply to Olexander Sosna, Chairman of SUZERO, said that he would pass on the complaints to Delafield in that administratively External Affairs had "no responsibility in regard to the International Service." The lobbying effort continued unabated for at least a year and a half, and Delafield, at the request of External Affairs, sent a detailed dossier on the Ukrainian Affair to External Affairs on August 7, 1957. But that did not end the controversy, internally or externally.

External Affairs, for its part, carried out its own analysis of the situation at the Ukrainian Section. One confidential memorandum (August 27, 1957) declares that "the tendency to intrigue, to attribute to an opponent, and to violence in public expression is not uncommon to émigrés of Slav origin."[10] The memorandum drawn up by the European Division at External argues that the manifestation of a Ukrainian-Canadian interest in the Ukrainian Service with a significant degree of intrigue, was a fact of life to which External Affairs had to find a lasting means of adjustment. By the end of 1957, External Affairs suggested a number of compromises to defuse the controversy by extending to the Ukrainian community "the right to consultation." One suggestion called for the Ukrainian-Canadian Committee to set up a small body of representatives to meet regularly with the International Service. External, however, wanted to deal essentially with the right kind of people, those who lived in Canada since 1939, "long enough ... to have acquired some feeling for the Canadian way of life and work." In effect, External was taking a defensive posture; it acknowledged that establishing a Ukrainian Service was an internal political decision that was nevertheless unfortunate from a foreign policy perspective; it wanted to contain the activities of the Ukrainian Service and was highly critical of Ukrainian programming; it sought to contain the lobbying of the Ukrainian community.

While all this was going on, the Ukrainian Section under the direction of Chipman, was falling into the prescribed programming pattern. Chipman's appointment to succeed Panchuk followed consultations between Delafield and External Affairs. Chipman recalled years later that he was not aware of the intricate behind-the-scenes manoeuvres.[11]

> I was told it was easier to have me learn sufficient Ukrainian, as I did later on learn Russian, than to take a European Ukrainian and teach him to be a Canadian

> journalist. The first task was to see that our broadcasts were journalistically correct but that also meant an end to all the Anti-Russian snide remarks that seemed to creep into so many [Ukrainian] translations of scripts and into news and interviews.

Chipman's first priority was to bring to an end what he called "the Ukrainian Section's ... own propaganda war ... which had nothing to do with communism and fascism."[12] He was troubled by the anti-Russian line that was essentially McCarthy-type primitive anti-communism. Somebody would be interviewed and asked what he did before the revolution and after the revolution. "Why did you come to Canada, to choose freedom?" The rhetoric was considered primitive, not thoughtful. Chipman recalled that the Canadian Ukrainian Congress in Winnipeg was monitoring the activities of the Ukrainian Section at all times and, he felt, it wanted what could almost be called a Voice of Free Ukraine.

Chipman was brought in to make sure that a "free Ukraine" policy would not be identified with the International Service. The challenge to turn this situation around was formidable. While not all the people in the Ukrainian Section were professional journalists, "they were very bright." As Chipman pointed out, they were not born in Canada and "saw things differently."[13]

> They had a view of communism which wasn't mine obviously because it was one formed in Europe where they were born and they suffered ... Their policy was very much the Dulles kind of policy; we should be pushing for an independent Ukrainian state ... the best way to forward the breakdown of Soviet power was to forward the emergent nationalities among them, most principally, the Ukrainian.

Chipman found that the Ukrainian Section sought to give legitimacy, and to Canadianize the revolutionary viewpoint by quoting prominent Canadians, including Senators and Members of Parliament; "they gave it a kind of journalistic gloss." Chipman worked on repairing fences with the Ukrainian community and made numerous trips to Winnipeg for meetings with the Ukrainian-Canadian Committee, seeking their understanding for what the International Service was all about. He found sympathetic understanding but "the pressures always continued." There was the continued lobbying,criticism of International Service in Ukrainian-language newspapers and speeches about the un-Canadian voice of the International Service.

The controversy surrounding the Ukrainian Section took a peculiar twist on June 3, 1957, with the unexpected visit to Montreal by a delegation which included a personal representative of the Mayor of Buffalo (NY). Both the Mayor, Steven Pankow, and his representative, Wolodmyr Chopyk, were Americans of Ukrainian origin. The City of Buffalo had decided that the International Service broadcasts to the Ukraine were the best from any part of the free world and the Buffalo delegation brought Delafield a citation of merit and a golden key to the city. The *Montreal Star*, in an editorial on June 5, 1957, *CBC International Gets An Accolade*, extended congratulations to Delafield and his staff and to External Affairs.[14] The *Ukrainian Voice* (Winnipeg) saw things very differently in an editorial page article (June 19, 1957), accusing the Buffalo delegation of making mischief; "they were meddling in what was not their business. Who prompted them to do it?"[15] The Winnipeg paper referred to the International Service broadcasts to the Ukraine as "simply terrible" and said it was a waste of money "to broadcast such nonsense behind the Iron Curtain."

The eventual solution after a while was that Chipman became the head of both the Russian and Ukrainian sections. He considered this a wise move in that Canada was broadcasting to one state -- the Soviet Union -- in that country's two main languages.

The Ukrainian controversy came at a time when External Affairs was reversing gears in its psychological warfare policy in broadcasts to Eastern Europe. After years of behind the scenes direction in the Cold War battle to influence minds in Eastern Europe, in a memorandum dated January 11, 1956, Peter Roberts of External Affairs describes a visit to International Service to discuss Canadian policies in Europe with Delafield, Mr. Pidgeon and various section heads.[16]

The discussions were chiefly concerned with "External's preference for relaxation of tensions in Eastern Europe as opposed to the 'no holds barred' attitude of some the section heads." External Affairs prepared memoranda dealing with the choice of subjects, methods of criticism and general tone for broadcasts to the Soviet Union which were also to be applied to broadcasts to other Eastern European countries. One such memorandum made the argument that the Canadian broadcasts should be uniquely Canadian and not simply a review of events with the coverage slanted obviously to justify the Western case; "the credibility and balance" of the International Service news was especially important in settling the tone of the broadcasts. The memorandum suggested essentially that there be a return to the policies of Ira Dilworth in the late 1940s.

> The listener expects to hear about Canadian ideas when he tunes in on a Canadian broadcast and if his attention can be secured by the quality of the broadcasts and his curiosity satisfied by the information we give him them there is some hope that he will discover after a while that our ideas arequite reasonable and that they shed quite a new light on his own Government's statements and policies. If, however, our attack on Communism is taken out of the Canadian context, develops a tone quite different from that of commentaries on Canada and news broadcasts so that it bears a distinct 'propaganda' label, then we may lose most of our listeners because we are asking them, before they have any idea of what we are like and how we think, either to join with us in an outright general condemnation of their Government and its philosophy or to be denounced themselves.

It would take some time, five years or so, before the change of policy direction suggested by External Affairs would take hold. An unfortunate broadcasting lesson of the 1950s was that propaganda had developed a momentum of its own.

Lobster Festival

Definition: Let the Reds go after each other like the lobsters in a tank.

On the afternoon of February 8, 1955, A.J. Andrew of the Political Coordination Section at External Affairs placed an urgent phone call to Willie Chevalier, the head of policy at the International Service in Montreal, about the startling development in Moscow: Mr. Malenkov had resigned. Andrew's advice -- confirmed in a confidential letter the same day from the Under Secretary of State to Delafield -- asked the International Service to provide two separate streams of coverage of the power change in Moscow: "one in the nature of a news commentary and the other in the nature of a propaganda effort."[17]

The suggestions for the contents of the news commentary were quite specific and offered eight points that should be taken into account. External Affairs noted that while Malenkov's resignation was surprising, it was not an "entirely unforeseen development" and should be viewed as the culmination of a long process which began when Nakita Khrushchev became First Secretary in September 1953.[18] This was followed by the gradual removal of the "Opposition": Beriya (head of KGB), Bagirov, Arturinov (the latter two were Party bosses in Azerbaijan and Armenia and had a record of opposition to Khrushchev, especially in agricultural policy matters) and the side-tracking of Mikoyan who had pressed for the pro-consumer concessions initiated by Malenkov when he came to power. External saw these developments as having brought about the reversal of some liberal economic trends initiated by Malenkov. The Department advised that International Service commentary should include references to statements by various Western leaders, including Prime Minister Lester Pearson, to the effect that the international atmosphere had improved since Stalin's death and it was hoped that this trend would no be altered as a result of the power changes in the Moscow government.

The "separate" propaganda initiative tied to the Malenkov resignation gave rise to what was to become known as *The Lobster Festival*. External wanted International Service to review some of Malenkov's public statements (e.g., New Years' messages in 1954 and 1955) and point out that he had promoted a more liberal policy, especially concessions to peasants and consumers. Soviet listeners were to be reminded that they would be worse off as a result of Malkenkov's resignation. Ewart Prince, who had worked in the Prime Minister's Office before he had gone to International Service, was preparing a couple of propaganda scripts which should then be teletyped to Robert Redford, the International Service representative in Ottawa, who would secretly hand deliver them to the Department.

Nine days later, on February 17, the Under Secretary of State sent a SECRET letter to Delafield and an analysis of the change of Prime Minister in Moscow and the propaganda opportunities this presented.[19] The object was "to exploit Communist contradictions in answer to Communist attempts at what they call Capitalist contradictions." The Under Secretary of State stressed the importance of keeping the propaganda operation "distant and separate from any presentation of Canadian government policy."

The Department provided International Service with studies that pointed to "soft spots" in the Soviet Union and the secret initiative should be calculated "to hit the soft spots" and should be identified with the script writer and not reflecting Canadian opinion. Ottawa wanted to see the scripts before they were broadcast. The propaganda initiative developed a momentum of its own and

External Affairs arranged for a secret Ottawa meeting on March 14th with senior International Service officials in the Small Conference Room in the East Block, to discuss *The Lobster Festival*."[20] Delafield was asked to bring along Chripounoff, the head of the Russian Section, although this was contrary to International Service policy which excluded those of foreign background from highly confidential matters. Minutes of the meeting show that Chripounoff did not attend. The International Service was represented by its Director (Delafield), his assistant (Pidgeon), the Policy Director (Chevalier) and a senior writer (Chipman). External Affairs was also represented by four officials (Andrew, Southam, Williamson and Trottier). By the time the Ottawa meeting took place, the views of External Affairs had crystallized on the power change in Moscow and had been spelled out in dispatches from the Minister for External Affairs (March 8) to the Canadian High Commissioner in London and the Canadian delegation to the North Atlantic Council in Paris.[21] The choice between Malenkov and Khrushchev was no longer seen as differences in Soviet internal matters but differences in foreign policy.

External's propaganda operation was based on the argument that Krushchev's victory over Malenkov had tipped the scales in favour of closer Sino-Soviet ties against the rest of the Western world. What was going on in Moscow was, according to External Affairs, a struggle "between Asianism and Europeanism" in the Soviet Union which has roots on both continents.

At the March 14 meeting with International Service officials, Andrew immediately got to the heart of the matter: the objective of *The Lobster Festival* was to try to divide Russia from China and/or woo Russia away from China.[22] The Minister had been fully briefed about the operation which had the formal approval of the Under Secretary of State. Delafield and Pidgeon raised questions about *The Lobster Festival* scenario and suggested that the internal affairs of the Soviet Union might have been the key reason for the Khrushchev rise to power rather than Sino-Soviet policy. The strongest reservations and doubts about External Affairs were in answer to doubts raised by Chipman, the External Affairs officials declared that "the established plausibility and not the truth of the analysis was the important thing to keep in mind." The International Service officials continued to express concerns and thought it was necessary to be sure of the facts, otherwise there was the risk that the radio operation, if groundless, might backfire and discredit the International Service. Andrew's reply was to re-emphasize that there was sufficient plausibility in the External Affairs' version. It was envisaged that the listeners to and those receiving reports of the Canadian programs were well placed Russians; they would have their own fears and suspicions of China. The propaganda operation would build on these fears. At the same time, the International Service was cautioned against giving a racial "yellow vs. white" slant to the broadcasts. One of the central arguments was the cost factor of the Sino-Soviet ties which involved a flow of Soviet resources to China at the expense of living standards in the USSR.

The Lobster Festival was to be introduced discreetly. It was felt that if all the Iron Curtain sections would begin the propaganda line at the same time, "like runners in a race," it would be too obvious that this was a concerted and planned operation. *The Lobster Festival* began in the Russian Section and the other broadcasts to Eastern Europe were brought in gradually, one by one. The propaganda operation was to last several months and the BBC was approached to partake. Regardless of the BBC stand, the Minister was informed on March 9 that *The Lobster Festival* -- a major Canadian initiative, had already begun.[23]

Some 30 years later, Chipman, who had attended the March 14, 1955 planning meeting at External Affairs, said it was difficult to take *The Lobster Festival* seriously: "we thought anybody who had come out with ... a name like this was somebody ... fit for the CIA or the Deuxième Bureaux." Chipman, who wrote some of the Festival scripts, said he was sure that he must have had some profound thoughts about "this absurdity." The Festival did not last very long and the External Affairs official who had put it together commented rather bitterly in a memorandum that International Service had responded to his views with the rapidity and subtlety of turtles. Andrew was replaced by P.M. Roberts in the Policy Coordination Section at External Affairs and the new thinking was that International Service should cool it.

External Affairs was developing a new outlook on broadcasting to the Soviet Union. R.A.D. Ford, who was at the time in the Department's European Division, drew his colleagues' attention to a Harrison Salisbury article in the *New York Times* on American propaganda. The US had adopted a new and softer tone in the broadcasts to Eastern Europe. Inspired by the article, External Affairs wrote to International Service that it proposed to make similar changes.

Chevalier and Nemec replied that if the cold war was to become less intense, the propaganda broadcasters would have to moderate their tone or run the risk of putting propaganda material in the hands of the Soviets. Both the International Service and External Affairs were now launched on the long road of changing the tone of Canadian broadcasters. The International Service wanted to provide factual reporting of the news, with detailed comments on life and conditions in the West which was perceived as an effective defence against Communism during a "cold peace."

CHAPTER XIV

THE SEARCH FOR DETENTE

The 1960s was a period of decompression in the relationship between the International Service and External Affairs. There were three main reasons for the more realistic interaction described by the Department as "regular and harmonious": the Désy formula had not worked and, in fact, was detrimental to the shortwave operation; and the waning interest of External Affairs in utilizing the International Service for psychological warfare.

One of the characteristics of the Delafield era (1953-1972) was that he was never hesitant to take orders, but he frequently did not pass them on. His direct influence in broadcasting content was minimal and he played his relationship with External Affairs by the rules. Since much of the documentation, letters of policy advice and analysis of highly sensitive situations was classified as "Secret" and "Confidential", he kept it that way.[1] Those who had access to secrets worth knowing, kept them secret. The somewhat larger group cleared for access to confidential documents, read the documents with interest -- and a sense of belonging to the in-group -- but was overwhelmed by the quantity of the documentation, with complex explanations couched in diplomatic language. There were some dispatches that were brutally frank, but External Affairs reemphasized the secret and sensitive nature of the material.

Commentaries were normally prepared in two or three hours, and often in less time, and writers seldom had access to the "material of enlightenment." Willie Chevalier, the noted journalist who was Policy Coordinator for some years, complained to one External Affairs official that he himself was not well informed about secret policy dimensions in that Delafield had a "sticky desk," the documents were stuck to the Director's desk until they were due for return.[2] While the Chevalier comment is perhaps an exaggeration, Edward Prince, John Svedman and Arthur Pidgeon, each of them in charge of policy at one time or another, had clearance and were known to lock themselves up with confidential documents. The contents, however, were hardly ever passed on the stable of commentators. As one long-time writer for the International Service observed: "In about a dozen years of writing commentaries, press reviews and news backgrounders, four or five times a week, I never saw a confidential report or received any detailed briefing other than general comments. In all those years, Arthur Pidgeon, who was then second to Delafield, talked to me once about a minor phrase, 'an academic question,' which he thought had detracted from the script."

An examination of the files containing Secret and Confidential dispatches and memoranda, provides insights on foreign policy formulation and explanations for various positions, but often enough there were departmental requests that the topics not become subjects of commentaries or that there be 'non-committal fence sitting.' (One External Affairs official, critical of this, noted that fence sitting was never a dignified position.) Désy wanted access to everything, especially if it was very secret, and as a senior ambassador he was entitled.

After Désy, External Affairs had misgivings about some of the material it was sending to Montreal, though not because of concerns about Delafield and Pidgeon who had top clearance. A British embassy official in Washington, Mr. Watson, on a visit to Ottawa, commented that "journalists were always hungry for secret information and even if they were involved in psychological warfare they did not need to know 'too much'; brief them on what you want and they will do the job." External Affairs had stopped sending Top Secret material in the 1950s, and the "need to know" practice evolved into the forwarding of documents to Montreal. The heavy flow of documents, however, continued and there were two diplomatic mail bag deliveries every week. This "need to know" practice showed up in other areas: when Arthur Pidgeon, long a favourite with External Affairs, was sent by the International Service on a liaison mission to the B.B.C., External Affairs decided not to put him in contact with British Foreign Office officials.

Daily telephone calls between External Affairs and the International Service had become the principal instrument of liaison. In 1960, however, there was a change in the telephone communication system; land lines, which were relatively secure, were replaced by a microwave system subject to easy interception. As a result, the liaison system changed in September 1960, with weekly exchange visits between Montreal and Ottawa by representatives from External Affairs and the International Service respectively. This was cumbersome because of the critical time factor in writing commentaries tied to news developments. Also, External Affairs officers were reluctant to ride the trains between Ottawa and Montreal on a weekly basis.

Over the next two years, or so, a streamlined liaison system developed. This revised systems, based on documentation and practices, was written up[3] for Sidney Freifeld who had taken over as head of the Liaison Service Section (made up of Policy Coordination and the Press section).

The Department was providing guidance to the International Service in three fields:

- selection of broadcast target areas;

- Eastern European program policy;
- current international affairs.

Political commentaries were submitted by the International Service each week for the Department's information and possible comment. Program reports were also submitted to Ottawa weekly so that External Affairs could judge their quality and content.

External Affairs had three ways of "assisting" the International Service:

- Documents. Classified documents were mailed daily on a "need to know" basis up to but not including TOP SECRET. Overly sensitive documents were not sent.
- Visits. A member of External Affairs Liaison Service visited Montreal every three weeks. Delafield went to Ottawa on an irregular basis, Pidgeon every month, Prince and Svedman on alternating weeks.
- Phone. The phone contact was used only for exceptionally urgent developments. The calls were placed through Operator 1000 -- a secure land line service -- reserved normally for cabinet ministers and senior officials.

External Affairs wanted to ensure that the broadcasts gave the correct impression of Canadian foreign policy. This was the basis for the close and continuing consultative relationship with briefings that provided highly confidential information; senior Departmental officials were consulted when there were doubts. Liaison contacts with International Service, thus, differed markedly from those with the press in Ottawa.

By 1965, External Affairs policies in relation to the International Service were in sharp contrast to those of the days of the Lobster Festival, ten years earlier. When Freifeld headed the Liaison Section, the contacts served mostly as guidance to be borne in mind in preparing commentaries. The International Service had the final responsibility for its political commentaries. The Department saw its liaison activities as "partly positive in ensuring that the basic themes of Canadian foreign policy are accurately and adequately reflected in political commentaries and partly negative in making sure that CBC-International Service stay on firm ground when commenting."

The decompression process in the interaction between External Affairs and the International Service was, tied to the search for detente and the thawing in the cold war. In January 1959, the Department asked the International Service to cool it; ease off or cease political warfare broadcasts to Eastern Europe.[4] The Canadian diplomatic missions in Prague, Warsaw, Moscow and Budapest supported this position; the consensus was that anti-communist polemics were not useful but positive presentation of western thought and accomplishment would be worthwhile. It was precisely this policy ten years earlier by Ira Dilworth that contributed in his being viewed with disfavour by the Prime Minister and the Minister for External Affairs and led to his replacement by Jean Désy. At that time the diplomatic missions in Eastern Europe wanted Canadian broadcasting to be a Cold War warrior in the full sense.

The adoption of the Dilworth philosophy in the 1960s is reflected in a dispatch from David Johnson at the Moscow embassy.

> ... The key to Canadian broadcasting to the Soviet Union had to be the almost pathological curiosity which almost most Russians have about the outside world. Russians are well aware that the official information available to them about other countries is inaccurate or incomplete. Their interest is less in politics than day to day living.

The advice from the Moscow embassy was to give the Russians more information about things Canadian: Canadian houses, cars, clothing, books, films, working conditions, trade unions, theatres, sports and so on. Propaganda directed at the Soviet regime, Johnson wrote, would often meet with indifference on the part of the listeners, and not infrequently with hostility. He also thought that the Soviet authorities might stop jamming Canadian broadcasts if we had more acceptable programming.

In the decade of the 1960s and well into the 1970s the International Service commented on world affairs with a "natural Canadian bias and reflected Canadian attitudes," as expressed in large part by editorial comments in newspapers and in official statements. The emphasis was on national and international news and doing what the International Service could do better than any other international broadcaster: providing information about Canada, projecting Canadian cultural life and transmitting Canadian views on global affairs. An unusually interest in programs which illustrated the atmosphere in the mid-1960s, is the Keresky interview.

Kerensky

About June 1, 1964, Alexander Kerensky, the first Russian leader after the February 1917 revolution, had an important date in New York with Carrol Chipman, the head of the Russian Section of the International Service. Kerensky, who was living in New York in exile, had suffered a bad fall that morning but pulled himself together for the meeting with Chipman and another member of the Russian Section. The meeting had been arranged some weeks earlier during a visit by Kerensky to Canada where he made a speech.[5]

The meeting took place at the CBC studios in New York and lasted for nearly four hours. It was essentially a debriefing of Kerensky for the eight months that he was in power until his government was ousted in the Communist Revolution of October 1917. Kerensky was interviewed virtually every day of his leadership between February and October. The absorbing story was split into a dozen programs and the CBC-International Service announced to its listeners that it would be broadcasting 30 minute excerpts on Sundays.

After the first segment was aired, External Affairs made an urgent phone call to Chipman. Ambassador Ford in Moscow had been summoned by Foreign Minister Andrei Gromyko and scolded. Chipman considered the Kerensky interview so interesting that he had thought of sending it to the Soviet Academy of Science, History Department. Chipman sent a memo to Delafield, describing the Kerensky interview as an impeccable piece of journalism, very relevant and interesting, historical, and of no propaganda value; "we were just giving the listeners something wethought they should be interested in."[6] External Affairs passed on this message to Ambassador Ford. External Affairs accepted the Chipman position and the Kerensky series continued as scheduled.

The Kerensky incident reflected the careful position of External in relation to the International Service in the mid 1960s: it advised, it criticized but if did not seek to have the final word. As Chipman recalled 20 years later, External Affairs was eager to establish a separation in the public's mind -- in Canada and abroad -- of the separation between the Canadian government and Canadian broadcasting. In Chipman's view, Ottawa realized that governmental censorship would undermine the credibility of the broadcasting operation and prove politically embarrassing.

The calming atmosphere prevailing at External Affairs did not mean that all was well for the International Services; in fact, it was in more trouble than ever before. The decade of the 1960s began with fiscal restraints in Ottawa and the International Service was an attractive target for Treasury Board. There was another critical problem, also tied to funds, in that the shortwave transmitters at Sackville had become obsolete.

The Treasury Board

On January 8, 1960 -- as the International Service was preparing special programs in celebration of its 15th birthday -- the Secretary of the Treasury Board sent a letter to Norman Robertson, the Under-Secretary of State at External Affairs, noting that the ministers wanted a report on the International Service that would help them "todetermine whether or not it should be continued and if so, what the future scale of the operation might be."

A team of senior External Affairs officials, headed by Marcel Cadieux, promptly met with International Service. Director Delafield, on January 21st and 28th, to be briefed on International Service activities which now included one television program every two weeks for wide distribution in Britain over BBC and in Europe over Eurovision. By May 1960, External Affairs had concluded that shortwave broadcasting was important for Canada and that the International Service was performing a useful function in promoting goodwill towards Canada through the presentation of an objective picture of Canada and Canadian viewpoints on international affairs.

The way External Affairs saw it, the International Service was virtually Canada's only means of reaching Eastern Europe. To abolish Canadian shortwave broadcasting would merely be playing Russia's game for them; the Soviet authorities would see the end of the broadcasts as a vindication of their jamming activities. Yet another major argument for retention of the service was that Canada had implied responsibility within NATO's program of information and propaganda. Over the previous five years, or so, Ottawa had rejected initiatives that would have resulted in a centrally-directed NATO information program and argued that each member country of the alliance should have its own initiative. External felt that abandoning Ottawa's broadcast venture would prompt questions in NATO Council.

The Treasury Board wanted even further cuts, "an occupational disease in the organization." Arthur Blanchette, the head of the Liaison Service Section at External, in a memorandum to Cadieux on October 5, 1960, reported that he had been visited by J. Fortier, the Treasury Board officer in charge of radio affairs who stressed "three main desirabilia." Firstly, abolition of broadcasts in English, French and German; secondly, abolition of the Latin American Section (Spanish Portuguese); and thirdly, External Affairs financial control over the International Service.[7]

The third of the Treasury Board proposals was not grounded in fiscal restraints but brought into question the independence not only of the International Service but also the parent organization, the CBC, an alarming proposition. Blanchette's memorandum (Restricted) is revealing:[8]

> Regarding External Affairs financial control over the CBC-International Service, instead of trying to argue our case further, I decided to ask him point blank why Treasury Board always kept coming back to that point in the face of our obvious refusal. He said the reason was quite simple. Treasury would like to express the same control over the CBC and the CBC-International Service as it does over Government departments. Under the existing CBC set-up, this is impossible. To place the CBC-International Service under External's financial control would, I gather, be viewed by Treasury as the thin edge of the wedge for some such arrangement (under another Government department) for the entire C.B.C. Mr. Fortier did not pursue the matter further yesterday, but I am pretty sure that Treasury will come back to this question.

At no point in the Blanchette-Fortier conversation did the Treasury Board official mention the Eastern European Section, except *en passant* when Fortier asked whether it would be possible to abolish broadcasts in Ukrainian. Blanchette thought the Department "would view such a possibility with equanimity, but ... doubted whether the Ukrainian colony in Canada and perhaps the Government itself would so view it."[9]

Treasury Board considered broadcasts in English and French expendable, but Blanchette emphasized that valuable exchange material was involved, there was the prestige factor and there were likely to be complaints from internal Canadian sources. Regarding German, External thought this would attract criticism from NATO if broadcasts in that language disappeared. Regarding Latin America, it was pointed out that the then Minister for External Affairs, Howard Green, would favour an increase rather than a decrease in programming.

The International Service budget was cut in 1961 to $1.7 million, a decrease of a whopping $300,000. Major transmission changes went into effect on January 29, 1961; overnight five services to Western Europe were dropped: Norwegian, Swedish, Danish, Dutch and Italian. Twenty-one employees were laid off.

The time freed up on the transmitters was used for broadcasting to Africa in English and French. This was done on the cheap, without new money or staff: the English and French broadcasts to Europe were re-broadcast for the African Service. To give the programs an African touch, interviews with students and visitors from Africa were inserted. The Canadian signal was strong throughout the continent south of the Sahara and proved especially useful during the Canadian participation in the United Nations' peace-keeping venture in the Congo.

What was surprising after the budget cuts, which had muted the Voice of Canada, was that the International Service remained an important player in world radio. It was broadcasting for 12 hours a day in 11 languages and the letters pouring into Montreal showed that there were attentive and interested listeners at the receiving end. It was nosmall miracle that the two 50 Kilowatt transmitters of 1940s vintage were still doing a fair job although the airwaves had become far more crowded and most countries were using more powerful transmitters. Canada, which had started out with one of the clearest voices in the world in February 1945, was still being heard, but not easily.

To attract listeners, an international broadcaster must provide a service which can be heard consistently and without difficulty in the target area. The signal strength has to be competitive with other signals aiming at the same area. While it is unrealistic to expect the CBC to compete with such powerful broadcasters as the British Broadcasting Corporation and the Voice of America in numbers of transmitters, there are, however, minimum levels which can be regarded as acceptable. In broadcasts to Eastern Europe, the International Service was complementary rather than competing with the Voice of America and BBC transmissions as part of the western effort to penetrate the Iron Curtain. To enhance the likelihood of the Canadian broadcasts reaching the Soviet Union, the International Service entered a relay agreement with the BBC to rebroadcast some of the Canadian transmissions from Daventry.

In 1960, when the two original 50 Kw transmitters had reached the end of their dependable life, Canada was making do with obsolete equipment. In the search for replacement parts, the International Service found out in April 1961 that RCA Victor had shipped a 50 Kilowatt transmitter -- similar to the ones at Sackville -- to the Venezuelan government in 1948. This unused transmitter had never been installed and was stored at a Caracas warehouse. Its value in 1948 was $100,000 and Canada bought it "as is, where is," for a bargain $35,000. It cost another $1,500 to ship the transmitter toSackville. The "Venezuelan transmitter" was to be used for replacement parts but it was in good condition and became the third Sackville transmitter in September 1962. The total cost, including duty and installation, was $75,000.

But Canada's voice was fading. Among the many countries with more powerful installations were eight African nations (recently independent), Egypt, Iraq, India, Japan, Colombia, Argentina, Cuba, Pakistan and Curacao.

In 1970, the International Service was still making do with the three 50 Kw transmitters at Sackville and in the "dog eat dog" competition of international broadcasting, Canada was losing frequencies forced off air by more powerful transmitters. For example, one International Service signal to Europe was lost to Israel, Radio Nederland's 260 kw. transmitter on Bonaire forced off the air on International Service transmission to South America: Radio Moscow knocked off two International Service channels and Radio Pakistan using a 250 Kw transmitter was displacing one of the Canadian signals to Europe. These displacements were legitimate in that Canada was not making efficient use of the frequencies.

There were significant shifts in the Soviet Union's jamming priorities. The Russians first suspended the jamming of the BBC in 1956 on the day when the Soviet leaders -- Khrushchev and Bulganin -- landed in London for an official visit. During the Hungarian uprising, jamming resumed. In 1959, Khrushchev's visit to the United States brought about the suspension of jamming the Voice of America broadcasts. The Soviet authorities unsuccessfully sought some censorship rights over Voice of America and BBC broadcasts. Nevertheless, Washington and London introduced sufficient self-restraint in their broadcasts; both the BBC and Voice of America provided the Soviet Union with transcripts of broadcasts.

In August 1960, Under-Secretary of State for External Affairs, Cadieux, in a dispatch to the Canadian embassy in Moscow, noted that while there had been "an improvement recently in International Service programs, there is undeniably still room for improvement." Cadieux did not think that Moscow would be willing at that time to lift their jamming of Canadian broadcasts on the basis of script materia,l and taking up de-jamming discussions would prejudice later opportunities. The Under-Secretary of State was hopeful, however, that "by autumn CBC-International Service broadcasts might ... achieve a sufficient degree of objectivity and unobjectionableness to justify a formal approach to Mr. Zhukov [the Soviet Minister of Cultural Relations].

At that time, Ottawa was negotiating a cultural agreement with the Soviet Union. External Affairs was "happy to note" that a series of direct exchanges had been taking place between the International Service and the Soviet radio and TV authorities. These broadcast exchanges were stepping-stones to the broader cultural agreement.

CHAPTER XV

FROM DELAFIELD TO BROWN

The 1970s began with an abundance of optimism at the International Service. The budgetary absorbtion of the external broadcaster into the CBC in 1968 gave confidence that there would no longer be threats of sudden death; if there were government cuts in the offing they would be shared equitably across the corporation.

There was good news along many fronts: a time of growth and expansion was about to begin. There was also a change of name: the International Service officially became Radio Canada International -- RCI.

RCI celebrated its 25th birthday in 1970 and the government joined the festivities. The Post Office, on June 1, 1971, brought out a 15-cent stamp -- the price of overseas airmail at the time -- to celebrate Canada's involvement in international broadcasting. The impressive stamp, in three colours, was designed by Burton Kramer of Toronto; it showed a pattern of six maple leaves radiating out from the centre. On the top left it read "Le Monde aux Écoutes -- Speaking to the World"; on the right top, "Radio Canada International." The stamp created favourable publicity at home and was of special interest to stamp collectors all over the world who listened regularly to International Stamp Corner, one of the popular programs.

When the CBC consolidated its Montreal broadcast facilities in the 23-story Maison de Radio Canada, RCI broadcast the first transmission from this state-of-the-art broadcasting centre on June 19, 1972. At the time RCI employed 180 people, occupied four floors of the Maison de Radio Canada in Montreal, plus offices and production facilities in Ottawa and Toronto, the shortwave plant in Sackville and two shortwave monitoring stations at Stanley Corner, near Ottawa and Westham Island, near Vancouver, RCI's operating budget was $5 Million and another $5 Million was being spent on new transmitter installations.

The most reassuring sign that there was a future for the external broadcaster was the building project underway at Sackville, N.B. On November 7, 1971 two 250 kw transmitters were inaugurated; they were five times more powerful than the old transmitters which had long become obsolete. The Canadian radio signal in Europe and Africa was again competitive with the transmissions from other countries. In 1974, the additional 250 kw transmitters were on stream.

The expanded transmitter facilities at Sackville placed canada in a better position to enter barter arrangements. For nearly 15 years, Canada had a highly successful arrangement with the BBC to re-transmit RCI programs from the British shortwave facilities at Daventry, first into the heartland of the Soviet Union and later into other Eastern European countries. The agreement with the BBC was formalized in the 1960s and enlarged to carry Canadian programs to Africa. These arrangements proved so successful that Canada eventually built two 300 kw transmitters in Britain for the BBC to relay Canadian programming well into the 21st. century.

In 1972, RCI entered a somewhat similar barter arrangement with Deutsche Welle which gave Canada access to West German Transmitters at Sines in Portugal to relay broadcasts to Eastern Europe. In return, Deutsche Welle was given access to the RCI shortwave transmitters at Sackville for a clear signal into North America and the Caribbean. (The agreement also called for Canada to use the West German transmitters located in Malta but the Maltese government forbade RCI transmissions from its territories following a diplomatic dispute between Ottawa and Malta over unrelated issues.)

Canada's invigorated voice -- it could now be heard much clearer in Eastern Europe, Africa and the Middle East -- attracted millions of new listeners; the number of letters and post cards pouring into RCI headquarters jumped from 50,000 to 80,000. Canada's largest audience was in Eastern Europe, especially the Soviet Union, but it became more expensive and difficult for the listeners in Eastern Europe to send letters to the West. One Czech listener switched to the telegram which was almost as cheap as a letter. Although there were only 75 letters a month from listeners in the Soviet Union -- about the same number as received by the BBC -- there were many indicators that the Canadian message was getting through. One of the most valuable reports came from Kol Israel which collected information from immigrants to Israelarriving from the Soviet Union: they described RCI programming as gaining popularity; the listeners emphasized they heard items about Jewish life in Canada, the Jewish diaspora and praised the news bulletins. About one out of three immigrants had listened to RCI before they left the Soviet Union. Other surveys by the BBC, the Voice of America and refugee organizations in Europe showed similarly gratifying results about the RCI penetration; an estimated six million persons in the Soviet Union were reportedly listening to Canada at least once a week.

The letters from listeners reflected audience approval. In all language services, the RCI transmissions began with a comprehensive bulletin of international and Canadian news, followed by news commentaries, backgrounders, cultural talks and sports. There were musical programs, listeners clubs and stamp collectors' discussions.

The RCI newsroom, which had been the strong point of the service since its earliest days, was almost always singled out for praise. As one letter writer commented: "I appreciate your news; its impartiality is quite a change from most shortwave broadcasts. The lack of blatant propaganda is most refreshing." Similar messages came in thousands of letters in 11 languages from all over the world.

There was recognition of RCI achievements from many sources. Radio Sweden honoured RCI and its producer Alan Yates for the best coverage of the United Nations Environment Conference heldin Stockholm in the summer of 1972. RCI's German section was voted four years in a row as the most popular shortwave service heard in Germany; 500 letters a week were pouring in from listeners in Germany requesting songs, asking questions about Canada or commenting on programs. In a survey conducted among French language shortwave listeners in France, Belgium, Switzerland and Algeria by the Association des Clubs de Réception-Radio, RCI was chosen the favourite international broadcaster.

The head of the Latin American Section, Pedro Marcos Bilbao, was honoured in Madrid for the second time with the ONDAS prize as the best foreign producer of spanish programs outside Spain. Bilbao had an all-encompassing view of the world; he had spent 20 years as an officer and captain in the Spanish Navy, worked for the BBC external service and as a war correspondent in Europe, wrote and produced plays on the London stage and was named a Fellow of Britain's Royal Astronomical Society for his writing on science. He came to RCI's Latin American section in 1952 and over the following 20 years produced numerous award-winning programs that are still aired in some Latin American countries, four decades later. They include Bilbao's radio series *Christopher Columbus* and *Let Us Rediscover America*.

Although a relatively modest operation, RCI was recognized as a world class broadcaster. Its impressive shortwave programming, augmented by a remarkably innovative transcription service, projected Canada effectively. The display of dynamism inthe early 1970s came at a time of change and renewal.

Charles Delafield, who had stayed at the helm for two decades was preparing for retirement. For the first time, it would be the CBC that was clearly selecting a new director; all the previous directors -- Aylen, Dilworth, Phelps, Desy and Delafield -- had been either approved or actually imposed by External Affairs. The CBC head office saw the Delafield retirement as an opportunity for a new relationship with its external broadcasting arm.

The Task Force

The CBC, which had long kept its distance in order to safeguard its own autonomy, viewed RCI with some suspicion; it had little knowledge of what was going on in Montreal. The CBC, in 1972, ordered a broad-based formal study on the future of RCI. Betty Zimmerman, the Director of International Relations at CBC head office in Ottawa, chaired the Task Force; the other members -- Alan Brown, Jean-Lucien Caron and Brian Townsley -- were from RCI. The Task Force Report of May 9, 1973 made 31 recommendations which dealt with every aspect of operations, ranging from RCI's relationship with the government, to program content and languages of transmission.[1]

The Task Force seemed to be happy with the operation; it wanted RCI to remain in Montreal and not move to Ottawa; it proposed bigger and better programming and additional languageservices in Japanese and Chinese. All this would require additional funding which was not available. Two of the Task Force members, Alan Brown and Betty Zimmerman would become the heads of RCI in the 1970s.

Change At The Top

Delafield retired in 1973, the year of the Task Force Report. The CBC search committee for a new RCI head included four Vice Presidents. It was a highly bureaucratic procedure: 15 persons from inside the CBC and four from outside were considered for the position. Those from inside the CBC were rated in six categories that included managerial leadership, bilingual skills and professional qualifications.[2] (Those from outside the corporation were not rated and never given serious consideration.) The Vice Presidents recommended two names: Jack Craine and Alan Brown.

Jack Craine was described as the most ideal candidate "on all counts"; he was a proven entity in Canadian broadcasting whose first full-time job with the CBC was in 1950 at the International Service. In recommending Craine, the Vice Presidents said he should not be given the job: he was too valuable to the corporation to be sent to RCI.3 The Vice Presidents also mentioned Betty Zimmerman because she presented the CBC with an opportunity to make the first ever appointment of a woman at a senior executive post. But the decision was made togo with Alan Brown, although he was not rated highly in leadership and flexibility. It was an astute assessment of the new director.

Alan Brown

Brown was 53, an extraordinary charming man, attractive in a boyish way; he was also introspective and often displayed mood changes. During World War II, he served in the Royal Canadian Air Force which awarded him the Distinguished Flying Cross. After the war, Brown returned to the University of Toronto for a degree in English Literature. He became a CBC radio producer in 1952 and later worked with Jack Craine at the Armed Forces radio station in Europe. When Brown returned to Canada in 1967 as program director for the CBC English Radio Network, he was fluent in French, German and Spanish. He was instrumental in launching the popular program, *As It Happens*. Brown later spent two years at Information Canada, the short-lived government information service. In 1972, he joined RCI and was promptly named to the Task Force.

Brown had a much respected and deserved reputation as a translator of French literary works into English for which he was awarded the Canada Council prize in 1974.

Brown's takeover from Delafield was, at first, perceived as a breath of fresh air, just as Delafield was seen as a good choice after Desy. But it turned out a difficult job for Brownwhose reorganization included the appointment of a brash young Executive Assistant, Ted England. (This appointment was reminiscent of Desy bringing in Yvon Beaulne as his Chargé d'Affaires in 1952.) After two decades of predictable, if not always inspiring, leadership under Delafield, England proposed changes that struck at the very heart of RCI operations as they had evolved over the long haul. A new power structure surfaced; it unleashed resentments that plagued accident-prone Alan Brown's tenure.

CHAPTER XVI

THE SOVIET TRAP

External Affairs was obviously pleased by RCI's detachment from cold war activities. For Canada's external broadcaster, the drift out of the cold war business had begun around 1958. It was a gradual transition. By the time Alan Brown had taken over from Delafield, RCI had already adapted to new realities; there was little contact with External Affairs which no longer acted as if RCI was an agent -- albeit erratic at times -- in Canada's foreign policy.

Canada's commitment to the North Atlantic Alliance had become diluted and Ottawa itself was less involved internationally. This was reflected in RCI programming, which at the insistence of Ottawa, stopped placing the spotlight on the East Bloc countries.[1] Furthermore, the diplomatic unity of NATO -- which for so many years had priority in programming considerations and had at times resulted in a distorted picture of the world, was no longer a raison d'être. Program exchanges between RCI and Radio Moscow, initiated in the 1960s had developed into the radio equivalent of the ping-pong diplomacy used by China to foster links with Western countries. RCI was at the forefront of the radio diplomacy.

The Soviet Union, which regarded virtually all foreign broadcasting to its population as an unfriendly intrusion, hadits own reasons to dislike Canada; the only country in the world that had a Ukrainian Service which Moscow regarded as a support structure for Ukrainian separatism. But in the atmosphere of detente, RCI and Radio Moscow had developed good relations; in fact, the radio interactions had contributed to better relations between Ottawa and Moscow.

RCI was spared from jamming in 1971 when there was renewed Soviet hostility for Russian language broadcasts; the transmissions from the BBC and Radio Liberty (U.S.) were jammed. There was reason in the Soviet madness: RCI's policy towards Eastern Europe was politically correct; "we had a very rigid policy -- we never interfered in Russian affairs." While RCI did not originate criticism of the Soviet Union in the broadcasts, it did carry news stories and press reviews that reflected Canadian critical opinions on controversial issues in international relations (e.g., USSR policy on emigration and refusenicks).

Some programs were indeed innocuous. For example, every Tuesday, there were readings in Russian from *Encyclopedia Canadiana*. The popular program had started five years earlier with the letter "A" and had reached

"M" by 1971. Letters from Russian listeners showed an enormous interest in facts; there were requests for tourist information, picture postcards, booklets on Canada. One letter writer from Central Soviet Asia was sent sheet music for Beethoven's *Moonlight Sonata*, as she had requested.

Radio diplomacy in Canada-USSR relations focused on the exchange of programs. Radio Moscow and Radio Kiev were featuring RCI programs in Russian and Ukrainian dealing with sports, music, culture and trade at a time when there was still heavy jamming of foreign broadcasts. The Canadian Ambassador in Moscow, R.A.D. Ford, reported that on March 3, 1973 Radio Moscow broadcasted a 20-minute program on singer Gordon Lightfoot. The next day, Radio Moscow featured an RCI program on Robert Goulet in a Sunday evening transmission heard across the Soviet Union.

RCI tapes, with a heavy emphasis on music, hockey, cultural exchanges, diplomatic visits, and talks about Canadian industry and scientific achievements, were shipped regularly to the Soviet Union. Radio Moscow, for its part, was supplying Canada with equally impressive programs that were heard on the CBC network. The only grating programs were those dealing with hockey; the Soviet announcers invariably referred to the Canadian hockey players as hooligans.

In March 1975, Carroll Chipman, RCI's Supervisor of Eastern European programming, went to Eastern Europe for talks with broadcast officials in Moscow, Kiev, Warsaw and Budapest. Chipman had visited the Soviet Union 10 years earlier when he played a key role in initiating the CBC Radio Moscow program exchanges. He was struck by the change in atmosphere: "it was more friendly and we could have frank exchanges without getting at each others' throats."[2]

Chipman, amiable and open, never sought to be politically correct. He had the self-confidence to speak his mind and replied strongly when Soviet officials criticized Canadian shortwave programming; they regarded it as negative; worse than the Voice of America and the BBC. Alexander Yevstasiev, a deputy chairman of the state Committee for TV and Radio, told Chipman that the RCI programs were considered negative. Holding up a sheet of paper, Yevstasiev said that the Soviet Union was "like a page of great achievements"; he then folded a corner of the paper and added: "you take this tiny corner and seek out what you consider the bad parts."[3]

The Soviet officials were well prepared; they had a red binder which contained transcripts of RCI programs in Russian. Yevstasiev cited as an example an RCI story based on an article by *Toronto Sun* editor, Peter Worthington. The story was about the abuse heaped on Israeli athletes at the 1974 University Olympiad in Moscow; the Israeli students were given a rough time on the field; they were hissed and squealed at; the jeering was widespread. Chipman, while agreeing that the tone of the story was somewhat rough, the point of the story was valid. There was a great deal of sympathy for israeli sportsmen after the tragedy at the Munich Olympics and the story reflected Canadian concern lest something of that sort be repeated. RCI, in addition to its news coverage, ran a review of some editorials in Canadian newspapers saying that if this was the way the Soviets are going to treat people in the Olympics, maybe we have to rethink Moscow's selection as the site for the 1980 Games.

Yevstasiev was adamant in his criticism of the Canadian program; he said the Olympiad incident was "a provocation by Russian Zionists." He also thought that RCI was being most annoying by spending so much time on the question of Jewish emigrating stories on Solzhenitsyn and reports on Soviet refusenichs: "We do not see your programs contributing to the detente which is supported by both our governments.[1]

Chipman explained that Canada was keen on detente but saw no contradiction between criticism and good relations: "We would not indulge in self-censorship to avoid offending Soviet sensibilities." On the question of emigration from the Soviet Union, RCI's job involved "reflecting Canadian concern; we are not in the business to reflect Soviet policy. So, there is, inevitably, criticism of Soviet policy." Chipman considered his response a valuable illustration of Canadian democracy. For Moscow, this was not the end of the story.

In the next few months, there were three major Soviet thrusts to undermine RCI. Two of them were initiated by the Soviet ambassador in Ottawa and the third was launched through the Soviet magazine, *TRUD*.[4]

At a cocktail party in Ottawa, Ambassador Alexander Yakovlev complained informally to External Affairs officials about the Canadian radio programs: they were offensive -- worse than the BBC and Radio Liberty (U.S.) -- and said nothing about Canada. The Ambassador seemed to be especially distressed about the RCI programs during Soviet Foreign Minister Andrei Gromyko's visit to Ottawa in the fall of 1975.

In response to the request for information from External Affairs, Carroll Chipman sent a note on December 3, 1975 to Bill Hooper and Alex Christoff of the Eastern European Division of External Affairs describing the RCI Russian programs, before, during and after the Gromyko visit. There were no requests by External Affairs to change the Russian and Ukrainian programs: it was more an exchange of views. Chipman presented the journalistic interest while External expressed the diplomatic point of view. Often, the interests did not coincide.

Two weeks later, on December 18, 1975, Ambassador Yakovlev went public. The *Ottawa Citizen* carried a front page headline story in which Mr. Yakovlev labelled as subversive the RCI broadcasts to Russia. RCI Director Brown's reply was also carried in the *Ottawa Citizen*: the Ukrainian and Russian language broadcasts were designed "for the general public not for the Soviet embassy in Canada." Brown described RCI's news programs as balanced and added that the activities of certain dissident groups in Canada -- reported in RCI programs -- may be of interest to their countries of origin.

The Soviet ambassador gave his interview to the *Ottawa Citizen* during a protest outside the embassy. Five women dressed in prison clothes were parading with signs saying: "Silent vigil in defence of Ukrainian women prisoners of conscience."

The Moscow attacks on Canadian broadcasts gained momentum. On March 20, 1976, the magazine *TRUD* said that the RCI programs, with the opening words "Govorit Kanada" (This is Canada) did not reflect the friendship of Soviet-Canadian relations espoused by Prime Minister Trudeau: "Judging by the broadcasts, one could think that the Canadian people are peevish and even aggressive non-friends." The *TRUD* article, widely disseminated by news agencies, cynical in tone, poked fun at what it described as Canada's distorted righteous view of itself and its slanderous criticism of the Soviet Union. *TRUD* attacked RCI's Russian and Ukrainian announcers by name, describing them as fascists, drunks, and criminals. "The Russian and Ukrainian radio became a shelter for swindlers who had altogether genuine reasons for hating the Soviet people, inasmuch as the traitor always hates what he betrayed." *TRUD* had inside information about the Russian and Ukrainian broadcasts; among those it attacked was Schuman, "traitor to his homeland, who abandoned his family and other dear ones in search of the 'sweet' life abroad. At the time of the *TRUD* article, the Schuman affair was about to become public in Canada.

The Schuman Affair

Schuman first came to the attention of RCI in July 1972 through an urban and witty letter to Chipman, inquiring about employment possibilities. He was a soviet Russian, that is, of the post-revolutionary period and described himself as a refugee, not a political renegade. He had left the Soviet Union legally when he visited his ailing father who was a disillusioned German Jewish Bolshevik who had gone back to East Germany to die. Schuman then went on to West Germany with a group of students and never returned.

Schuman's life story, as told to Chipman and Assistant RCI Director Karl Renner in an interview on Friday, August 1, 1972, provided an intriguing background.[5] He had had a taste of Western values in India, where he had been a Soviet aid officer, who spoke three Indian languages fluently. As a student in Moscow, he had helped edit Hindi and Gujarati text in the Radio Moscow service.

Schuman came to work for RCI in 1973 and lived up to many promises. Chipman described him as "an able man, though not amiable; abrasive, but then refreshing." He was "terribly hard working" and thus created "unfair jealousies on the part of some members of the Russian Section who also occasionally muttered anti-semitic comments -- and so you would defend him." His good work habits were so upsetting to some of his colleagues in the Russian section that "he was charged with being a KGB agent -- anevident absurdity." Schuman had been cleared by RCMP, which screened all RCI applicants. Chipman regarded him as "a healthy breath of fresh air."

One day, Chipman and Schuman were walking together to the cafeteria on the ground floor of the Radio-Canada building. Chipman was on his way to meet a new candidate for a freelance position who was approaching the cafeteria from the other end of the corridor. The prospective candidate got excited when he saw Schuman and called out, "Yury." Schuman was obviously upset, "rushed into a corner and later came back in a tizzy." He had a long chat with Chipman.

The next day, Chipman met with an RCMP officer whom Schuman had called. His cover had been blown. The RCMP officer confirmed Schuman's story. "His name was false, his whole history, except for his Indian experience, was a fabrication. His father was not a Jew, or an old Bolshevik, or a German." Schuman had not left for Canada from Germany; in fact, "he had been a Soviet officer."

The freelance candidate and Schuman knew each other from the special language school at Moscow University where the KGB trained its foreign agents. The RCMP was concerned about Schuman's security.

Chipman was bitter that he and the CBC had been duped with the active consent of the RCMP. There was no Schuman; he was another man. Accompanying his application to the CBC was an authorized translation of Thomas C. Schuman's Moscow University transcript, signed by the rector. It was the RCMP that gaveSchuman a false name, and a false history. Chipman believed that it was Canada's own security people "who must have fabricated the document" which Schuman presented for employment in a Crown Corporation. Neither Chipman nor Brown -- both had top security clearance -- had been advised of Schuman's true identity.

Chipman's view was that Schuman was a deliberate plant for he learned from Schuman himself "that his normal reporting to his protectors included information about the journalistic contact other section members had with all sorts of Soviet delegations, cultural, industrial, scientific, maritime.'' This meant that Schuman had a double duty: ''to serve RCI journalistically, and to serve the Canadian security services for a political purpose. Even the most honest man -- and our man isn't -- would suffer from the conflict ... he could never be a straight journalist.

Chipman's assessment of Schuman was that he ''was an enormously able, highly intelligent man, a shallow and empty human being, entirely self-centred, acutely perceptive, engaging when he wants to be, quite devoid of conscience, ruthlessly malicious.''[6] It is not implausible, Chipman thought, that Schuman was also working for the KGB, after all, there had been some notorious KGB plants in Radio Liberty in the 1970s.

RCI was determined to get rid of Schuman and enticed him to resign with an offer of freelance work which would take him all over Canada. Schuman was uncooperative, drank at the Press Club in Montreal's Mount Royal Hotel where he described RCI as soft on communism. He gave an interview with reporters in which he talked about his past: it made front page headlines in a number of Canadian newspapers.

The Cossitt Affair

The CBC and Ottawa were still feeling the after-shocks of the Schuman Affair when the devastating Cossitt Affair erupted. Tom Cossitt, the Progressive Conservative Member of Parliament for Leeds, accused External Affairs of censoring RCI programs to pacify Moscow. RCI, which for so many months had to defend itself from the Soviet attacks from the left, was now faced with an ideological barrage from the right. It was a no-win dilemma for RCI Director Brown who was becoming increasingly isolated; his employees were leaking documents.

Brown had been quick to defend the Russian and Ukrainian services publicly but privately he was unhappy with many of the foreign language sections, especially the Eastern European. An anonymous outside evaluator had been highly critical of a Russian program. The evaluation ordered by Ted England, Brown's Administrative Officer -- made some preposterous assertions that were later described as anti-christian, anti-semitic, anti-Canadian and anti-democratic. RCI staff saw the review as a hatchet job in support of the Brown-England agenda of restructuring RCI.

Three weeks after the *TRUD* article in March 1976, Brown issued a highly controversial memorandum on program reforms. It provided for centralization and bureaucratization to eliminate what Brown called "programming abuses."[7] Brown's memorandum was reminiscent of the kind of orders handed down by Jean Desy 25 years earlier, except that the ideological pendulum had swung in the other direction. Brown banned in-house writing, no commentary writing by RCI staff; no more so-called "news backgrounders." The news, which had always been the crown jewel of RCI programs, could no longer be adapted by any sections nor could news stories be shortened, expanded or clarified, they had to be translated exactly as they came from the English and French newsrooms. A lineup sheet -- issued by the newsroom -- listed the sequence of stories; there could be no deviation. There were other controls to ensure conformity in the programming cross languages. Differences in listener interests in different parts of the world were disregarded.

There was outrage among RCI staff. The Assistant Program Director, Axel Thorgeson, wrote a memo on June 1, 1976, in which he raised questions about why RCI should not take note of religious holidays as suggested by the evaluator; Thorgeson also wondered why it was permissable to discuss Canadian anti-Vietnam protests in broadcasts to the United States but there could not be stories about anti-Soviet protests in the Russian and Ukrainian broadcasts. In effect, Thorgeson touched a sensitive nerve. There was talk in the corridors at RCI and at External Affairs of anti-americanism overtones in RCI broadcasts.

Carroll Chipman, who had played a major role in Canadianizing the Eastern European programming, was opposed to the Brown policies. As Chipman put it after both he and Brown had retired from RCI:[8]

> There was a complete division of views between myself and Alan Brown.... He felt that you could run a journalistic enterprise but still pull your punches and I felt you couldn't. You couldn't broadcast to the Soviet Union and keep always diplomatic thought in mind ... we mustn't be too harsh ... we mustn't be too mean ... because it might hurt their feelings, it might destroy detente.

Cossitt's allegations created consternation at the CBC and External Affairs. RCI newscasts provided coverage of the drawn out controversy about itself. On August 26, 1976 the head story in the RCI news began as follows:

> The Canadian Department of External Affairs has rejected allegations that it imposed censorship on overseas radio broadcasts beamed from Canada.

The same newscast quoted CBC President Al Johnson as denying that RCI was censoring its own programs; he called the Cossitt allegations a lie. Mr. Cossitt, for his part, told Parliament that the CBC President was either lying or ignorant and should retract his denial or be fired.

In the fall of 1976, CBC President Johnson received a highly critical 90-page *Report* on RCI.[9] Authored by Ted England, the *Report* projected an often distorted picture. Brown's marginalcomments on his own copy showed that he agreed with some of England's most problematic remarks. (England was under the false impression that the CBC President also had commissioned the *Report*, would prepare a summary for Cabinet.)

The England *Report* and Brown's marginal notes indicated they were paranoid about the Eastern European sections, especially the Russian and Ukrainian. Their concern was that the staff could not be trusted; England considered the programs largely propaganda, reflecting strongly anti-communist views of the foreign-born broadcasters.

It is noteworthy that some of these same "anti-communists" were regarded as untrustworthy and probably "pro-communist" by Desy when he was cleaning out RCI for External Affairs 25 years earlier. The pendulum was swinging wildly and threatened to ruin the reputations of loyal CBC staff. England thought they were too old, he described their background as pre-revolutionary Russia, because of their foreign birth there cold be no thorough security checks; they spoke old Russian; they did not know much about Canada; they were quarrelsome and engaged in verbal abuse and even fist fights. Their major sin seemed to be their "foreignness," although most had been in Canada for 30 years. England was especially critical of Canadian broadcasts to the Ukraine; an activity he likened to France broadcasting to separatists in Quebec.

The way England saw it, the Latin American sections -- Spanish and Portuguese -- were nearly as bad as the Eastern sections. He did not find the language of spain suitable for Latin America, besides no one Spanish accent was suitable for all of Spanish speaking Latin America; nor was he happy with the Portuguese dialect in the programs to Brazil.

The England Report recommended the abolition of broadcasts in Russian, Ukrainian, Czech, Slovak, Polish, Hungarian.

In 1978, the government cut the CBC budget by $71 Million and President Al Johnson, in turn, cut the RCI budget by $1.5 Million. Alan Brown's reaction was somewhat muted; he thought that RCI could be "more efficient with a selective reduction in staff.'' Some of the builders of RCI took early retirement.

These were the last days of Brown's unhappy tenure at RCI. When the CBC offered him early retirement, Brown returned to a successful career in translating literary works from French to English. Brown was replaced by Betty Zimmerman.

CHAPTER XVII

THE ZIMMERMAN VOICE

Betty Zimmerman arrived at Radio Canada International in July 1979 with a glittering reputation in international communications. She had replaced the ailing Marshall McLuhan on UNESCO's 16-member International Commission for the Study of Communications Problems -- known more familiarly as the MacBride Commission. (The Commission's report, *Many Voices, One World*, was published in 1981.) The CBC Vice Presidents who had passed her over in favour of Alan Brown five years earlier, could hardly contain their enthusiasm. Her credentials included strong production experience in broadcasting, film and theatre as well as proven executive skills as the CBC's Director of International Relations.

In Zimmerman's view, RCI needed fixing at the top. She set out to restore the image of RCI tarnished by Soviet entrapment, CBC budget cuts, the RCMP caper of placing a former KGB agent in the Russian service, and the Cossitt Affair.

Zimmerman's self-confidence and sparkling personality helped to change the atmosphere of gloom and doom created by the 30 percent budget cut and layoffs in 1978. She had chaired the CBC Task Force on RCI in 1973 and, more than anyone else, knew its strengths and weaknesses.[1] Zimmerman did not interfere in programming; on the contrary, she respected the creativeintegrity of the editors, writers, producers and announcers in all language sections. Her second-in-command, Allan Familiant, had been at RCI for many years and had worked his way up a slippery pole; his own background as an editor and producer at RCI and before that at the United Nations made him a knowledgeable and hard-nosed director of programming. Zimmerman and Familiant were never good friends but each respected the other's special skills; they were an effective team.

RCI had developed strong survival skills and had remained a dynamic and innovative broadcaster even under the trying conditions of the previous five years. The broadcasts from Montreal were striking a responsive chord; it was estimated that between 12 million to 16 million listeners heard RCI at least once a week.[2] Equally important, RCI had the respect of other international broadcasters who were interested in cooperative ventures, including joint transmitter projects, program exchanges and barter arrangements for transmitter time. Zimmerman and Familiant were especially good at deal-making.

Zimmerman's vision of the broadcast world was bigger than RCI's traditional emphasis on Europe and the Americas; she sought to develop the Asian potential and give expression to Canada's Pacific personality. Familiant, who was born in Shanghai and speaks Chinese, supported the Asian thrust.[3]

One of Zimmerman's strengths was her knowledge of the CBC head office in Ottawa; she held the highest executive position a woman could achieve in the 1970s. She had access to the President and his Vice Presidents; she knew that most of the CBC top hierarchy was at best indifferent to RCI and she set out to change this situation. Although Zimmerman maintained an apartment in Montreal where she spent about three days a week, her principal home remained in Ottawa. CBC President Al Johnson, who had little use for RCI, and his successor Pierre Juneau, saw more of Zimmerman than they wanted. Zimmerman, for her part insisted that she be heard and was not hesitant to raise her voice; gossip had it that Johnson put cotton in his ears when Zimmerman came calling.

Zimmerman was unhappy with the undefined relationship between the CBC and External Affairs in the operation of RCI. From the beginning, there had been a requirement for consultation, but the changing meaning of "consultation" over the years had created problems for the government, the CBC and RCI. Zimmerman was astounded when she learned that CBC presidents had never discussed with External Affairs the meaning of consultation.

At the insistence of Zimmerman, CBC President Johnson met with Under-Secretary of State, Allan Gotlieb, resulting in an exchange of letters on the scope of the consultation process.[4] This cleared the way for the CBC Board of Directors to approve the RCI mandate that continues to this day. It declared that External Affairs policies form the basis for decisions on RCI target and language priorities, "but programming and editorial policies are wholly the responsibility of the CBC." Zimmerman had achieved her first goal; she ensured that External Affairs could not interfere in news and information operations, if it were so inclined.

The 1981 Federal Cultural Policy Review (Applebaum-Hébert) supported this arrangement when it declared:[5]

> It is imperative that the editorial independence of Radio Canada International be maintained in any new financial arrangements that may arise from changes in the operation of the Canadian Broadcasting Corporation.

But five years later, The Task Force on Broadcasting Policy (Caplan-Sauvageau) recommended that External Affairs should assume the cost of operating RCI. The well-intended recommendation was not enthusiastically received. The stated reason was that listeners may be suspicious about the editorial autonomy of a government financed operation. There was also a second reason, RCI has had bad experiences -- cuts in funding and attempts to close it down -- when it was financed directly by the government.

External Affairs was comfortable in its more clearly-defined role which limited it to advising on the choice of languages and target areas for broadcasts. In December 1980, External declared that RCI's resources reflected Canada's external interests but it wanted some fine tuning: the Caribbean, Latin America and the Middle East should move up the priority ladder, right after Eastern Europe; broadcasting to Asia could be delayed.

Four years later, External Affairs changed its mind: While Eastern Europe remained the top priority, broadcasting to the Pacific rim and to the Middle East were now of higher priority than other regions. The new priorities were reconfirmed in 1986when External Affairs again stressed the importance of broadcasting to Japan, China, India and Soviet Asia.

RCI had External Affairs' support for Asian broadcasting but it did not have the money. In the late 1970s, the Voice of America had offered to lease cheaply to RCI three powerful transmitters on the California coast but the budget cuts at the time aborted the project. Unsuccessful RCI experiments in broadcasting to Asia from Vancouver suggested that other avenues would have to be considered. The best solution was to relay the programs by satellite to shortwave transmitters closer to the target areas which were now Japan, China, India and Soviet Asia. Radio Netherlands faced similar problems and approached RCI about building jointly a powerful transmitter in the Philippines which would provide strong signals into most Asian regions. The cost was prohibitive for RCI; the project required a $40 million investment, half immediately and the other half over the next five years.

Zimmerman set out to broadcast to Asia on the cheap. In 1984, RCI introduced a weekly Japanese language program sent by satellite to a private station in Japan for rebroadcast over shortwave to audiences throughout the country. RCI had to pay for this broadcast as well as for an English language weekly program transmitted over medium wave in Hong Kong. These ventures attracted large audiences and served as pilot projects for a full-fledged Asian service.[6]

Zimmerman initiated negotiations with Japan's public broadcaster, NHK, for a barter arrangement which would give RCI access to the powerful shortwave complex at Yamata in exchange for Japanese use of the Sackville transmitters for transmissions to the United States and Latin America. Japan, however, needed to amend its broadcasting laws in the Diet before this could be realized; Zimmerman waited patiently, reminding the Japanese from time to time to get on with the job. When the Diet passed the necessary legislation, RCI was ready.

On April 4, 1988, Canada launched an extensive shortwave service -- 25 hours of programming a week -- to Asia and the Pacific rim in English, French, Japanese, Russian and Ukrainian using the Yamata transmitters. In short order, RCI entered into similar barter agreements with Radio Bejing and Radio South Korea. A whole new world opened up for RCI; it became an important actor in Asian broadcasting with strong signals into huge population centres in China, India, Pakistan, Indonesia, Philippines and Soviet Asia. The broadcasts in Russian and Ukrainian to Soviet Asia were transmitted at the same time that the European regions of the USSR were receiving RCI programs. Canada had powerful new entry points into the Soviet Union. The Ukrainian language service to Soviet Asia was a wasted effort because there are few Ukrainians in the region and was largely 'lip service' to be politically correct for Canada's Ukrainian population.

The barter process -- economical sharing of transmitter resources -- developed a momentum of its own. RCI entered agreements with Radio Austria and Deutsche Welle for shortwave broadcasts to Arab lands and with Radio Monte Carlo for prime time use of its standard wave transmitter in Cyprus that provides one of the strongest signals into the countries adjoining the Eastern Mediterranean. There had been other initiatives over the years that amplified the Canadian voice; Radio Antilles in Montserrat rebroadcast RCI programs in the Caribbean; BBC transmitters in Berlin carried RCI programs on AM and FM, and a private station in Hong Kong rebroadcast a weekly program.

Zimmerman was a great negotiator whether she was dealing with foreign broadcasters or the CBC. Part of her style was keeping meticulous records and preparing supporting documents. Her own background may have contributed to this. She is the Christian Science daughter of a Jewish father and Icelandic mother, both of whom had decided to bring up their child in Manitoba in what they regarded as a neutral religion. At Christmas time, she visited her mother's relatives; Pesach was spent with the father's family. She had an open mind, always insistent on putting forward her own case as best she could. If there was to be compromise, it would come after she had her say. In effect, Zimmerman had a firm grip on RCI's rudder; there was a sense of direction in her policies.

On a yearly basis, she brought forward a review of RCI in light of the changing broadcast and technological environment; itwas a ten-year plan, annually revised. The document was always "cabinet ready," if RCI were called on to justify its existence at the highest level, it had its case ready in the top drawer.

Zimmerman was sufficiently convincing to receive funding for transmitter renewal; the three 50 Kw transmitters of 1940s vintage were replaced by modern 100 Kw transmitters. The CBC also provided $3 million dollars for an antenna designed specifically for an additional new band (13 MHz) made available through international agreement to deal with heavy congestion in shortwave broadcasting.

Zimmerman was the first RCI director who paid attention to history; Alan Brown, her predecessor, ran into difficulties largely because he did not appreciate the evolvement of the organization. Brown sought change in the context of modernization and did not consider past experience. Delafield, for his part, was walking history; he had been at RCI for 22 years; he had seen everything and found himself accommodating everything. Delafield was not an agent of change, rather he responded reluctantly when change was imposed from outside.

The Voice of Canada changed dramatically in the 10 years that Zimmerman was at the helm. She retired in 1989.

Andrew Simon became the eighth Executive Director of RCI in January 1989. One of his principal objectives was to continue Zimmerman's efforts to enhance RCI's position within the CBC parent organization. The CBC's prime interests are four basic operations: the French and English services in radio andtelevision. As Simon saw it: "RCI -- the fifth medium -- gets overlooked."[7]

The CBC's Priorities and Allocations Committee (PAC), headed at the time by Tony Manera, was not sensitive to the needs of RCI, and PAC was allocating funds according to need. It was not easy for RCI to make itself heard in the corridors of the CBC power. Also, very few Canadians knew about the external broadcaster. The Voice of Canada was operating in a virtual vacuum at home.

The Hungarian born Simon, was a graduate of Montreal's Concordia University and post-graduate work at the Boston University School of Public Communications. He had a caring attitude toward RCI, going back to his student days when he served as a guide at the CBC and always brought his groups to see the RCI operation. He had been with the CBC for 27 years and had good credentials in radio programming. His achievements include the launching of *Cross Country Checkup*, one of the CBC's most popular and durable radio programs. He liked to point out that he had much experience in fixing broadcast problems from his previous positions in Montreal, Toronto and Calgary. He was a broadcast repair man.

There was little, however, at RCI that required fixing. This did not discourage Simon from initiating changes which created more problems than they solved. In particular, he stepped into quick-sand when he sought to integrate the French and English news operations. This issue quickly became caught up in the farlarger question of language rights and the interest of the French Fact in Canadian external broadcasting.

For many years, French had been a language of translation for RCI news; English was the *lingua Franca* that held the different language sections together. This was true in René Lévesque's time at RCI and continued for perhaps 20 years. The achievement of equal language status during Quebec's quiet revolution also brought a strong sense of Quebec nationalism in the French newsroom.

This sensitive topic was raised by Ted England in his report to CBC President Johnson in 1976:[8]

> The French section, which originally was created to broadcast to occupied France, has always had a problem reflecting the Quebec nationalism in the Canadian framework for foreign audiences.

The report states further that during the FLQ crisis in October 1970, "The French section was encouraged to play down the crisis and only minimal coverage was given in the news." There is, however, no evidence of censorship at RCI during the FLQ crisis, although there was enhanced accountability in that the then Director of Information, Lucien Coté, spent long hours, late into the evening, keeping tabs on what RCI was broadcasting. This was probably true for all news operation in Canada, especially after the War Measures Act was invoked.

Simon's effort to integrate the French and English news operations was designed to bring out target area specialization with the news specifically tailored to the interests of theaudience, an approach that had prevailed 30 years earlier. Whatever Simon's good intentions, the reorganization produced his first major crisis; French language newspapers saw it as an invasion of linguistic autonomy. Laval University Professor Florain Sauvageau, a noted Canadian communications authority, who co-chaired the Caplan-Sauvageaun Report, was brought in to study the news operation and eventually the planned reorganization was abandoned. The controversy embarrassed the CBC.

A second crisis for Simon developed out of an External Affairs recommendation that German broadcasts be discontinued and the resources used for the long planned Arabic service. This resulted in protests from some sectors of

Canada's German community and was seen by RCI's German language staff as an unacceptable treatment of a language section that had helped to pioneer shortwave broadcasting and was held up as an example of one of the best sections of RCI which had won numerous awards for excellence. Canadian newspapers criticized External Affairs Minister Joe Clark for the decision to discard German, and Simon kept the controversy alive by seeking alternate funding through a private foundation, and possibly advertising. This never materialized. The collapse of the Berlin Wall and the eventual reunification of Germany were factors in External Affairs' decision to postpone the closing of the German section. The controversy created some embarrassment for External Affairs Minister Clark.

Simon became problem prone within RCI itself in that he became overly involved in details, big ones and little ones. His intentions were good. His perceptions of problems relating to programming and meeting audience expectations were designed to make RCI "less institutional and more relevant"; he wanted to apply some of the advances of domestic radio in Canada. He did not get very far.

CHAPTER XVIII

THE FINAL CHAPTER

Between 1990 and 1995, Radio Canada International was struck by lightening four times. This pattern of disaster is almost predictable. As Keith Spicer, the Chairman of the Canadian Radio-television and Telecommunications Commission (CRTC), pointed out in 1994, "The history of Radio Canada International has been a series of intermittent terrors with reprieves at the last minute for a few years and then it starts all over again with a new breed of politicians who again do not know about it."[1] Spicer, a strong supporter of RCI, was only half correct; the threat to RCI comes partly from the government and in an equal amount from the CBC itself. For nearly three decades in its 50-year history, RCI has been the stepchild of both the CBC and External Affairs.

On November 23, 1990, CBC Vice-President Michael McEwen was in Montreal on corporation business. He phoned RCI Executive Director Andrew Simon to ask for a lift to Dorval Airport. It was a strange request; McEwen could have easily taken a taxi but he wanted to talk. Simon picked up McEwen in front of the Sheraton Hotel on René Lévesque Boulevard and after exchanging pleasantries, heard a devastating message.[2]

> For your information, a final decision has yet to be made, but it is very much within the realm of possibility that RCI will be discontinued.

McEwen thought that the external broadcasting service, which was under his jurisdiction, would be closed down within a few weeks.

An outraged and disbelieving Simon grabbed the steering wheel to make sure he did not run off the road. He asked McEwen to repeat what he had said. McEwen again said that "a final decision had not been made, but it is quite possible." Just how bad the situation was can be deducted from McEwen's next remark; he asked Simon if he knew anyone who might be interested in buying used transmitter equipment from Sackville. Simon did not know anyone.

The possible closing down of RCI, McEwen explained, was part of massive CBC budget cuts in the offing, including layoffs. McEwen wanted to know the implications of the sudden death, especially what would happen to the radio frequencies used by RCI. Also, there was the matter of a transmitter exchange agreement with shortwave broadcasters in Britain, Japan, China, South Korea, Germany and Austria. From all appearances, the game was over; there were about 10 days left to save RCI. Simon was instructed to keep quiet.

Even as McEwen and Simon were talking, word began to leak in Ottawa that RCI would be shut down. A local TV station in the capital carried a story and the *Ottawa Citizen* featured a front page headline story, which the paper confirmed in a telephone call to Simon at RCI headquarters in Montreal. The Liberal Member of Parliament, Sheila Finestone, then the Opposition critic for communications, was ready with questions on the floor of the House of Commons. External Affairs Minister, Joe Clark, in adifficult situation on which he had not been briefed, placed a call to the departmental officer in charge, De Montigny Marchand, who was on a visit to Rome. According to reports, Marchand was livid that CBC President Gerard Veilleux was taking this move without full consultations. The CBC President explained that he had held several meetings with External Affairs officials about his intentions but indications were that key figures at the Department were not informed. Simon says that not only was External Affairs not consulted, "it was not even aware of the decision to close or even the possibility of closing. They were not aware of that decision at the highest level of the ministry."

Almost immediately after the word leaked out, the many friends of RCI around the world, including the BBC, became part of an international lobby for RCI. Alva Clark of St. Lucia, Secretary General of the Commonwealth Broadcasting Association, rallied to the RCI cause. The international broadcasting personalities found it hard to believe that Canada was planning to shut down its highly regarded shortwave station after 47 years on the air. Hundreds of faxes poured into the offices of Prime Minister Mulroney, External Affairs Minister Clark, Communications Minister Marcel Masse and CBC President Veilleux. Canadian newspapers were also coming out in strong support; on Friday, November 30, the *Montreal Gazette*'s lead editorial was headlined: "Don't Silence Canada's Voice." The paper argued that RCI is part of the core of the CBC's mission. To kill it would be a grievous error.

There were second thoughts in Ottawa, especially after a confrontational session between DeMontigny Marchand of External Affairs and CBC President Veilleux. On December 4th, McEwen, in a telephone conversation with Simon hinted that RCI might escape immediate death. This was confirmed the next day when Veilleux announced that the CBC could no longer pay for RCI after March 31, 1991, but he added that because of the international importance of the service, the government had indicated it would "consider alternate ways of financing." In effect, the CBC was no longer financially responsible for RCI; if the government wanted shortwave broadcasting service it would have to pay for it, otherwise the service would be dead.

Veilleux's statement on RCI's future was part of his grim announcement that the CBC was reducing its spending by $108 million and laying off eleven hundred, about 10 percent of the total CBC staff. The corporation was in big trouble because of a drop in television advertising revenues caused by the recession and the cumulative impact of several years of reductions in Parliamentary grants to the CBC. The CBC President was in an impossible situation: he was closing down important local television operations, including Windsor and Calgary; he could hardly ask the CBC Board of Directors who represent provincial interests to approve closing broadcast operations in their home provinces, but keep open the international operation about which they knew very little, if anything at all. RCI was the best kept secret in the CBC.

Veilleux knew little about RCI; he does not recall having ever listened to the Voice of Canada in his travels abroad. When the CBC named him President, he received the same briefings from the same people who had advised his predecessors at the helm of the broadcasting corporation. Not since the days of Davidson Dunton, who was one of the godfathers of the shortwave broadcasting service, has RCI had a truly interested protector in the power structure at the CBC.

One former president of the CBC never knew RCI existed. Al Johnson is remembered at RCI for having referred to Canada's international broadcaster as an 'ancillary service' and treated it as such. Pierre Juneau, Veilleux's predecessor, reportedly always had RCI first on his list when budget cuts were considered. Veilleux followed in this pattern, but instead of threatening, actually did it. His decision was based on the premise that the CBC must fulfill its primary mandate -- the French and English services in radio and television -- and anything else was beyond its means and had to fall by the wayside.

Before he left the CBC, Veilleux praised RCI for its dynamism; he admitted that he had not fully appreciated the marvellous things it was doing.[3] He was even more impressed at how well it coped with so little money. Nevertheless, he felt he had made the right decision; there had been little choice, the realities of the politics of Canadian broadcasting made it impossible for the CBC to fund an external broadcasting service while it wasreducing services at home and television stations were being closed all across the country. The CBC's Board of Directors had authorized Veilleux to terminate the operation of RCI by April 1, 1991, except in the event that the government assigned funds for the continuation of the service. The CBC took a similar position on the parliamentary channel which is now funded by Canada's cable industry.

Veilleux's December 5th announcement, which at least provided for 16 weeks of additional life for RCI, was greeted with a sigh of relief at RCI headquarters in Montreal, but there was at the same time a realistic concern about the future. As Simon put it on the day when the shortwave service was spared:

> It's sort of heartening ... but on the negative side, we're a little bit anxious ... we'll be happier when they announce the exact methods of financing.

Events later proved Simon had good reason to be anxious. For the time being, however, RCI was saved again, at the last moment.

In the coming weeks, there were negotiations between External Affairs, represented largely by Peter Daniel, the Assistant Deputy Minister for Communications and Information, and the CBC represented by McEwen and Terry Hargreaves, senior advisor to Veilleux. They all knew each other well. Daniels was a CBC correspondent before he joined External Affairs. Simon and Familiant were not involved directly in the talks on RCI's fate although Vice-President McEwen consulted with them.

It was clear from the outset that External Affairs had no intention of paying $22 million a year to maintain RCI; in fact, it did not want the money to come from its own budget which was also under pressure. The government was looking towards a number of Departments, especially those that have an interest in international publicity, to volunteer funds for RCI, but none was forthcoming. There was, however, $7 million that had become available from the cancellation of the Opera House project in Toronto.

External Affairs sent two officers (with special interest in money matters) to Montreal to establish the cost for what was dubbed "the Lights On" scenario. This meant that the government's primary interest was to protect the shortwave radio frequencies used by Canada for its international broadcasts. RCI was on the air 232 hours per week and the Canadian occupied frequencies could be protected with a neutral sound, a hum, a slewing signal or by plugging into the regular CBC network shows. The problem is, of course, that listeners to international broadcasting could be terribly offended if Canada were just making noise on the air and interfering with listening to broadcasts from other countries.

Negotiating the Future

Simon and Familiant prepared eight different scenarios for RCI's future. They ranged from total closure which required one time dismantling changes; a "lights on" scenario where RCI would serve as a rebroadcaster of domestic French and English CBC programs at a cost of $8 million; to continuing the service as before for $22 million. Other options included a seven language service including French and English for about $14 million. Only four of the eight options were presented by CBC to the External Affairs negotiators, who recommended one option to a cabinet committee. RCI officials were bitter that they were not allowed to take part in the negotiating process; the CBC felt that they were 'too personally' involved.

The negotiating process was not going anywhere. The Department of External Affairs declined to finance RCI; it was facing its own budget cuts which already required some retrenchment in its diplomatic activities. The game plan was that several departments of government, especially those that had direct interest in promoting Canada abroad, would contribute voluntarily. This approach did not work; there were laudatory statements about the good work RCI was doing but it was cheap talk; there was no money forthcoming.

The media, for its part, had kept the RCI story before the public by publishing from time to time sympathetic stories, editorials and letters to the editor. These projected an image of RCI as a 'gem', an essential force of Canadian broadcasting, the ambassador on the airwaves; Canada's voice of reason in the powerful international radio sphere, a voice that speaks wisely and truthfully, a voice that furthered foreign policy interestsand stimulated exports. Those words of support in the French and English press did not appear to be reaching the negotiators for RCI's future.

Accident prone RCI, however, had a lucky break. Prime Minister Mulroney was visiting his Quebec home town of Baie Comeau when a reporter, who had worked for RCI at one time, asked him about RCI. The Prime Minister said emphatically that he would not let the shortwave service die. This off-the-cuff pledge -- "I guarantee that RCI will survive" -- created a moment of panic in the Prime Minister's Office, his officials sought a solution to support Mulroney's unexpected commitment. Within a week, a deal was in place. It kept RCI alive ... but barely.

The Gutted Service

The decision by the government was to finance a service that could provide broadcasting in five foreign languages -- Russian, Ukrainian, Arabic, Chinese and Spanish -- plus rebroadcasting of French and English programs from the CBC domestic networks. The French and English programs would be of interest mainly to Canadians travelling abroad. Canada had, thus, virtually abandoned all broadcasting to foreign audiences in its own official languages except for a few newscasts. The cost for this gutted RCI was service was $12.5 million; it would have cost an additional million dollars to maintain French and English services.

The government decision was announced to the staff on March 22 and was followed up by a press release from then External Affairs Minister Joe Clark. CBC, recalling the criticisms that followed the December 1990 cuts when TV stations across Canada went off the air without saying goodbye, allowed RCI one broadcast day to inform its listeners. In all the language services that would be abandoned, the announcers made their formal statements of closing. They apologized to millions of listeners around the world for funding cuts which they said were forced by the Mulroney government. The Prime Minister was upset by the rebellious action -- his spokesperson expressed astonishment at RCI's decision to trumpet such embarrassing news. In fact, the Prime Minister's press secretary observed that the final decision had not been taken on the RCI package; it sounded like a threat that RCI may yet go under. *The Windsor Star* proclaimed in a front page headline, "CBC EMBARRASSES MULRONEY AROUND THE WORLD."

The effects of the cuts were devastating. Broadcasts to foreign audiences were dropped in nine of the 14 languages: French, English, German, Japanese, Polish, Hungarian, Czech, Slovak and Portuguese (Brazil). The decision to close the Japanese service came at a bad time; the Prime Minister was preparing for an official visit to Japan that included the inauguration of a new Canadian embassy building in Tokyo. Japanese shortwave listeners had mounted a letter-writing campaign urging Canada to maintain RCI's service which was the fourth most popular foreign shortwave service in Japan. Atsuchi Konno, editor-in-chief of the Japan BLC Federation, (Japan's largest association of broadcast listeners) pointed out that the demise of RCI's programs in Japanese "will cut off our only source of information on Canada."

In addition to closing nine language operations, the cuts brought to an end other RCI services including Recorded Programs, Current Affairs, the Reference Library, and the Documentation Centre.

Of the 193 positions in RCI, only 100 remained. At Montreal headquarters, more than half the staff were laid off. The Russian section was reduced from eleven to four persons, and the Ukrainian staff which previously had five, now had four. Nearly all middle management positions were wiped out: manager of communications, manager of program operations; manager of financial administration; supervisor of current affairs; and manager of worldwide programming. The reference library staff was reduced from seven to one. Untouched by the cuts was the entire 38 member engineering division, which included the two engineers in Montreal, the 24 staff at the Sackville transmitting station, and the seven persons at the shortwave monitoring station in Ottawa.

The Executive Director, Andrew Simon, was placed on early retirement. He had made noises when he was told that RCI would be closed down, and in the process, had annoyed CBC President Veilleux, Vice-President McEwen, External Affairs Minister Clark and Prime Minister Mulroney. There was much admiration at RCI for his fighting spirit that had politicized what was to have been a quiet end to RCI. Program Director Familiant was made the Acting Executive Director -- a position he occupied for some months.

In April, 1991, External Affairs drew up a Memorandum of Understanding. It stipulated that RCI would be on the air for 232 hours a week (the same amount as before the cuts) and all of the shortwave frequencies used by Canada would be utilized and maintained. There would be a mere 28 hours a week of foreign language programming in Russian, Ukrainian, Chinese, Arabic and Spanish (for Latin America). The remaining 204 hours would be used equally for French and English rebroadcasts from the CBC networks. These broadcasts in Canada's official languages can best be described as, *As It Happens* programming because *As It happens* in English, and *Le Magazine Économique* in French are repeated several times a day to various world regions. Both are programs designed for domestic audiences; they are "not an effective way to attract an international audience." As the Senate Committee on Communications pointed out:[4]

> These programs are ... predominantly about current events that very much deal with the so-called realities and qualities of Canadian life, but do not adequately deal with Canadian culture.

Foreign audiences neither understand nor are they interested in most of the CBC domestic programming. Asking listeners around the world to eavesdrop on Canadian programming is presumptuous.

Acting Director Familiant moved almost immediately to rebuild RCI. His priority project was to reintroduce at least an element of French and English broadcasting; it was embarrassing that the Voice of Canada neglected Canada's official languages while most other international broadcasters are heavy in French and English programming. There was no problem with newscasts since the newsroom was supplying English and French news for translation by the five foreign language sections. One English and one French program were put together almost on a voluntary basis by staff for broadcasting to all target areas. While this generic program called *Spectrum Actualités* was not targeted for any specific audience, at least it was a start for reintroducing the official languages.

The CBC, for its part, was viewing RCI in a more favourable light now that the government was paying for it. President Veilleux appointed a veteran broadcaster, Terry Hargreaves, who had previously headed the Parliamentary Channel, as Executive Director of RCI. Hargreaves was a senior advisor to the CBC President and had represented him in the negotiations with External Affairs about the future of RCI; he was very much aware of the problems of the international broadcaster in relation to both the CBC and the government. Furthermore, Hargreaves knew Ottawa -- the political sector and the CBC.

Hargreaves and Familiant were a strong team -- the best that could be put together. They worked closely and complemented each other's strengths. They embarked on highly successful projects that kept alive the reputation of the Voice of Canada; and they did it without additional funding. Following the precedent set by Zimmerman,RCI set out to negotiate for time on foreign transmitters; except, this time it was on foreign domestic radio.

China provided the first opening for RCI on domestic radio. The program, *Everyday English*, was first introduced in 1990; it comprised English language lessons in a 40-part series, each segment running for 30 minutes on stations in Beijing, Xian, Shanghai and Guangzhou. The books that accompanied the radio lessons were snapped up immediately and despite numerous reprints, it was impossible to keep up with the demand. Because of popular request, the language lessons were repeated several times a week; millions of people in China were learning to speak English with a Canadian accent. For Canada, the payoff was that the language lessons focus on Canada; its geography, culture, politics, business life, scientific achievements that illustrate the vibrance of this country. The language lessons, in a subtle manner, are raising the profile of Canada as a country capable of supplying sophisticated technological products in addition to raw materials.

In 1994, RCI introduced a new series of English language lessons broadcast in about 20 cities across China. The lessons feature Mark Rowswell, who is with the Canadian Embassy and speaks fluent Mandarin. Rowswell is also a Mandarin comedian and has been on Chinese television; he is known throughout China as *Dashan* the comedian. No one in China suspected that learning English could be so much fun.

In addition to the language lessons, stations in four major cities broadcast once a week in Chinese a program devoted exclusively to Canadian artists playing classical music. This helps to raise the Canadian cultural profile in China. RCI programs on business are heard in three cities in Mandarin. A Canadian business program in Cantonese is featured in Guangzhou; it is heard at a choice time throughout the entire Pearl River Delta area.

The Chinese experience has been the catalyst for a Canadian cultural invasion of Russia, the Ukraine, Poland, among other former communist countries. There was much good will towards the Voice of Canada in the post-communist era; it was considered more palatable to carry Canada's voice than the Voice of America or the British Broadcasting Corporation. Consequently, RCI was given air time while the 'big power' broadcasters had to pay if they wanted similar air time on Russian domestic radio. Canada thus had a jump start and a free ride.

RCI succeeded in placing English language lessons on local stations in more than 25 major Russian cities including Moscow, St. Petersburg, Vladivostok and Perm. The stations in the 25 cities also broadcast an RCI-produced series of programs in Russian that explain characteristics of democracy, entrepreneurship and the environment. The series called "My delayem tak" was separately funded by Foreign Affirs. In other parts of the former Soviet Union, RCI's English language lessons and classical music programs are heard on the national networks of Estonia, Lithuania, Latvia, Moldova, Kazakhstan and the Ukraine. Ukraine has a special feeling about Canada because RCI was, for four decades, one of the few broadcasters in the world with a Ukrainian Service. In 1994, RCI moved into Belarus, Georgia, Azerbaijan, Armenia and Kyrghyzstan.

In Latin America, RCI also found local outlets for its English language lessons as well as Spanish programs on 50 stations in more than a dozen countries. This was followed by the establishment of a radio relationship with Africa. In Namibia, RCI produced English lessons are used in eight local languages. These programs, widely promoted in schools and the business community, were broadcast nation-wide.

An especially popular RCI program that is broadcast on all continents features top Canadian pop hits. Once a month a high quality tape is distributed to 300 radio stations that carry the *Pick of the Pops*. Yet another RCI venture distributed for local broadcasting is a weekly mini-documentary on Canadian affairs in English, French, and Spanish. Twenty-nine stations in Russia and in the Societ successor states carry the weekly selection in Russian, "Kanadskaya Panorama".

The RCI ventures in language lessons, musical programs ranging from classical to pop hits, and mini-documentaries are impressive achievements. These operations have cost very little; the air time on the foreign domestic stations was free. But in the republics of the former Soviet Union, other broadcasters were bidding for air time, and the free ride had a limited life span.

It would be self-defeating if projects of this kind became the main objective of the Voice of Canada. These programs are largely public relations for Canada abroad; the contents have to be politically correct and as Veilleux observed just before he gave up the presidency of the CBC: Does RCI want to become an English language teacher?[5]

Language teaching was traditionally used as listeners bait by the BBC in its shortwave service; the hope was that the interest in learning English would bring the audience to the news and public affairs programs. (The Voice of America, in its shortwave service, has programs in slow English, suitable for listeners who need more time to digest the messages.)

RCI programs on foreign domestic stations should be an important supplemental enterprise; it should not be allowed to divert attention from the main challenge of serving as the Voice of Canada. Such a voice has to pay its own way to protect its autonomy. The Voice of Canada must largely speak for itself, using its own transmitters.

RCI is an international broadcaster because of its shortwave service that seeks out targeted populations where it is in the interest of Canada to be heard. This costs money and was a matter examined by the Senate Committee on Transportation and Communications in the spring of 1994. The Senators were enormously impressed with what RCI was accomplishing on very little money. The funding at the time was about $14 million and shrinking. The government was not living up to its commitments. The Senators considered asking the government to tripple RCI's budget. But in the end, the Committee recommended that the funding be restored to what it was in 1990 -- before the devastating cuts. This would mean that RCI would receive over $20million a year and could therefore restore the seven languages dropped in 1991. The committee wanted broadcasting restored to Central Europe and Japan.

The prospects for this scenario are nil. The government continued to chip away at RCI's funds in line with the general policy of small reductions everywhere. For RCI, small reductions are actually big, because half of its funding goes toward transmitter maintenance and other fixed costs. This means that all cuts come from the already inadequate funds that maintain the five foreign language services.

Then, lightening struck for the third time. The Minister of Finance, Paul Martin, in his February 1995 Budget placed RCI under the financial control of the CBC. This came at a time when the CBC's own budget was facing serious cuts immediately and even more devastating cuts over the following three years. If the CBC could not afford RCI in 1991, it could afford it even less in 1995. This again raised the ultimate question asked so often in the fifty-year history of RCI: "will it survive?"

One of RCI's main problems is that it has few friends in Canada; most Canadians do not know it exists. This invisibility is part of the tradition of RCI which, for many years, did its utmost to maintain a low profile. Established under the War Measures Act in World War II, it was seen as a useful weapon in that war. The CBC was holding off meaningfull involvement with its international broadcasting arm until the war was won. The golden years of RCI at peace did not last long; by 1948 cold war politics resulted in the mobilization of RCI for psychological warfare, a practice that increased in intensity for about a decade. The debacle of the *Lobster Festival* which sought to play Russia against China came at a time when the tide was turning. Canada had become disenchanted with cold war politics and alarmed about the consequences. It took five years to shape RCI into a cold war instrument and it took another five years for the demobilization from psychological warfare to take effect.

It was during the cold war that RCI became truly invisible. The CBC was uncomfortable with the psychological warfare warrior. External Affairs which sought to control external broadcasting to promote foreign policy interest, nevertheless wanted to avoid public scrutiny of its activities. Only when questions were raised in Parliament or in the media did External Affairs talk. It usually hung RCI out to dry; when there was public criticism, External Affairs distanced itself from RCI publicly. Among the early deserters of the RCI ship was Lester Pearson; he worked hard to build it but later sought to give it away to the United Nations. RCI, over the years, promoted Pearson's image more than any other public or artistic personality; more than Oscar Peterson, Glen Gould, Maureen Forester and more recently, Leonard Cohen. The radio promotion of Pearson was not a distortion; as External Affairs Minister and later as Prime Minister, Pearson was involved in the bread and butter stories of RCI newscasts and commentaries. During the Suez crisis in 1956, RCI stayed on the air around the clock; the Voice of Canada was at the time the most authoritative radio broadcaster describing the Suez events and the Pearson role in establishing UN peacekeeping for which he was awarded the Nobel Peace Prize.

Pearson personally admired RCI but it was the politics of Canadian broadcasting that turned him away from it; he found the ethnic lobbying for more aggressive cold war broadcasting counter-productive in terms of international peace and equally important, in terms of the politics of his Liberal party. External Affairs always advised RCI to keep a low profile; when Montreal station CJAD asked for sample tapes of RCI broadcasts, the decision was taken not to make them available.

On the numerous occasions when RCI was facing closing, it was Canada's ethnic communities and the listeners abroad who were the best friends. The listeners, who have a choice from the offerings of well over one hundred international broadcasters, have consistently liked what they heard from Canada. This is as true today as it was half a century ago. Even in the worst days of the cold war, RCI was not easily contained; its enthusiastic voice was always a voice of reason. Compared to other broadcasters, RCI performed well; it always avoided the worst features of propaganda and distortion.

RCI is largely a story of missed opportunities. Canada could have been a world leader in international broadcasting if it had had greater confidence in Fessenden, the Canadian inventor of voice radio. There were good reasons for Canada, so closely linked to American broadcasting offerings, to have extended its voice internationally in the 1930s. By the time RCI went on the air on Christmas Day in 1944, it was a late entrant but it had the loudest voice into Europe. The phenomenal success and growth of RCI in the early years was curtailed by government restraints.

The director of RCI plays a shaping role for the organization. Peter Aylen the builder left a smooth working operation. Ira Dilworth fought successfully to prevent funding cuts; he also fought for the free press principle in the early days of the cold war; he was not a compromiser. The diplomat, Jean Désy, had a devastating effect on RCI morale; he was there for only eighteen months and despite his autocratic behaviour, he could not fully implement his rightist views. He shocked External Affairs when he refused to carry a story on Tito when the Yugoslav leader was visiting Britain and had tea with the Queen. Désy told External Affairs: "Once a communist, always a communist." He had no intention of "rehabilitating" Tito. The gentle Charles Delafield stayed far too long and is best remembered for benign leadership; a policy so badly needed after Désy. But Delafield was not a fighter and when External Affairs decided on cuts or even threatened closing the operation, Delafield was not as heavily involved as other RCI staffers who fought the great battles for survival. More recently, Brown, Zimmerman, Simon and Hargreaves have each left their mark at RCI. Zimmerman was especially successful -- with the help of Familiant -- in expanding the RCI presence globally through bartering for transmission time.

The battle to keep the Voice of Canada on the international airwaves continues as new technology is introduced. In the 1990s, in broadcasting to Canadians serving with United Nations, peacekeeping missions in the Middle

East, in Somalia and in the formerYugoslavia, RCI was using direct satellite transmissions to maintain Canada's entertainment and information link with the forces. RCI was testing the future technology for international broadcasting even as it was facing threats to its very existence. If there is one outstanding characteristic about RCI, it is optimism. The voice of Canada has always projected this image to listeners abroad.

ENDNOTES

CHAPTER I

1 It was a short test broadcast. The regular transmissions started on Feb. 25, 1945.
2 Letter from Prime Minister Mackenzie King to President Franklin D. Roosevelt, dated January 9, 1943. At the end of the two page letter, the Prime Minister added by hand: "With warmest personal regards, I am yours sincerely." MG 26 Jl, Volume 349, pages 301496-301497.
3 Minutes of the Cabinet War Committee, January 13, 1943.

CHAPTER II

1 Bumpus, Bernard and Skelt, Barbara, *Seventy Years of International Broadcasting*, Paris: UNESCO, 1984, p.7.
2 Ibid.
3 Ibid. p.13.
4 V.I., Lenin, Collected Works, vol. 33, pp. 360-361, Moscow: Progress. Lenin in cited in Bumpus and Skelt, Seventy Years, op. cit. p.7.
5 BBC. The Radio Supplement, 17 July, 1925, cited in Bumpus and Skelt, *Seventy Years*, op.cit., p.8.
6 Bumpus and Skelt, *Seventy Years*, op.cit. p.9.
7 For a discussion on the Diamond Jubilee broadcast, see E. Austin Weir, *The Struggle for National Broadcasting in Canada*, Toronto: McClelland and Stewart, 1965, pp.35-40.
8 Bumpus and Skelt, *Seventy Years*, op.cit, pp. 9-14.
9 Gerard Mansell, *Let Truth Be Told*, London: Weidenfeld and Nicolson, 1984, p.22.
10 Bumpus and Skelt, *Seventy Years*, op.cit, p.17.
11 See Charles Rolo, *Radio Goes to War*.

CHAPTER III

1 Transcript from recording of program.
2 Ibid.
3 This theme comes up in correspondence and is discussed in newspaper articles and book. See, for example, Gary Evans, *John Grierson and the National Film Board: The Politics of Wartime Propaganda*, Toronto: University of Toronto Press, 1984.
4 Report. *The Inquiry Into National Broadcasting*. CRTC, 1977.

5 Austin Weir, *The Struggle for National Broadcasting in Canada*, Toronto: McClelland and Stewart, 1965. For an excellent historical account, see Frank W. Peers, *The Politics of Canadian Broadcasting*, Toronto: University of Toronto Press, 1969.

6 *Re Regulation and Control of Radio Communication* (1932) A.C.304.

CHAPTER IV

1 For a discussion of Brockington's career at the CBC, see Frank Peers, *The Politics of Canadian Broadcasting*, Toronto: University of Toronto Press, 1969.

2 Ibid, pp. 202-7 and pp. 301-3.

3 CBC Engineering Division. Preliminary Studies on the Location of a Canadian Shortwave Station, 1934.

4 Minutes of fourth meeting of the CBC Board of Governors, March 15, 1937.

5 Report by Donald Manson on building a shortwave facility, July 26, 1937.

6 Minutes of the fifth meeting of the CBC Board of Governors, Quebec City, August 5-7, 1937.

7 Letter from Brockington to King, October 6, 1937.

8 Ibid.

9 Ibid.

10 Memorandum from Bushnell to Gladstone Murray.

11 Ibid.

CHAPTER V

1 *The Financial Post*, October 21, 1939.

2 Ibid.

3 Ibid, December 9.

4 *Regina Star*, December 12 and December 22, 1940.

5 *Winnipeg Tribune*, December 27, 1939.

6 Ibid.

7 *Windsor Tribune*, November 24, 1939.

8 Minutes of the Cabinet War Committee, October 10, 1940.

9 Minutes of the Cabinet War Committee, November 5, 1940.

10 CBC internal memorandum from Frigon to Murray, July 13, 1940.

11 Memorandum from Norman Robertson to Prime Minister King, September 25, 1941.

CHAPTER VI

1 For an examination of the activities of the Bureau of Public Information and the Wartime Information Board, see L.A.D. Stephens, "Study of Canadian Government Information Abroad 1942-1972." Unpublished document. Department of External Affairs, March 1977, especially Chapter I, pp. 1-11.

2 The Wartime Information Board was established by Order-in-Council P.C. 8099, September 8, 1942. The CBC International Service was provided for in Order-in-Council P.C. 8168, 18 September, 1942.

3 Letter from Lester Pearson to Norman Robertson, June 30, 1943. Excerpts from the letter are cited in Stephens, "Study of Government Information Abroad," *op.cit*.

4 *Ibid*. When the war ended, the Wartime Information Board disappeared on September 28, 1945. Dunton returned to his peace-time job as editor of the Montreal *Standard* until his appointment at the age of 33 as the first full time chairman of the CBC.

5 External Affairs memorandum "Psychological Warfare", July 3, 1945.

6 Letter from Saul Rae to Stone, April 20, 1943.

7 Saul Rae provided an account of the Bush House meeting in a detailed letter on April 22, 1943.

8 Ibid.

9 Intelligence Report, December 1943.

CHAPTER VII

1 For a history of the American involvement in the War of words, see Holly Cowan Shulman, *The Voice of America*, Madison: University of Wisconsin Press, 1990.

2 Letter from James Thompson to prime Minister King, December 27, 1942.

3 Ibid.

4 Memorandum from Lester Pearson (Washington) to Norman Robertson, November 3, 1942.

5 Frank Peers, *The Politics of Canadian Broadcasting*, Toronto: University of Toronto Press, 1969, p.332.

6 Memorandum from Norman Robertson to Lester Pearson, December 1942.
7 Teletype from Secretary of State to Lester Pearson, March 4, 1943.
8 Memorandum from Secretary of State to War productions Minister, May 19, 1943.
9 February 16, 1944.
10 Peter Aylen interview (on tape).
11 Ibid.
12 Gerard Arthur interview (on tape).
13 Mavor Moore interview (on tape).
14 Peter Aylen interview.

CHAPTER VIII

1 Peter Aylen interview (on tape).
2 Ibid.
3 Stuart Griffiths, "International Shortwave Broadcasting in Canada", *Canadian Geographical Journal*, November 1946, p.13.
4 Written text of broadcast in English, translated into Czech.
5 International Service files, 1944.
6 Aylen interview.
7 Ibid.
8 Eric Koch interview.
9 Transcript of broadcast.
10 Holly Cowan Shulman, *The Voice of America*, Madison: The University of Wisconsin Press, 1990, pp. 28-30.
11 Interview with Mavor Moore, June 1990.
12 Stuart Griffiths, "International Shortwave Broadcasting in Canada", *op.cit.* p.9.
13 Ibid., p.13.

CHAPTER IX

1 Order-in-Council P.C. 8186, September 18, 1942.
2 L.A.D. Stephens, "Study of Canadian Government Information Abroad 1942-1972." Unpublished document. Department of External Affairs, March 1977, Chapter V, p.4.
3 Minutes of Government - CBC Shortwave Advisory Committee,June 22, 1944.
The CBC was represented at the meeting in the East Block office of

Norman Robertson, the Undersecretary of State for External Affairs, by a powerful team: Dr. Frigon, who was then the Acting General Manager of the CBC, Donald Manson, the Chief Executive Assistant, Bushnell, the General Supervisor of Programmes and Peter Aylen who was the Supervisor-designate for the International Service. Also attending were Davidson Dunton, the General Manager of the War Information Board and Glazebrook of External Affairs.

4 External Affairs Memorandum (secret), January 18, 1945, from G.W. McCracken to E.G. Smith.

5 Ibid.

6 Ibid.

7 Notes on the conversation between Aylen and MacDermot February 17, 1945, at the International Service in Montreal. The notes were drawn up two days later.

8 Peter Aylen interviewed by Gary Marcuse (taped). Transcript p.10.

9 Ibid., p.11.

10 Ibid., p.12.

11 Ibid., p.13.

12 Ibid., p.12.

13 Ibid.

14 External Affairs Memorandum prepared for Soward, July 5, 1946.

15 Memorandum from G.C. Andrew to Lester Pearson, March 28, 1947.

16 Ibid.

CHAPTER X

1 Memorandum from Charles Delafield to Tom Fairley, January 5, 1948.

2 Minutes of the Advisory Committee of the CBC International Service, February 15, 1948.

3 Letter from Macdonnell to Walter Schmolka, Prague, March 5, 1948.

4 Ibid.

5 Memorandum from Saul Rae to Marcel Cadieux, March 22, 1948.

6 Minutes of "Political Warfare" meeting, April 16, 1948. The minutes are dated April 19, 1948.

7 Ibid.

8 Ibid.

9 Ibid.

10 Ibid.

11 Ibid.

12 Ibid.

13 The meeting with Sir Ian Jacob was attended by Michael Barkway (BBC Canadian Representative), Escott Reid, George Glazebrook, Saul Rae, G.A. Southam, B.H. Hicks and Davidson Dunton (CBC).
14 Minutes of meeting with Sir Ian Jacob, June 21, 1948. The minutes were prepared two days later and are dated June 23, 1948.
15 External Affairs memorandum from E. Reid to Watkins, April 29, 1948.
16 External Affairs memorandum from Allan Anderson to Saul Rae, September 18, 1948.
17 External Affairs memorandum from Rogers to Pearson, February 18, 1949.
19 Tom Benson interview, taped (1981).

CHAPTER XI

1 This is a frequently repeated theme.
2 External Affairs memorandum prepared by Assistant Under-Secretary Jules Léger, July 6, 1950.
3 Ibid.
4 L.A.D. Stephens, "Study of Canadian Government Information Abroad", Unpublished study. March 1977, p.8.
5 John McCordick interview on tape (transcript).
6 Ritchie made a report of his Montreal visit in a memorandum dated March 19, 1951.
7 Ibid.
8 English text of inaugural broadcast.
9 Dispatches (Secret) from Secretary of State for External Affairs to the Canadian High Commissioner in London and the Canadian ambassador in Washington, "Ukrainian nationalism and Psychological Warfare", January 22, 1951.
10 Ibid.
11 Ibid.
12 Ibid.
13 Dispatch from Canadian embassy in Washington, March 31, 1951.
14 Dispatch (Secret) from Chargé d'Affaires in Moscow to Secretary of State, "New Broadcasts to the Soviet Union". May 31, 1951.
15 Memorandum (Secret) prepared for Charles Ritchie, "Ukrainian Broadcasts by CBC-IS", October 23, 1951.
16 Dilworth letter to Harris, March 21, 1953.

17 Ibid.

CHAPTER XII

1 Eric Koch commenting on Désy in interview with author.
2 Jean Éthier-Blais in interview with author.
3 Interview with author.
4 Éthier-Blais interview.
5 Ibid.
6 Pearson interview.
7 John Hilliker, *Canada's Department of External Affairs: The Early Years*, 1909-1946, Montreal: McGill-Queen's Press, 1990.
8 Ibid., p.318.
9 External Affairs Memorandum by Charles Ritchie, May 29, 1951.
10 Ibid.
11 Beaulne presented this view to a Parliamentary Committee.
12 Transcript of Beaulne interview in 1956.
13 Ibid.
14 Ibid.
15 Sidney Freifeld in conversation with author.
16 Letter from Désy to Pearson, May 26, 1953.
17 Stephens, "Study of Canadian Government Information Abroad", op.cit., p.12.
18 Charles Ritchie, *Diplomatic Passport*, Toronto: Macmillan of Canada, 1981, p.58.

CHAPTER XIII

1 Dispatch from Chargé d'Affaires in Prague to External Affairs, November 30, 1951.
2 External Affairs memorandum for Under-Secretary, January 15, 1952.
3 A.D.P. Harvey to Chargé d'Affaires in Prague, January 12, 1952.
4 Dispatch (Secret) from Canadian embassy in Washington to External Affairs, January 21, 1952.
6 Transcript of July 1, 1952 broadcast.
7 Dana Wilgress letter to Jean Désy, June 18, 1953.
8 Memorandum from Désy to Panchuck, June 23, 1953.
9 Chipman interview (transcript).
10 External Affairs Memorandum, European Division, August 27, 1957.

11 Chipman interview (transcript).
12 Ibid.
13 Ibid.
14 *Montreal Star*, June 5, 1957.
15 *Ukrainian Voice*, June 19, 1957.
16 External Affairs memorandum on visit to Montreal, January 11, 1956.
17 Letter (Confidential) from Under Secretary of State to Charles Delafield, February 8, 1955.
18 Ibid.
19 Letter (Secret) from Under-Secretary of State (signed R.M. Macdonnell) to Charles Delafield, February 17, 1955.
20 Letter (Confidential) from Under-Secretary of State (signed A.J. Andrew) to Charles Delafield, March 10, 1955. Attached to the letter was the agenda for the March 14, 1955 meeting and two memoranda (Nos. 1 and 2) to CBC-IS providing analyses of Moscow power change.
21 Dispatch (Confidential) from Secretary of State for External Affairs to High Commissioner, London. March 8, 1955. Similar Dispatch to Canadian Delegation to North Atlantic Council, Paris, March 8, 1955.
22 Minutes of a meeting, January 14, 1955, between CBC-IS and External Affairs representatives.
23 Memorandum to Minister for External Affairs, March 9, 1955.
24 Chipman interview (1984), transcript.

CHAPTER XIV

1 External Affairs Memorandum for D.B. Hicks to Weshof re: Conversation with W. Chevalier, December 6, 1955.
2 Ibid.
3 External Affairs Memorandum on liaison with the International Service prepared for Sidney Freifeld, April 25, 1963.
4 External Affairs Memorandum authored by T.C. Hammond, P.G. Dobell and G.P. Kidd, January 23, 1959.
5 Carroll Chipman correspondence with Alexander Derensky, May 1964.
6 Chipman interview recounting RCI history, 1984.
7 External Affairs memorandum. Arthur Blauchette to Marcel Cadieux, October 5, 1960.

8 Ibid. The implications of the memorandum are discussed in L.A.D. Stephens, *Study of Canadian Government Information Abroad 1942-1972*, Unpublished study. March 1977, pp. 26-27.

9 Ibid.

CHAPTER XV

1 Report. Radio Canada International Task Force. CBC Publications. May 9, 1973.

2 CBC Search Committee for International Service Director, files, 1973.

3 Ibid.

CHAPTER XVI

1 Humorous documents discuss the advantages of balanced coverage of international affairs. Canadian missions in Eastern Europe felt that anti-communist polemics were counter productive. The policy of detente in broadcasting was formulated in an External Affairs memorandum, January 23, 1959.

2 Chipman made a written report on his journey to Eastern Europe. The discussion here is based on undated copies of the report and notes in Chipman's files. Chipman discusses the trip in taped interviews. the author interviewed Chipman on numerous occasions.

3 Ibid.

4 *Trud*, March 20, 1976.

5 Details of the Schuman Affair came largely from the Chipman files. The CBC head office requested a detailed account. Chipman also discusses his bitterness over being duped by the RCMP in taped interviews and in private discussions with the author. The author also met with Schuman.

6 Ibid.

7 RCI internal document. Memorandum from Alan Brown to service management. The memorandum, dated May 12, 1976, introduces a new structure designed to help RCI "reflect abroad a consistent approach to Canadian and international events." It deals with news, in-house writing, press reviews and commentaries.

8 Chipman interview, on tape.

9 *Report*. Radio Canada International: Language and Target Area Study.

CHAPTER XVII

1 *Report*. Radio Canada International Task Force, CBC Publication. May 9, 1973.
2 For many years, RCI carried out audience research, some of it in cooperation with other international broadcasters. Audience figures are not always regarded as reliable and are seen as approximations. Reduction in language services resulted in large audience losses. For a recent comment on audience, see *Report*. Standing Senate Committee on Transport and Communications, June 1994.
3 Interview with author.
4
5 CBC, *Radio Canada International Reading Out to the World*, Queen's Printer for Canada, Ottawa, 1993, p.16.
6 Interview with Betty Zimmerman.
7 Interview with Andrew Simon.
8 *Report*. Radio Canada International: Language and Target Area Study. Unpublished report prepared by Ted England for the president of the CBC, 1976.

CHAPTER XVIII

1 *Report*. Standing Senate Committee on Transport and Communications on the mandate of Funding Radio Canada International, June 1994. Keith Spicer appeared before the committee as a private citizen.
2 Details of Andrew Simon's interaction with Michael McEwen came from Simon's presentation to the Senate Committee on Transport and Communication on April 20, 1994. Michael McEwen appeared before the Committee on April 19, 1994.
3 Interview with author.
4 *Report*. Senate Committee on Transport and Communications, *op.cit*.
5 Interview with author.

INDEX OF NAMES